DIVIDED TIME

For Helen

Divided Time

Gender, paid employment and domestic labour

RICHARD LAYTE
Nuffield College, University of Oxford

Ashgate

Aldershot • Brookfield USA • Singapore • Sydney

© Richard Layte 1999

Published by
Ashgate Publishing Ltd
Gower House
Croft Road
Aldershot
Hants GU11 3HR
England

Ashgate Publishing Company
Old Post Road
Brookfield
Vermont 05036
USA

British Library Cataloguing in Publication Data
Layte, Richard
    Divided time : gender, paid employment and domestic labour
    1. Sexual division of labour - Great Britain 2. Sex role -
    Great Britain 3. Households - Great Britain
    I. Title
    306.3'615'0941

Library of Congress Catalog Card Number: 98-73762

ISBN 1 84014 397 5

Printed and bound by Athenaeum Press, Ltd.,
Gateshead, Tyne & Wear.

Contents

List of Figures and Tables

Acknowledgements

I would like to give my thanks to the fellows of Nuffield College for their generosity in awarding me the studentship for the doctorate upon which this book is based (Layte 1996). Jay Gershuny was my DPhil supervisor for a relatively short period, but in that time he had a great influence on my thinking and I am sure he will recognise some of his own ideas here. Similarly, Susan McRae gave me a great deal of practical advice in her short stint as supervisor. Special thanks must be given however, to Gordon Marshall and Carolyn Vogler for their long term support and hard work. Both were extremely generous in the amount of time they spent making my arguments clearer and more rigorous. I would also like to thank Duncan Gallie for his sound advice and support, both during the writing of the original thesis and since then as a colleague. Martin Range and Jane Roberts were amazingly patient with my questions on computing and requests for data and Clive Payne and David Firth have been great sources of statistical advice. A number of (ex)students at Nuffield College offered practical advice and support during my years there. May Tam and Sheila Jacobs deserve special recognition for their advice on certain technical issues as well as for their friendship and Anand Menon, Crispin Jenkinson, Mathew and Jayne Humphrey, Penny and Steve Moyle, Katherine Rake and Juliet Dowsett have been great friends and thought provoking colleagues throughout. My mother and father deserve much more than I can express here; they have always provided unflinching support and patience. Finally, I would like to thank Helen Russell for her support and insightful criticisms over the years. The original thesis and this book would have been impossible without her.

Oxford, July 1998.

Introduction

This book explores how households *work*. Everyday, households create the fabric and texture of their lives through their paid employment and household work. In so doing they largely determine the quality of their life and their experience of it. Yet, although there have been a number of excellent British studies of the domestic division of labour and how this is combined with paid employment, these tend to have been small scale (e.g. Gregson and Lowe 1994; Morris 1993; Oakley 1974; Wheelock 1990; Yeandle 1984), or have concentrated on the role of the household in industrial restructuring (Pahl 1984, 1985) and ignored the interaction and negotiation of partners within the household[1]. Using data from a British survey in the late 1980s, this book investigates how couples within households decide the amount of time each partner will devote to paid employment and household work and what factors shape these decisions. It examines to what degree we can view households as unified decision making entities with household work 'strategies', or whether individuals within households seek to do more or less of certain types of work. The division of work has implications for partners' sense of equity, thus the book also looks at how fair partners feel their work load is and whether inequitable shares of work lead to dissatisfaction and conflict.

Unlike in Britain, there have been several studies in North America which have investigated the processes of household production[2] using social surveys that have yielded valuable insights into the relationship between partners' paid and unpaid work contributions. However, as I will show, these studies have been limited by inadequate theoretical approaches. If we want to study the division of domestic labour, we need to have a theoretical framework which allows us to study the division of work as a *productive* process influenced by cost/benefit behaviour, whilst also recognising that it is shaped by structured conceptions of *gendered* work roles. Previous studies have tried unsuccessfully to combine these types of analysis. For example, Sarah Berk (1985) found that Becker's (1976) economic theory of the allocation of time explained some of the variation in the division of domestic labour between partners, but she also found, contrary to Becker's theory, that if female partners work more hours in the labour market, or have a greater income, male partners do not generally do more domestic work. This suggests that partners (or at least one partner), are not 'maximising' in the manner Becker's theory proposes. To explain why this is so, Berk invokes an interactionist theory of 'symbolic displays'. This states that partners have a 'preference' for certain types of domestic work over others, a preference derived from the social roles that they are enacting. The question is, where does this preference come from? Attitudes toward work roles vary across the population, so how do we account for this? More importantly, if this theoretical framework is to hold, when and why do people switch from the maximising rationality of the economic theory to the cultural rationality of the sociological theory?

However, there is a cure for this theoretical schizophrenia if we make a theoretical and methodological jump. First of all, we need to move away from seeing social and cultural structures as external constraints in the shape of 'norms' or 'roles' and instead see them as the organising rules and resources (Giddens 1978, 1979, 1984) or social and economic capital (Bourdieu 1990), which people use to *frame*, or *understand* their decisions and choices in situations of scarcity. This means that we need to show why it is people understand their situation as they do (the *structuring* of rules and resources) and when and why this understanding will change. But how do we access these rules and resources? I propose that we also make a methodological and theoretical jump toward analysing behaviour as the outcome of longitudinal rather than cross-sectional processes. If we are to uncover the structured rules and resources that underlie behaviour and choices, we need to accept that peoples' definitions of a situation will differ because of the material, habitual and cultural baggage that they bring with them. These can only be accessed by examining peoples work and life histories.

The Social Change in Economic Life Initiative (from here on referred to as SCELI) data sets will be used to examine the relationship between the gender attitudes of partners, their material circumstances, the division of labour and their work and life histories. The SCELI data set is the result of a programme of research funded by the Economic and Social Research Council (ESRC) carried out in two phases, the first, or 'Main Survey' in 1986 and the second, or 'Household and Community Survey', a year later. The research was carried out in six urban labour markets: Aberdeen, Coventry, Kirkcaldy, Northampton, Rochdale and Swindon. Most importantly for this study, SCELI contains life and work-history data for 6111 adults and the findings of a time-budget survey for a subset of these respondents. These two sources of data are complemented by questions on general attitudes and material circumstances at both the individual and household level.

Looking at the book in more detail, chapter one will examine both the economic and sociological theories of the determinants of the domestic division of labour. The chapter will show how research using these theories has failed to arrive at any conclusive answers about the structuring of household work because they have incompletely conceptualised the relationship between the material reality of household life and the wider socio-cultural context. To put it another way, we need to establish gender in the household as a grounded product of the partners experiences of specific socio-economic situations. The aim is not to produce an overarching theory of society or gender, but to set up certain hypotheses that can be tested empirically in the following chapters. The main finding of this chapter is that, although economic theories of the household allow us to look at domestic work as a 'productive' process from which we can create predictive models, they are ultimately found wanting in that they cannot take into account the cultural influences on the way domestic work is divided. A new theoretical approach is then laid out in skeleton form and specific hypotheses generated that can be tested empirically. A first set of hypotheses revolve around the attitudes, socio-economic position and relationship between partners. The second set will relate to the importance of life and work-history for the present arrangements of the partners.

Chapter two examines the types of data available in the SCELI data sets and gives some descriptive statistics before going on to look at the advantages and disadvantages of the different ways that domestic work can be measured. The chapter includes an examination of the different types of data that are available in the SCELI data sets and suggests that these data can be usefully augmented with more qualitative findings from existing studies.

Chapter three then sets out to test whether the economic theory of the household (in the form of the new home economic approach) is a sufficient theoretical framework within which to analyse the patterns found in the SCELI data set. The main finding of the chapter is that the new home economic theory is a good predictor of some of the patterns found, but that it ultimately fails to explain why some men do not do more domestic work as their spouses do increasing amounts of paid work. In conclusion, the chapter points to the need for the framework outlined briefly in chapter one which can encompass cultural factors such as attitudes toward gender work roles in a meaningful manner.

Chapter four begins the process of developing this framework by examining the theoretical literature on the relationship between gender role attitudes and actual behaviour. It then goes on to analyse the data in the SCELI survey on attitudes, their social patterning and their relationship with the work status of the male and female partners.

Chapter five sets out to relate attitudes to the actual behaviour of respondents in the SCELI survey. More specifically, the chapter investigates whether and how the woman's degree of attachment to the domestic role, leads to her performing a greater proportion of the domestic work. Previous work has also suggested that it is not the woman's attitudes that are important in defining her proportion of domestic labour, but those of her spouse, since the man must agree to take on the tasks that the woman does not do. Thus chapter examines whether partners' regard their proportion of domestic work as fair and the reasons they give for inequalities. The last part of the chapter extends this analysis by showing the relative importance of the partners' attitudes in defining their proportion of domestic work.

Chapter six looks for the origins of the partners' social attitudes and domestic work practices in their life and work-histories. As explained earlier, one of the main threads of this book is the role that the past experiences of partners plays in shaping their attitudes, beliefs and practices in the present. This approach is very important since it allows us to better understand where the structured beliefs about the 'gendered' nature of work roles come from, through which economic constraints (i.e. time and resource constraints) are refracted. In this way we can avoid accepting 'gender' as a homogenous cultural system. Moreover, we can also look at the effect that different histories of paid work have on the type of domestic work arrangements that partners practice. Changing circumstances within the household and in the labour market, create pressure for domestic work practices to change as well, but this is unlikely to happen immediately. This means that present work practices and attitudes will bear the marks of past paid work circumstances. One of the great problems in sociology is to explain the taken for granted ways of achieving certain ends that people use in everyday life and the assumptions they make about them. By using work histories we can get a better picture of where these 'habitual' forms of behaviour come from.

Chapter seven uses both qualitative and quantitative evidence to examine the relationship between paid work, unpaid work, attitudes and partners' satisfaction with and conflict over the domestic division of labour. As Hakim (1989) has shown, women seem to express greater levels of satisfaction with what would seem to be objectively bad jobs and inequitable divisions of domestic labour. Yet as others such as Brannen and Moss (1991) have shown, if researchers use more informal, or in-depth techniques, women tend to express more ambivalent and less satisfied responses. With this in mind, the chapter examines the findings of previous qualitative studies on women's satisfaction with domestic work and interprets these through the theoretical schema laid out in chapter one. Findings from the qualitative material are then used to construct a number of specific hypotheses about domestic labour and satisfaction that are tested using quantitative evidence from the SCELI survey.

Notes

[1] Exceptions are Gershuny (1982; 1994), Horrell (1994) and Warde and Hetherington (1993), although these papers have all looked at specific issues rather than been general treatments of the subject.

[2] C.f. Berk and Berk 1980; S.F.Berk 1980, 1985; Brines 1993, 1994; England and Farkas 1986; Geerken and Gove 1983; Pleck 1985.

1 The Theoretical Context: In Search of a Usable Framework

In this chapter, I examine the literature on the domestic division of labour from the last thirty years or so from both the UK and North America. My argument is that a coherent theoretical framework has been conspicuous in its absence from writings on the subject in the UK, although much of the sociology of the family, and later the household, has studied the subject. The north American literature on the other hand, has spawned three major schools of theoretical thinking that have, upon different premises, erected rigorous models of the household that have had varying degrees of success in empirical tests. Yet, as innovative and useful as these theories have been, they have suffered from theoretical problems that have limited their explanatory power in empirical analysis. This chapter describes the history and impact of these theoretical difficulties before going on to present a limited theory of the household which attempts to transcend these problems and in the process construct a set of hypotheses which the rest of the book will go on to test empirically. There are two main arguments in this chapter: firstly, past theoretical approaches cannot adequately combine cost/benefit and value oriented behaviour in the same model. To do this we need to develop a new theory of choice. Secondly, the chapter then argues that this is only possible if we adopt a longitudinal, rather than a cross-sectional approach to our explanations of the division of domestic work.

British Sociology of the Family and the Nature of Household Work

The last thirty years has witnessed a distinct shift in how British sociologists think about the household and domestic work. Until the early 1970s, the household was taken as a unitary concept, based upon consensus and collective decision making. As such, it was assumed that all the members of the household shared the same standard of living, and that the division of family roles by gender was self-evident. This unproblematic view of the household rendered inequalities in power invisible and saw conflict in the household as pathological. To a sociology that was still deeply steeped in functionalist theory (Parsons 1949, 1956), the family was uncritically taken as 'a good thing' that served the interests of both the individuals within it (irrespective of sex), and those of society at large.

Although studies such as that of Bott (1957) took issue with Parsons' notion of the universality of the instrumental/expressive division between husbands and wives, and instead linked it to the closeness of kin networks, gender roles were still not seen as problematic. In the same way, although Young and Willmott (1957, 1973) gave the differences identified by Bott a temporal dimension by arguing that a new and more 'companionate' type of relationship was emerging between men and women (and thus a greater sharing of domestic tasks), they were much more interested in the possible effects of these structural changes and thus did not attempt to look at the processes involved or the conflicts that may have ensued.

Doubts about this optimistic interpretation of the family were first expressed in studies such as that by Pahl and Pahl (1971), who examined the strain for middle class wives when the ideal of sharing in marriage was contradicted by the primacy attached to the husband's paid work, and the unequal division of labour that resulted. But the real sea-change in British sociology occurred with Oakley's *Sociology of Housework* (1974), which looked explicitly at housework as *work*. It is hard now to appreciate how great a change in perspective this move was, but it sensitised sociology to the labour involved in housework tasks, and women's attitudes to them. Such a move shed light upon the implicit sexism within sociology itself and allowed the processes within households and between partners to be portrayed as structured inequality, even oppression, rather than as a 'natural' part of a monolithic institution called 'the family'. However, the study of domestic labour remained within the remit of the 'sociology of the family' and the satisfactions and dissatisfactions of married life. Moreover, the dynamics of the relationship between partners remained largely implicit, and as the role of the 'housewife' (sic) remained essentially female the question of how the roles and obligations within the household were distributed remained unasked.

Oakley's evidence of inequity in the division of domestic tasks in Britain added to that of feminist researchers in North America (Robinson et al 1972; Vanek 1974; Meissner *et al* 1975) and directly confronted the optimistic picture outlined by Young and Willmott (1973). It did not, however, lead to increased investigation of the mechanisms in the household that led to this inequality. Instead, feminist scholars became increasingly embroiled in the 'domestic labour debate' (c.f. Finch & Groves 1983), seeking to develop theories of gender inequality which linked unpaid domestic labour to the system of paid labour and the capitalist economy at large. The empirical research that was carried out in the later part of the 1970s and the early 1980s (of which there was very little) also failed to develop any theoretical notion of the dynamics of the household (Martin & Roberts 1984; Yeandle 1984; Morris 1985, 1988).

With the rise of male mass unemployment and the continued growth of female part time (and later full time) employment in the 1980s, this emphasis on the formal (usually masculine) paid sphere became untenable. The work of Ray Pahl (1984) is important here as the first of a number of studies that have reoriented sociology toward the household as the central focus of study. From being a 'black-box' that supplied labour power to the paid sphere, and in turn consumed its products, the household became the focus of study to both sociologists and economists who wanted to understand the ways in which people respond to, and in turn, mould the wider economic situation. Like Oakley's redefinition of housework as work, this shift in perspective brought home to researchers the active role which the members of the household played in producing the lived material reality. Yet, although full of ethnographic detail on the relationships between the household members and both the formal and informal work spheres, Pahl largely failed to explore the relations between spouses and concentrated more upon what he termed the 'household strategies' in use (c.f. Wallace 1993)[1]. Thus, the possibility that members of households may in fact have different interests and strategies was not taken into account. Instead, a largely implicit theory of the household as a joint-decision making unit rendered invisible inequities in both the distribution of work and resources. Moreover, even though feminist researchers initially focused upon the household 'as the theatre of many aspects of the relationship between men and women' (Morris 1988, p337) the relationship of the partners was only given descriptive analysis and no attempt was made to assess systematically just how partners negotiated roles between themselves. From this review it is plain that there has been no real attempt to produce a coherent theoretical schema about how the household 'works' in the British literature. At best, theoretical stances have been *ad hoc*; at worst, implicit or missing completely.

US 'Theories of the Family' and the 'Problem' of Culture

In the following sections, I want to outline three rather broad, but I think distinct, types of theories that have arisen in the American literature seeking to explain the structure of household 'work'; namely, 'resource theory' (which I have amalgamated with exchange theory), 'dependency theory', and 'human capital theory of household time allocation'. There are overlaps between theories, but at the heart of each lies a particular and specific logic that explains the inequalities that have been found in the division of household tasks. Before going on to examine resource theory, I want to look first at the theoretical context from which this, the earliest of the theories presented here, emerged. By doing so, I hope to bring into shaper relief the 'problem' which resource theory was attempting to deal with and, I believe the origin of its failure to combine within its explanation of the domestic division of labour an understanding of culturally meaningful social action with economic (scarcity related; cost/benefit) behaviour.

As with early British sociology, American theories of the domestic division of labour emerged from the shadow of functionalist social theory. The label 'functionalist' as applied to the study of the family can encompass a wide variety of perspectives among which there is not necessarily any high degree of agreement, but there are assumptions which are common to them all that are crucial to our understanding of the later theories. Although Murdock (1949), Coser (1964) and Goode (1964) all contributed much to the functionalist analysis of the family, it was the seminal work of Parsons and Bales (1956) that organised a range of topics such as the role of the family in industrial society and the socialisation process within a single theoretical perspective. Because of this, they not only provided a framework to argue within or against, but also largely defined the rules within which people argued. Central to Parsons and Bales' argument was the intricate relationship between the family subsystem and the wider social system. Bales' experimental work on the structure of small groups had shown that in all small groups there is a tendency for some person or persons to take on leadership roles and for others to take on more subordinate roles. More specifically, he argued that groups tended to differentiate along two intersecting axes: a vertical axis based on differentiation of power and a horizontal axis based on the distinction between instrumental and expressive roles. Parsons applied this finding to the small group of the family and tried to show that the sex specific roles that this spawned - the mother in the expressive role and the father in the instrumental - was a functional response to the wider needs of the social system. For the system as a whole, such differentiation allowed the family to fulfil the reproductive, socialisation and economic functions necessary to sustain the wider society. But it also functioned for the benefit of the members of the family individually in that it 'stabilised the adult personalities of the population of the society' (Parsons and Bales 1956, p17). Parsons great contribution to the sociology of the family was in linking Freudian theory of personality development to Bales' findings; thence to the roles that spouses filled; and, finally, to the needs of the wider social system. Parsons showed that the development of functionally differentiated roles fitted neatly into Freud's theory of the universal oedipal complex and the identification of male and female children with the parent of their sex and the roles that they fulfilled. The theory thus rested upon the psychological theories of Freud, combined with the sociological idea of the internalisation of structured normative orientations. Parsons' and Bales' theory is cleverly constructed and seems to offer a theoretical framework within which we can analyse peoples decisions about how they organise domestic work. Unfortunately, the link between sociology and psychology in the theory is made in such a way that we are left with a model of human action which cannot respond to changing circumstances: the model is deterministic. In the introduction to this book, I stated that, to be of use to us, any theory should allow us to analyse choice under circumstances of scarcity, i.e. people should be able to respond to changes in the costs or benefits of a particular course of action. Parsons' and Bales' theory is, however, based upon a 'value theory of choice', thus, choices can only be made within the remit of the values given by the culture within which the person making the choice has been socialised. We can see why if we analyse Parsons' and Bales' model of social action as a three stage process.

In the first stage, an actor discriminates among different 'objects' within its environment; these can be of a social (what Freud would have called the 'alter ego') or physical nature (objects). The actor also assesses the significance of each of these objects for the 'gratification' of their needs, these being an outcome of the Freudian 'drives' that each person possesses. But, importantly, these drives are combined in the second stage of the model with 'values' internalised via the process of socialisation such that the person can differentiate among the alternative 'objects' (first stage) via their 'need dispositions', one of which is to comply with 'situationally adequate rules' of behaviour. The clever part of the theory is that when we come to the third stage of the model, the choice or behaviour stage, Parsons and Bales have made sure that values govern the definition of the situation in both a normative and a motivational sense. Thus, people will have similar and reciprocal expectations of each other because of their internalisation of the groups 'social system', but they also *want* to do what is expected of them. The primary aim of the theory is to get round the Hobbsian problem of social order (i.e. individual innate drives will inevitably cause social disorder) with a social *and* normative drive. The problem is that the model cannot accommodate aspects of scarcity or cost/benefit since changes in demand can only be modelled as changes in 'need-dispositions'. Given constant preferences from the social structure and innate drives, changes in relative prices cannot be accommodated.

If we leave the problem of combining Parsons' and Bales' theory with economic reasoning aside for one moment, there is another basic problem with the theory: it is essentially static in terms of the way it views social roles and their relationship to normative orientations. Such a theory could not survive the developments that followed in the wake of women's increased participation in paid work that had begun to occur in the 1950s. In reading Parsons and Bales, we are constantly left with the impression that what is, must be because of the vital functions which are being fulfilled. That Parsons shows little concern for the range of human variability and potentiality is illustrated in the following passage

> Put very schematically, a mature woman can love, sexually, only a man who takes his full place in the masculine world, above all in its occupational aspect, and who takes responsibility for a family; conversely the mature man can only love a woman who is really an adult, a full wife to him and a mother to his children (Parsons and Bales, 1956, p178).

4

Yet, in the 1960s, rising female employment was just one indication in US society that the old structures of prescribed social roles were lapsing (Scanzoni 1972; Brickman 1974). Sociologists were becoming convinced that the marital relationship in US society was changing from being 'fully structured', where 'the behaviour of each party is completely specified by prescribed social norms', to 'partially structured', in which 'rules constrain certain behaviours but leave others to the free choice of the parties' (Brickman 1974, p7). Now that marital relations seemed to be more free of normative constraint, and, moreover, sociologists were not blinded by an overarching explanation of the differences in spouses roles in the form of functionalist theory, where could they go for a conceptual structure which explained differential outcomes? One answer was to prescribe a new set of norms in the form of mutual support and affection, and hang on uncritically to the accepted division of labour which was still seen to a large extent as natural (Kimmel & Havens 1964). To many others though, the answer was to adopt the new social theories of such as Blau (1964), Thibaut and Kelley (1959) or Homans (1961), which looked at social relationships through the medium of 'exchange'.

This movement was picked up by two researchers on the family, Blood and Wolfe (1960) who asserted that marital power was no longer based on patriarchal notions, but rather on 'comparative resources'. Their book was to become hugely influential and precipitated a large literature based around what was to become known as 'resource theory'. Blood and Wolfe's thesis opened up the household to studies of conjugal power and decision making and led to more formal theoretical frameworks of exchange and choice. As I will now go on to show, this change in perspective was not entirely successful, primarily because, in the final analysis, sociologists had to step outside their theories of instrumental exchange to account for the specific social structure of domestic work. However, in doing this, they had to turn back to Parsonsian style overarching norms.

From Resource to Exchange Theory

Blood and Wolfe (1960) carried out a study of nine hundred families in the Detroit area of the US. Their chief concern was the distribution of power between husband and wife, and to measure this they asked the wife who made the final decision about such things as the job which the husband should take, whether the wife should work, where they should go on holiday, and so on. Against these data, they tested two models of the distribution of power, one based upon an 'ideological theory' and the other a 'resource theory'. Essentially, the ideological theory stated that the distribution of power would depend upon the norms held by the groups or subculture to which the family belonged, with Catholic and immigrant groups supposedly espousing more patriarchal norms than other groups. Their results showed virtually no support for this theory. When other relevant variables were controlled for, the fathers in Catholic families were found to have no more power than those in non-Catholic families, immigrant fathers no more than non-immigrants, and ill-educated fathers less power than educated. On the other hand, the resource theory received considerable support from the data. This theory held that

> the sources of power in so intimate a relationship as a marriage must be sought in the comparative resources which the husband and wife bring to the marriage....a resource may be defined as anything that one partner may make available to the other, helping

the latter satisfy his needs or attain his goals. The balance of power will be on the side of that partner who contributes the greater resources to the marriage' (Blood and Wolfe 1960, p12).

Blood and Wolfe defined resources as the education, income and degree of participation in the community that each partner attained. This would seem to offer a useful theory for understanding the specific negotiations and decisions arrived at by individual couples in the organisation of domestic life, and especially the distribution of their unpaid labour. The connection seems simple: the partner with the greater power, derived through resources attained and applicable outside the home, will do less housework within the home. This seems to imply that the division of labour between husbands and wives is decided by a negotiation between the partners who use whatever valued resources they can to strike the best deal on behalf of self-interest. Such a bargaining perspective also implies that housework is a source of disutility, an onerous activity one wishes to 'buy out of'. Thus, if the wife does more housework, it is because she has less power. However, Blood and Wolfe (1960) did not see this theoretical relationship leading to conflict or coercion, and did not, strangely enough, see 'resource bargaining' as an exchange situation. Instead, couples were simply 'optimising' the household utility by allocating their relative resources to different tasks. Thus

A few tasks.....require skills which may not be distributed equally in the family, nor easily learned. Hence they are best performed by whoever has the technical know-how. Some tasks....require muscular strength in which husbands usually surpass their wives. But most household tasks are humdrum and menial in nature; the chief resource they require is time. Usually the person with the most time is the wife - provided she isn't working outside the home. If she does work the husband incurs a moral obligation to help her out in what would otherwise be her exclusive task areas (Blood and Wolfe 1960, pp73-4).

To Blood and Wolfe then, the husband's relatively low contribution to domestic labour is not ideologically based, but a result of rational resource distribution. The use of the term 'moral obligation' points to Blood and Wolfe's continuing attachment to the functionalist notion of the family as a consensual unit, and this contributes in part to one of the theory's major flaws. Thus, firstly, the allocation of tasks in this theory is treated, as many critiques have noted, sometimes as an outcome, and at others as an indicator of power, rather than as a process requiring study and documentation (Heer 1963; Wilkening 1968; Blood 1963; Scanzoni 1979; Berk 1985). Are tasks allocated through the negotiation of the partners, each using their power as derived through their relative resources? Blood and Wolfe make no attempt to examine how 'power' relates to the minutiae of household arrangements. Thus as Berk has said

the perspective requires that one view the work of the household as a mirror - reflecting power relations - rather than as a window, revealing what and how everyday work is accomplished. The impression conveyed is that it is power and not the sustenance of families that is produced through household labour (Berk 1985, p12).

Secondly, Blood and Wolfe do not explicitly mention the alternatives open to each of the partners, but deal simply with the amounts contributed. The household is not a closed system away from the rest of the world, thus we need to have some idea of the perceived opportunity costs of alternatives. For example, although a husband may

6

contribute a very large income and the wife nothing, if the state provides a system of painless divorce and sufficient alimony, she has no financial reason to give in to his demands. Thirdly, what is the relation of resources to normative orientations in determining power outcomes? Blood and Wolfe's theory posits that partners accept the division of tasks that is specified by the 'rational' allocation of resources, yet they also say that a woman has to work only because of her 'no good' or incapacitated husband' (Blood and Wolfe 1960, p45). They also remark cryptically that 'a wife's work has significant repercussions on the husband'. These statements imply that couples have a normative interest in certain types of household arrangements over others.

In attempting to solve these problems, sociologists concentrated upon using a greater range of relevant resources, and showing how these were affected by the perceived opportunity costs of alternatives (e.g. Heer 1963). They also examined the relation of resources to normative orientations in determining power outcomes (e.g. Burr 1973; Cromwell and Olsen 1975) and the importance of unequal exchanges between partners (e.g. Bernard 1973; Safilios-Rothschild 1976). These changes led to the household being modelled within the more formal framework of exchange theory. In this form, the theory of the household shed the last vestiges of the consensus based and functional theory of Blood and Wolfe (1960) and went over to the rational choice theory of power. Thus, according to Heer (1963, p138)

> *In the revised theory, the greater the difference between the value to the wife of the resources contributed by the husband and the value to the wife of the resources which she might earn outside the existing marriage, the greater the power of her husband, and vice versa.*

From a theoretical point of view, Heer's formulation would seem to be a more parsimonious framework than Blood and Wolfe's. However, there are two main objections that Blood (1963) himself advanced against it that are important for my argument, but not quite in the way Blood thought. Resource theory is premised upon the idea that decision making and the division of household tasks are determined by the power each partner has, by virtue of their 'resources' such as their relative productivity (i.e. skill) and available time[2]. In Blood and Wolfe's formulation, 'power' did not infer exchange or negotiation (as in exchange theory) because, according to Blood, this would require people to be overly calculative and would require that they take the possibility of divorce or separation (as the final threat over compliance) explicitly into their calculations during negotiations (Blood 1963). Blood also disliked the idea that couples would be overly interested in the economic and monetary aspects of marriage, relative to those of mutual trust and co-operation. These are serious criticisms if we want to use the theory as a framework in which to model the division of household work.

Looking at the criticism that this theory is overly materialistic, it is true that the theory does assume that people value material factors and that these will make a difference in their decisions about whether to stay within the marriage or seek another, better alternative. But, the theory need not depend on this single axis of exchange alone. If, for example, we posit that women or men desire and value emotional support as much as, or more than material factors, we still have an exchange theory of power, but because the assumptions about men and women's values have changed our predictions would have to change too. If women value emotional support over material support, the theory as it stands would have to be discarded, but it could be replaced by one which predicted that husbands power varied with his degree of emotional support. If however, the original assumption holds, i.e., that people value material support as well as emotionality, the theory could stay intact and all we need do is deal with the later axis as a *ceteris paribus* clause (Heath 1976, p109).

Blood's first criticism is more troublesome for exchange theory, but not in the way Blood supposed. Blood states that couples in a marriage do not explicitly take divorce into consideration when negotiating. Yet, without such 'calculative' negotiation, how do couples arrive at the 'price' of exchange? If we want the theory to give us a framework within which we can model the division of domestic labour, we need to have alternatives that are available, even if the costs of switching to this alternative are high (Heer 1963). Exchange theorists reply that the actual rate of exchange will be guided by the alternatives available elsewhere, thus couples can bargain and use the threat of divorce if they like, but they do not have to. They could instead follow the 'norms' established by peers or kin and only consider divorce or separation (taking into account the costs involved) if they feel they are getting a worse 'bargain' than they could get elsewhere.

However, this is not a good solution since it either stays within the pecuniary exchange dyad (i.e. there are no better alternatives to the present) or it lapses into an 'over-socialised' model of the household which conforms to the 'traditional' division of tasks because of 'normative' constraints. It could be argued by the exchange theorists that the 'normative' level of the bargain is set by the prevailing 'market' for emotional support or material reward, but I don't think this is what they, or Blood meant by 'norms'. 'Norms' here mean culturally meaningful ways of acting that are generally followed by the wider community. But as with the functionalist theory that they were trying to leave behind, these norms are just static, homogenous belief systems that cannot accommodate changes in the price of alternatives, or change to new situations. Both alternatives are unsatisfactory: the social exchange answer cannot encompass any form of decision rationality outside of the exchange situation and the normative explanation lacks any relationship to the intentional, productive and practical lives of those it is said to affect.

Theoretically then, exchange theory has faults. Firstly, even if we stay within the context of pecuniary exchange, there are problems involved in measuring the price, or actual rate of exchange. Exchange theory models are about 'who makes the final decision', and this can be seen as a measure of the amount exchanged. Yet as Heath (1976, p111) rightly states, much more is exchanged in marriage than compliance. Domestic life is made up of thousands of individual actions that together provide the material basis of life. The task of measuring these individually, let alone combining them into a single index to give the rate of exchange, is a huge task and it is suspect as to whether people actually think like this in the first place. This is not a trivial problem that the theorist can relinquish. If people cannot make these valuations then the theory falls.

Secondly, the theory cannot decide whether it is a 'value' theory of choice or a 'rational' theory of choice, but is also incapable of combining the two approaches producing a rather schizophrenic result.

Economic Dependency Theory

The final sentence of the last section pointed to the problem of viewing the household as a static exchange situation where resources and obligations are used as tokens in the structuring of 'work'. As shown, such a theory inevitably falls back upon the monolithic normative system adhered to by functionalism, as a framework within which this exchange can take place. Lack of process aside, this type of theory has also been criticised for ignoring the differential power in heterosexual relationships between men and women usually derived from the male partner's provider role and social status. Although this criticism would seem to be taken into account by the resource theorists (do not the 'resources' of the husbands occupation and income encompass this?), their models are actually of a household system, rather than of a household in a social structure - a social structure moreover that is stratified by gender (c.f. Hakim 1979; Crompton and Mann 1986). Heer's (1963) attempt to introduce the opportunity costs of alternatives into the exchange model did not encompass such systematic differences in the alternatives of each sex, thus the 'resources' the authors see spouses 'bringing to their marriage', are in fact a *constitutive* part of the family, not a variable *explaining* differences in power between spouses. Decisions taken by individual couples need to be seen as taken within an overall social structure based on sexual divisions (men's power over women) of which marriage itself is an integral part or a contributory institution. In outline this is the economic dependency model. Whereas the two theories presented before were of complementarity and exchange between partners - a 'different but equal' model - the economic dependency model looks at the relationship between the sexes as one of structured inequality, exploitation and oppression. Although such a perspective would seem to merit an analysis of the roots of this relationship, in this section I will avoid trying to examine the mass of literature this would present (c.f. Finch and Groves 1983; Walby 1988, 1989; Finch 1993) and concentrate instead on the implications the theory has for the distribution of the household division of labour. My argument is that, as per the other theories examined so far, the economic dependency model is gender neutral in its explanation of the distribution of household work, except insofar as this exchange is permeated by the determining structure of 'patriarchy'.

Although, in the introduction to this chapter I stated that British authors writing on the sociology of the family, and later, the household had not attempted to draw up explicit theories of the mechanisms involved in the distribution of household labour, this, like all generalisations, is partly untrue. Economic dependency theory has its roots in the domestic labour debate of the 1970s in which many British (feminist) authors took part (c.f. Finch and Groves 1983). This debate set out to analyse the relationship between domestic labour and the capitalist system, but it also queried the nature of the relationship between the paid worker and the domestic worker. To simplify greatly, through voluminous exchanges, the debate split in to two: on the one hand there were those who looked at the advantages accruing to the individual paid labourer (as the beneficiaries of domestic labour), and on the other, those that stressed the gain to employers (capital) who could hold down the wage levels actually necessary to reproduce labour. To simplify this division even further, on the one hand there were those who stressed *capitalism* as the ultimate source of women's oppression, and on the other, those who gave *patriarchy* primacy. Hartmann's (1981) synthesis of these two approaches in the form of 'dual systems' theory laid the foundations upon which the more specific theory of economic dependency would emerge through the work of Acker (1988) and Delphy and Leonard (1986). These authors did not however formally test any hypothesis that emerges from their work empirically, thus I will use the work of an American author, Julie Brines (1993) to examine the empirical usefulness of the theory before making some critical observations.

Economic dependency theories of the household posit that housework remains 'women's work' as a consequence of the processes whereby household labour is provided in return for economic support. This 'trade' stipulates that the breadwinners are entitled to the domestic labour of those that are dependant upon them (him), in return for a share of their (his) earnings. Even if the dependant spouse is earning a wage, the theory posits that, insofar as this is insufficient to sustain the household, the dependant will be initiated into the reciprocal behaviour of supplying domestic work. Thus far, the theory seems to resemble the exchange theory of Scanzoni (1970), but dependency theorists do not see this relationship as a market exchange for two reasons. First, the model departs from an employment relation in that there is no calculable rate of exchange (Acker 1988; Walby 1986). Secondly, the main breadwinners and dependants are not in a position analogous to employers and employees who can enter a market for alternative partners with greater ease (England & Farkas 1986; Walby 1986). Exchange, or game theoretical processes are not applicable because

> *[O]ne can think of a marriage with the economic concept of a 'bilateral monopoly', at least in the period after extensive 'relationship-specific investments' have been made by each partner. After such investments in how to get along with a particular partner, one has no other potential partners with whom one has made such investments. Thus, each partner can be said to have a bilateral monopoly power over the other, because each partner is like a monopolist and a monopsonist with respect to the other. In this non-competitive situation, neo-classical economic theory cannot predict who will get what (England and McCreary 1987, p165).*

Primary earners however, have an advantage in this relationship. Money as a generalised resource (Blau 1964) is of use outside the relationship, whereas the relationship-specific investments of the domestic worker are not. Thus, because what the dependants have to offer in the bilateral exchange is illiquid, they are subject to a power imbalance that can induce them to work beyond the value of the support that they receive. This theory emerged in part through the attempt to situate the domestic division of labour within the existing theories of stratification (domestic labour debate), and it is instructive to see the theory in these terms, as Delphy and Leonard (1986, p62) argue

> *[I]f we were to use the same formal terms to analyse the family as have been developed for class analysis, namely, to see it as a 'structure of positions associated with a specific historical form of the social division of labour' (Goldthorpe 1983, p467), we think it would be recognised that the family is a social system in which subordinates work unpaid for a head (generally a husband/father) and are in return maintained by him (or provided with a contribution to their maintenance when they are in employment and earn some of their own keep).*

If we look at the implications of this theory, it is obvious that the dependants in this relationship can be expected to perform a significantly higher proportion of domestic tasks than the main breadwinner, and although a linear relationship cannot be established between housework and monetary support, we could expect that those who are less dependant to perform less housework, that is, if they have an outside wage. As in exchange theory, economic dependency theory assumes that domestic labour is performed because of the instrumental exchange relationship between the breadwinner and the dependant, and not because she/he has chosen to perform this work. The arguments against this assumption were made in the last section, and as there, this assumption is indicative of a theory that does not allow for different cultural choices, or preferences. Thus, if we look at the formal structure of the theory, it is quite easy to set up a model of the household based upon these assumptions that works irrespective of the sex of the persons involved. The question is, how well do such models fare in empirical tests? Useful in this respect is the work of Julie Brines (1993) who examined this theory using wave twenty of the Panel Study of Income Dynamics (PSID) from 1985 (Institute for Social Research 1985) which is based upon 5000 US families (households) first sampled in 1968.

In a very thorough test, based upon the implications just outlined, Brines found that some, albeit weak support was given to the theory. For instance, she found that for wives, the occupancy of the sole breadwinner role led them to spend significantly less time on housework compared to other women. However, the addition of a more finely grained measure of economic transfer showed this effect to be insignificant, whilst at the same time revealing that the share of earnings transferred between self and spouse has nearly two times the impact on wives housework time compared to that of husbands. In all, Brines shows that there are significant differences in the effects of support and dependency between male and female spouses, signifying that the mechanisms in operation are not gender neutral. This confirms, as the above quote from Delphy and Leonard suggests, that we should not assume that the theory can be applied without stepping out of the theoretical framework to seek an account in historical terms - specifically in regard to the effect of gender. Delphy and Leonard make it quite clear that, historically, it is women who have been incapacitated in the public sphere (e.g. because of the 'marriage bar' or sex discrimination in the type and rewards of occupations offered), and it is women who have been expected to perform domestic tasks in marriage.

As in the analysis of exchange and resource theory in the last section, we are left with the problem of how to conceptualise 'gender' as a variable in the construction of household work. The last section showed that resource and exchange theory were inadequate to the task of explaining the division of domestic tasks because they offered no way of combining social action with economic rationality. The dependant labour model of the division of domestic tasks was a product of the rise of the second wave of feminism in the latter part of the 1960s. This being so, it would seem logical that this model would have a much better conceptual hold on the concept of 'gender'. Since the late 1960s, the work of feminist authors has highlighted the unproblematic way in which sociology and the rest of the social sciences have conceptualised 'gender'. If not totally ignored, gender was, even up until the middle of the 1970s, seen as being a 'natural' aspect of persons and not something interesting in its own right or worthy of analysis. Oakley's (1974) study showed that the gendered distribution of work was far from unproblematic, but the problem remained as to how to conceptualise a personal attribute (i.e. one's sex) which had such widespread and profound *social* consequences. Janet Finch (1993, p235) has summed up the problem thus

In understanding gender relations, is it necessary or desirable to work towards a theory which will explain the subordination of women everywhere, living under different social and economic systems and across human history? Or is it sufficient to explain why men dominate women under specific historical circumstances and specific socio-economic conditions?

Since the early 1970s, explanations for women's generalised inequality have developed through several phases. From Marxist-feminist explanations, the debate has moved on to increasingly sophisticated variants of 'dual-systems theory' (Hartmann 1976; Walby 1986, 1990), where the interactions of capitalism and patriarchy are described in more and more detail. The problem is that such theories appear little more than description and leave as implicit the theoretical interpretations that should be made of it. As Rosemary Crompton observes (1989, p581)

To establish that many men will gain an advantage from their relationships with women restates what is already known, rather than demonstrates the existence of a 'system' of patriarchy. In making this argument against the use of the concept of 'patriarchy', it must be stressed that the reality of male oppression is not being disputed, but rather the theoretical interpretation which should be placed on it.

Given the widespread nature of sexual inequality, it is unsurprising that feminist sociologists have concentrated upon the 'structures' and institutional forms within which this has occurred. Some have realised that this carries the danger of being deterministic, but their answers take us no further forward. Thus, Maynard (1990, p 274) sees the need to

reinstate human 'agency' in the understanding of domination......[S]o it is not patriarchy, the 'system', which oppresses women...[this approach] stresses the existence of active agents who 'do' the oppressing.

But *why* do men, as the active agents oppress women? Maynard's answer is inadequate, since for her, 'structure' equals 'determinism', whereas 'human agency' sits beyond all influence and acts from some undefined 'preference' or 'will'. Maynard never actually escapes determinism as she has no option but to fall back either into essentialism or structural constraints when she attempts to explain why men should have these preferences in the first place. We are left with the situation that we saw in the last section: economic dependency theory supplies a framework within which we can analyse instrumental exchange based upon a particular economic decision rationality, but cannot explain why people may have varying degrees of commitment to certain types of culturally meaningful behaviour. Maynard, Walby and Acker, although all using complex theoretical devices, still have relatively little to say about the formation of men's and women's experiences at an individual level, yet *this is exactly what needs to be explained*. As some have pointed out (Connell 1985), 'gender' is not something 'out there' that has an ultimate base (at least not one we can apply in empirical research). Instead, it must be seen as the structurally located rules and resources (cultural and economic capital) which people utilise in the production of their daily lives. The different circumstances in which people live, and the different histories they have lived through both contribute to the patterning of the material circumstances (economic capital) and cultural rules and resources (cultural capital) that not only structure but also make possible their habits, routines and choices. This is not to say that these rules and resources are purely individual in nature, or that we must use methodological individualism to understand them. There are social patterns to these rules and resources and we must not forget that there are institutional forces that have shaped their history and will shape their future. However, when theorists such as Walby (1986) have concerned themselves with the formation of these rules and resources, they tend to have been in critiques of the role theories of socialisation that were touched upon in the last section. Again, this is understandable given that these theorists are attempting to understand gender relations that surpass the individual and have institutional form, but it does not help us gain an empirical understanding of their power in a particular instance. More seriously, the theory offers us no understanding of how obligations in the household are distributed, beyond the suggestion that the dependant members of the household will do more domestic work than the breadwinner. The question arises as to how tasks are distributed once a trade off is made between dependant and breadwinner. That is to say, we need a theory that offers a framework in which we can also analyse the productive aspects of the household.

In this section I have shown that economic dependency theory cannot act as a feasible framework within which to examine the domestic division of labour. In its formal structure, the theory offers the prospect of a solution, but this turns out to be inadequate empirically unless we step outside of the theory and account for gender differences through the notion of patriarchy. Unfortunately, 'patriarchy' or 'dual systems' theories of gender are conceptually weak, especially in empirical application, since they posit one unchanging set of cultural 'norms' or relations between the sexes. What we need to do is to introduce into our theories more dynamic conceptions of gender which take account of the differential experiences of individual men and women, which although structured, do still lead to differential outcomes. Moreover, economic dependency theory gives us little guidance as to how different kinds of domestic tasks are allocated. The next section looks at the sociological application of the human capital approach to the division of household time which seeks to answer just these questions.

The Human Capital Theory of Household Time Allocation

If nothing else, resource, exchange and economic dependency theories have at least encouraged sociologists to begin to understand the family as something other than a 'black-box' where socialisation occurred, and seemingly very little else. Unfortunately, the emphasis on power and resources, or power and dependency stopped them looking at the actual process of how everyday life is accomplished and work distributed in the household. In a sense, sociologists have produced an idealist sociology of family interactions where the way in which households meet their material needs is ignored. This is not true of the human capital theory of household time allocation, which has its routes in the work of Reid (1934), but has found its most powerful statement in the work of Becker (1976, 1981). The 'new home economics' (NHE) (Nerlove 1974), as it has been called, seeks to address one critical question: how do households allocate their resources to achieve the greatest possible well-being?[3] (Berk 1985, p23). In this section I will show how this question is used in the NHE to produce a framework which some authors have seen as offering the best theoretical framework yet for analysing the way households allocate the time of their members to different tasks. Although admitting that it is more useful in this respect than the resource, exchange or dependency theories that we have just examined, I will go to show that it suffers similar problems in empirical usage.

Whereas traditional microeconomic theory clearly distinguishes between the actions of firms and the actions of consumers, the NHE has conceptualised the household as a small firm in its own right, where production as well as consumption is organised along economic principles. Thus, in traditional economic theory, firms, motivated by the search for maximum profits, produce consumer goods (and capital goods); and consumers, motivated by the search for maximum utility, purchase these goods with the wages earned while selling their labour power to firms. To Becker (1976, p134) on the other hand

> *[the new home economics] approach views as the primary objects of consumer choice various entities, called commodities, from which utility is directly obtained. These commodities are produced by the consumer unit itself through the productive activity of combining purchased market goods and services with some of the household's own time. In this framework, all market goods are inputs used in production processes of the non-market sector.*

Thus, in the NHE, the combination of market goods and time is the immediate source of 'household utility'. These commodities can take many forms, from a cooked meal to a night in with a video, or from a made bed to a well brought up child. As with any small factory, the household is treated as the decision making unit, and Becker makes it explicit that it is the family's utility that is at issue, not that of any one member. Thus with the goal of utility maximisation, households seek the 'best' configuration of inputs, given opportunity costs and productivity (the household production function). This process of combining the inputs of goods and effort is, however, subject to the dual constraints of income and time. Without using the formal equations of Becker, we can define the 'optimal' allocation of time and income as Berk and Berk (1978, p434) do, as when:

> *the ratio of the 'worth' of household productivity equals the ratio of the 'worth' of market productivity. These results are analogous to the maximisation processes of consumers or firms and are therefore consistent with more general microeconomic theory.*

Therefore, although we can only expect households 'on the margin' to have fully maximised their available income and time (i.e. none), we can expect that it is the aim of all households to approximate maximisation. As such, the theory allows us to create a framework within which we can predict not only the type and duration of the households efforts (given that we can empirically operationalise the variables necessary), but we can also predict how changes in the level of resources, the costs of members time and price of other inputs will affect the efforts of household members.

The theory is parsimonious in its structure, starting from very simple assumptions and building from these to a more complex empirical model. Are the assumptions warranted though? Rather than attempt to present all the criticisms that can be found in the literature, I want here to concentrate on a few. Most troubling is the assumption that the household has a single utility function (the household production function). Since it is the household's well-being that is being maximised, not the well-being of any individual (in a multi-person household), there can be only one utility function. Becker himself did not like this unrealistic assumption, thus he put forward the concept (1981, pp172-201) of the altruistic head of the household whose own well being depends upon the well being of all the other family members. In effect, the well being of the other members of the household are, for the household head, just other household commodities, subject to all the concerns that govern optimal production. This has been criticised for being unrealistic in that it assumes members of the household will always be honest with the head in their dealings (e.g. Sawhill 1980; Ben-Porath 1982; Nerlove 1974). More serious is the defining away of conflict in the household over sources of utility and equity. In exchange theory this was of major concern, and, in defining it away, the processes of negotiation and decision making that occur within the household are ignored. In part, the last assumption is based upon another, more deeply embedded assumption in the NHE, that 'preferences are assumed not to change substantially over time, or to be very different between wealthy and poor persons, or even between persons in different societies and cultures' (Becker, 1976, p5). Presumably, this also implies that preferences do not differ between people of different sexes[4].

Note that in the theory and in its assumptions, nothing is said about the gender of the partners. Becker's deductive logic applies irrespective of the sex of the members of the household and dictates that in the long run, should one partner produce more of value in any given hour spent on market work than does the other, the former will increasingly specialise in market work and the latter in both housework and market work (or completely in housework). In empirical practice though, the implication is that it is the husband who will specialise in market work and the wife in housework and child care, a fact that is explained by Becker (1981) through a combination of efficiency and biology. He argues that a division of labour between employment and household work is more efficient than shared roles, and because women have a biological advantage over men in child care and nursing, it is more efficient for them to specialise in tasks that can be more readily combined with these. While it may be true that women have a biological advantage for nursing, it is doubtful that this could be taken to explain the extent of the division of labour by sex in both employment and housework. Such arbitrary justifications have led both sociologists and economists to criticise the NHE approach for its lack of attention to the normative and institutional constraints on the household division of labour (Nerlove 1974; Vanek, 1980; Hannan 1982; Berk & Berk 1983; Berk 1985).

As with exchange theory, it is clear that the new economic theory of the division of household labour has to reach outside its borders for ultimate grounding. This is understandable, given the simple premises upon which the theory is built, but is it impossible to thread more cultural orientations into this basically economic exchange? Richard Berk (1980) has tried to do this by positing 'norms' in the form of preferences as additional constraints (like income and time) on the division of work. Thus, the maximisation process proceeds only within the normative boundaries. This is a useful alteration to the original theory because it avoids the trap that some sociologists have set themselves by insisting that the division of work is down to 'tradition' (Ferber and Birnbaum 1977) and thus taking all choice and preference away from partners, but it is ultimately more troublesome in that preferences cannot differ between partners; if they do, the theory begins to collapse as the self-interest of partners takes over from the household production function. Moreover, in this altered theory, 'norms' are irrational constraints on maximisation of the household. This is a troubling assumption since it would write off all behaviour not explained by the economic theory to 'irrational factors'.

Theoretically then, it seems as if there are major problems inherent in the NHE approach that are difficult to ignore if we wish to include cultural influences on domestic practices. This is not to say that the theory has no value whatsoever or has no value to us. The theory has two major advantages over the other two theories so far presented in this chapter. The first is that it sets out a framework within which we can see the domestic work practices of a household as productive, rather than as constitutive of power relations or dependency. This is a great advance since it allows us to look directly at the patterns of work in the household. What is missing from many of the studies of the domestic division of labour is an account of the processes behind everyday household life. There are problems with the NHE approach, but its approach to the effects of relative productivity on time use gives us the tools to look at the material basis of life. The second advantage of the NHE approach is that it is based upon the micro-economic theory of choice, commonly known as 'subjective expected utility theory' (SEU) that makes it possible to combine it with a culturally formed theory of choice. If we look back to the section on resource or social exchange theory, the models there tried to combine a basic model of individual maximising behaviour with a functionalist theory of culturally determined choice. It was clear then that these theories could not individually account for the range of behaviours necessary, and yet they could not be conjoined to provide an explanatory framework either. In the same way, the section on dependency theory showed that this theory suffered a similar fate. The NHE theory on the other hand is a 'thin' theory that, in Becker's formulation anyway makes no attempt to secure itself outside of the boundaries of its limited economic assumptions (at least it does if we discard the superficial attempt at biological determinism). The theory is 'thin' because it does not pretend to describe cognitive processes. Rather, the theory is in the form of an 'as if' statement (e.g., the individual behaves 'as if....').Under the specific assumptions of the effects of relative productivity, there lies the SEU theory of scarcity-based choice that is more amenable to combination with a theory of cultural variability. If we analyse the SEU theory of choice as a three-stage process, as we did when assessing the 'value theory' of choice, we can get a better idea of how this combination can be achieved.

In the first stage, alternative choices or courses of action are identified, and the outcomes of each are examined. Each of these is then assigned a projected utility index number and outcomes are then ordered according to a transitive utility preference schedule (i.e. if preference is A>B>C therefore not C>A). In the second stage, each of the alternatives is then weighted by the subjective estimate of the risk (probability) of its occurrence. With the alternatives scored and ordered, the third stage is where the choice is made of the alternative with the highest subjective expected utility. The problem is that SEU theory can only be applied with the aid of three auxiliary assumptions (Lindenberg 1989) and it is these that are usually criticised[5], but which can open the way to a combination with a more sociologically oriented theory. All of the assumptions are related to the unbounded rationality of the actor and make the theory simpler to apply. First of all, the theory assumes that the actor can distinguish among as many choices in their utility function as the researcher cares to allow. Second, the subjective probabilities allotted by the actor to the risk of the choice occurring are a linear function of 'objective' probabilities, and thus the latter can be used as proxies for the former. Lastly, the 'invariance' assumption holds that alternatives will be cognized and evaluated in such a way that they will coincide with the objective descriptions. Thus if two alternatives are 'objectively' equivalent, they will also be subjectively equivalent, irrespective of their descriptions. Although these assumptions make the theory easier to apply in empirical practice, I think they are limiting to any theory that pertains to explaining the domestic division of labour. Fortunately, the replacement of these assumptions may allow us to formulate a new theoretical framework, and generate some meaningful propositions for the chapters ahead. The key to adding in what we can call cultural 'plasticity' to this model (Lindenberg 1989) is to be found in the replacement of these auxiliary assumptions since these can be altered to dovetail with a more sociologically informed approach to social action. This means that the NHE thesis is a useful theoretical framework from which we can work towards a theory that can properly encompass cultural factors. Before going on to do that, I would first like to examine some existing empirical applications of the theory.

There are quite a few studies that have looked at the NHE thesis from which we can assess the degree of support that the above hypothesis receives. All have used an indirect outcome of the NHE approach as the basis upon which to structure a test: that is, although the human capital model makes no explicit reference to the effect of earnings *per se*, a clear implication emerges if one takes a partner's actual or potential wage as a measure of the value of his or her time in the market. Granting some cross-couple variation in relative potential wages, even where one assumes sex differences in comparative advantage, joint utility maximisation, and optimisation at the margin, variation in the division of household labour should follow suit. Thus, as England and Farkas (1986, p95) have hypothesised, 'in couples where the wife's wage is close to that of her husband, wives will be engaged in more employment and the husband in more housework than in situations where the husband's wage is much greater than that of his wife.

One early study (Farkas 1976) found no support for the above hypothesis, a result replicated by Geerken and Gove (1983). The latter reported (p90) that 'the most striking result is the huge difference between the time the husband spends on housework, compared with the wife (even if the wife is employed); the drastic effect of the wife's employment status on her own level of housework; and the stability of the husbands housework time, whether the wife works or not'. A similar picture was also found by Coverman (1985). Perhaps the most prominent and persuasive study is that by Sarah Berk (1985), who carried out a rigorous test of the time allocation theory of the NHE. In her study, Berk found little variation in the division of household tasks, and that, of the variation that did exist, most could be explained through changes in the individual partner's part of the 'household pie'. The 'pie' is the total amount of domestic work being done by all of the members of the household, thus we can think of each persons contribution as a slice of the pie. Any increase in the market productivity of the female spouse was not matched by a take up of housework by the male, but absorbed by the female. Thus, rather than the man taking on some of the woman's tasks (i.e. taking on some of the woman's slice of the 'household pie') as the woman did more paid work, the woman did her existing tasks less often and the man's work load remained the same. More important to the division of tasks, was what Berk (1980, p185) called the:

> ....*vast (and largely uncharted) normative backdrop that influences the mechanisms by which work is apportioned to household members, and that renders household work relations, gender relations. Thus, as only one example, the total amount of work established for the household had a large and significant bearing on the wives' tasks and time. These findings cannot be dismissed simply by invoking some version of a 'natural order' - of either an economic or a biological variety.*

Berk's finding confirms the need for a conception of 'gender' in the NHE theory, but her answer (1985) is more theoretically informed than the 'preference' adjustment advocated by her husband Richard Berk (1980). The problem is how to conceptualise norms and cultural variables without invoking everything which Dennis Wrong (1961) said was 'wrong' about sociology, i.e. a determinist social or cultural structure within which individuals act out determinate roles. To do this, Berk turns to the interactionist sociology of West and Zimmerman, via that of Erving Goffman, and tries to combine their insight into the social construction of gender with the material production of what the new home economists called 'household use values'.

Berk argues following Erving Goffman (1977), that the partners in the household have gender identities that are the products of their socialisation. The theory of socialisation is well known in sociology, but as in Goffman's other work, the adoption of gender identities is not seen as a direct determinant of patterns of behaviour. Instead, roles are used in a 'dramatological' sense, as the basis for the ongoing construction of behaviour according to the prevailing circumstances and people encountered. But, to combine this with the materialist elements in the NHE of Becker, Berk shows how we must see the production of use values (i.e. household work, paid income) as just one side of the productive process. At the very moment that individuals in the household clean the sink, Hoover the floor, or more importantly negotiate who will do the task, they are also reproducing cultural conceptions of gender behaviour (or their perceived notion of 'proper' behaviour) and at the same time producing new ones. Their actions are not as Goffman (1977, p303) supposed displays of set gender activities, but more fluid interpretations. As West and Zimmerman (Quoted Berk 1985, p202.) state:

> .... gender displays pay homage to cultural conceptions of proper relationships between the sexes rather than as Goffman (1977, p71) notes, literally depicting them....Gender display....must be understood then, as a stance toward the conventions applicable to it rather than a precise predictor of how an individual will act....We argue that....accomplishing gender....refers to the ongoing task of rendering oneself accountably masculine or feminine.

This is a big advance over the one dimensional theory of Richard Berk, but I think that it has one critical problem: the notion of the active construction of gender displays rules out the use of power and the possibility of conflict between partners. This is a criticism often made of the interactionist approach, especially by more conflict oriented sociologists (Sprey 1979), but we cannot ignore the constrained nature of some social relations and certain contradictions inherent in the nature of marital and household relations. Berk (1985) writes as if the gendered practices that spouses pursue are fairly superficial relations that are always open to negotiation. This is not always so, and thus we need to add this dimension to any models that seek to analyse patterns of household labour.

To conclude this section, it is plain that the human capital approach to household time allocation is useful in the way in which it conceptualises domestic work as productive, and powerful in its predictive framework. However, it is also stunted by its weak conceptualisation of the cultural factors that shape the division of labour in the household. Attempts to correct this, notably by Sarah Berk (1978, 1980, 1985) have improved this blind spot in the original theory, but have introduced their own problems in the form of a present oriented, structurally bereft conception of the household that cannot cope easily with notions of conflict and power. Although

18

material circumstances are important, what is needed is a theoretical framework that allows us to combine economic 'behaviour' with social 'action' in a cohesive whole that does not break into idealist and materialist pieces at the first sign of an empirical problem. In the next section of this chapter I will outline a new framework that can accommodate these requirements.

Toward a Usable Theoretical Framework

In this section I want to try to develop a theoretical framework that will allow us to develop some propositions for the chapters ahead. This framework will be a variant of what Robert Merton called theories of the 'middle range', a rather vague description, but which nonetheless describes what I am trying to do: to develop a theory of choice that can combine economic and cultural rationality and link this with the person's work and life history. The theory should be linked to a general theory of choice that combines scarcity/cost-benefit analysis with cultural/meaningful behaviour in a form that allows us to define empirically testable propositions, but should not attempt to explain the historical, institutional and structural forces that have shaped the cultural perceptions or economic conditions that social actors make these choices within. Although very interesting and extremely important, these macro-level forces are well beyond the range of this book. In the last section I suggested that SEU theory could be used as the basis from which to build a theoretical position. The existing theory could be supplied with a new set of auxiliary assumptions that would then allow the 'plasticity' model of cultural choice to be added to the scarcity-based model. Just such a new set of assumptions have been put forward by Lindenberg (c.f. Lindenberg 1985, 1986, 1989) in the form of what he has called the 'discrimination model of probabilistic choice and framing' (Lindenberg 1989). In this section I want to describe this model and then explain the relationship of this model to the NHE theory of the household and put forward some specific propositions that can be tested in the chapters to come.

The main difference between the existing SEU theory and Lindenberg's discrimination model is the abandonment of the assumption that the individual is able to discriminate as many aspects and objects in the choice situation as the researcher feels is necessary. Thus, we are going to a model that sees actors as having bounded rationality. In Lindenberg's formulation, the discrimination model, unlike the value theory of choice and SEU theory, has four stages. In the first, as in SEU theory, the actor distinguishes between different courses of action and assigns to each of these a utility index in a transitive preference schedule. But, unlike SEU theory, the new model posits that people cannot distinguish between more than one main maximand at a time (i.e., they can only maximise along one dimension at any one time). This could be for a number of different reasons (e.g. span of attention, cognitive limitations), but is really an 'as if' clause that lets us introduce the first part of a more realistic model that includes cultural factors: the maximand is part of a 'frame' of the situation that defines what alternatives will be selected and the acceptable outcomes per alternative. The frame consists of a 'situational goal' and 'goal criteria' (Lindenberg 1989, p188) by which the outcomes of different courses of action can be judged according to the degree to which they have realised the situational goal. This is all beginning to sound a little parsonsian in its terminology, but we can see the idea of 'frames' as a logical clarification of the mainstream sociological idea of the importance of the 'definition of the situation'. Unlike economists, sociologists see the context and meaning given to a situation by the actors involved as crucial for understanding their behaviour and the idea of frames gives us a route to include these in our empirical models. To give a, perhaps overly simplistic example, we could view a man's 'frame' of himself as 'breadwinner' in the household as his situational 'goal' that he wants to be attained, and that the degree to which this is accomplished can be judged by the amount of paid work that his partner does in the labour market. These are the goal criteria, but they do not order the outcomes to the lowest overall costs incurred in attaining the goal (as would be stipulated by the assumption of unbounded rationality in SEU theory) such as the lost earnings of his partner relative to her productivity in the home (and thus lower standard of living for him) or more psychic outcomes such as her boredom and dissatisfaction. But, although these costs may not influence the definition of the choice situation, they will affect the choice of the means of attaining the goal, e.g., to minimise the opportunity costs of the female partner not working, but retaining his breadwinner role, he may persuade her that a better alternative is that she work part time.

The second stage of the model is identical to that of SEU theory: the actor will evaluate (or act as if to....) each of the alternatives and outcomes and assign each a probability of its occurrence. By summing the expected values per alternative the actor arrives at a subjective expected utility (value) index for each. The third stage of Lindenberg's model, on the other hand, differs markedly from SEU theory. Whereas in SEU theory, the third stage is a simple matter of the actor choosing the alternative with the highest subjective expected utility, in the Lindenberg model, they are expected to choose each alternative with a certain probability that is a function of the degree to which the individual discriminates between the alternatives. This sounds complex, but is in essence very simple. Moreover, it is the conceptual path through which we can enter cultural plasticity into the model that we are developing. If we go back to our example of the man whose main goal, or frame is to be the household breadwinner then he must decide upon the best alternative for attaining this goal. In assessing the alternatives and outcomes available, the man looks to find the alternative with the highest net utility compared to others, but this discrimination is weighted by a factor that indicates the individual's sensitivity to the difference at a particular moment. This weighting is the 'situational salience' of the main goal. What does this situational salience depend upon? According to Lindenberg's theory (1989, p188) it is the 'background' aspects of the situation that the actor brings to the context. Our man has to decide whether the costs of persuading his wife to stay at home and be a full time housewife are bearable given his own salary and their living standards. But, the level of cost that he is willing to bear will depend highly on the strength of his beliefs about the proper work roles of men and women. If the costs of living rise, or the household's (or individual's within it - though more of this later) tastes become more expensive, we can be sure that the decision will be assessed again. Likewise, we could expect that if the man receives social approval from his friends or family for his partner staying at home rather than working, then this will increase the motivational force of the situational goal, or frame.

Thus, as the situational salience of the goal decreases, the choice probability of the frame moves toward non-discrimination and vice versa. As the choice probability of the frame moves toward non-discrimination, we enter the fourth stage of Lindenberg's model. Here, the frame itself is evaluated and possibly replaced with another if the person can no longer discriminate between the alternatives that they face and the goal is no longer very useful for structuring the situation. In this situation, other types of frames may rise from the background characteristics to replace the existing one. But, since the salience of the old frame was small, it is likely that the most prominent background characteristic is a negative one (since it has pushed the existing frame towards non-discrimination). In this situation, Lindenberg states that the frame switch hypothesis is thus: when the choice probability approximates non-discrimination, the most prominent negative background aspect will become the new frame.

Thus, to go back to our fictitious example again, our potential or existing breadwinner may find that his concerns with the cost of his partner not working are now of equal weight to his beliefs that he really should be the main breadwinner, especially because in the community in which his partner and himself live has experienced an increasingly high level of male unemployment, but a growing level of female employment, which means that many of their friends and kin already live in households where the woman is the only wage earner. Recent years have also seen the rise of an attitude in the media and among some of their friends that it is fine for women to work if there are no small children in the house, so her working would not reflect on his ability to provide for a family (they have teenage children). In this situation of non-discrimination, the most prominent negative background aspect, that of a change in peoples' expectations of women (and indirectly men) becomes the main frame of reference, the definition of the situation that replaces that of the man as breadwinner.

We seem to have a way of entering cultural variables into our model of individual choice that still allows us to predict changes in behaviour if given changes occur in the relative prices/costs of other (notably more economic) variables. But how does this new theory fit in with the NHE theory that I outlined in the previous section of this chapter? The answer is that in some respects, very easily. As remarked upon earlier, the NHE thesis is based upon the SEU theory of choice from which the Lindenberg model is derived. Thus, the assumptions we have put forward can all sit easily with the economic rationality of the theory. The only problem is that, as Becker found, the NHE model of the household needs to assume that the household only has one utility, or production function. I criticised this heavily in an earlier section for its assumption that the head of the household always has the utility of others in the household in mind when making choices, but the problem arises as to how the household can be said to be coherent if we discard this assumption. In the example I used to illustrate the discrimination model I glossed over the role of the female partner in the decision process about whether she should work outside the home. Yet, the interaction of partners is of vital importance if we are to develop a usable sociological theory of the household division of labour. Our theoretical framework needs to encompass the power processes through which individual partners can shape household practices in their interests and to do this we need to include the individual utility curves. This is especially important if compliance is asked of one by the other. However, we need not fall into the situation that Becker, or the exchange theorists fell into, i.e. that the model becomes unworkable because individual maximisation inevitably leads to conflict between members of the household since we have given our models of choice production functions that can include social goods (i.e. they are social production functions). I am not suggesting that our models imply automatic harmony in household decision making (individual utility functions mean interests can diverge), but since actors can share the same beliefs about such social objects as the proper roles of men and women, they have the basis for a shared, 'social' basis of organisation, rather than an exchange relationship. Such a change to the NHE theory would entail a reworking of the logical structure that Gary Becker (1976) has put forward to include the possibility that partners could disagree about alternative courses of action (which I do not attempt to do here). This would also mean that the models would have to incorporate the differential amounts of leverage that partners could exert upon one another in this eventuality, but the model assumes actors have formed utility functions that can admit culturally formed ends.

Thus, unlike the value theory of choice that underpinned the resource or social exchange models of behaviour, or the less explicit model of dependency and patriarchy, we can model economic and cultural variables at the same time in an environment where economic rationality and cultural expectations mix at the same levels of importance. This sounds very promising, but where do these cultural variables actually come from? Are we just going to accept them as homogenous social facts that can be factored into the model? To do so would take us back down the path toward the determinist models that I have been criticising in this chapter. This is not a wise choice of route thus I suggest we make a conceptual jump: we need to take respondents past experiences and histories far more seriously since they provide us with what Gershuny (1994) has called a 'recursive model' of how people acquire the economic and cultural capital that shapes their approaches to such areas as the division of domestic labour. This is a very general statement, but it is important to realise that respondents past work and life histories are the key to an empirical application of cultural variables within a 'discrimination model'. Indeed, it is the second argument of this chapter that it is impossible to get an empirical hold upon the rationality that underpins certain choices without this approach.

What we see when we examine a person's work and life history are the socially structured 'rules and resources' (Giddens 1978, 1979, 1984) with which, and through which they now construct their lives. Although I have criticised Parsons' (1951) value theory of social action, his major insight was that people share (normative and motivational) cultural frameworks because they have shared experiences. This is very commonsensical, i.e. if people share the same social circumstances and cultural milieu they have the same experiences. But, whereas Parsons' saw this process as being grounded in the idea of 'internalisation' (via Freud and Durkheim), if we want to avoid determinism we have to see the process as grounded in social and linguistic reflexivity, an idea arrived at independently by Mead, Wittgenstein, and Heidegger. People are reciprocally (reflexively) linked through these experiences because they have similar expectations of each other and similar habits and tastes. Moreover, an argument could be made that this process leads to different nominal systems through which categories of objects (both natural and social) are defined and choices prioritised. This argument is less sure than the main one I am making, but would be interesting to develop since it would use many of the recent theories that have emerged from the sociology of science and epistemology to restructure the SEU assumption that subjective probabilities must be linear factors of objective probabilities. If we get back to the main argument, it is possible to describe the discrimination theory of frames in the mainstream language of both economics and sociology. In economic jargon, people who come from similar socio-economic circumstances or social groups share the same preference structures and social production functions. As Lindenberg states (1989, p190):

> *Where 'tastes' in economics are assumed as given in any situation and where 'values' are assumed as the product of socialisation in the past, instrumental goals are*

rationally connected to higher level goals given the constraints of the situation. In technical terms: utility functions turn into social production functions (c.f. Lindenberg 1986) and there is nothing idiosyncratic about production functions.

In sociological jargon, people share the same 'habitus' (Bourdieu 1990), 'life-world' (Schutz 1972) or 'index' (Garfinkel 1967) and this limits the indeterminacy of interactional or choice situations. Thus, in interaction and negotiation, people will define the situation in a similar manner and in choice situations they will want similar outcomes. This is not to say however that their interests in those choices will always coincide, but at least conceptually we have circumvented Becker's problem of having to have only one utility function. As Lindenberg states we have moved from 'man the role player' or 'man the consumer' to 'man the innovative producer'.

Although we cannot know the relationship of cultural variables to choices *a priori*, by empirical study we can seek to establish relationships between past experiences and present attitudes/behaviour. We can see peoples 'frames' as the outcome of experiences at various stages of peoples lives that shape the persons perception of specific objects (goals), or ranges of objects in their lives and thus lead them to follow certain choice paths or activities that only change when the pressure, or 'salience' of another frame becomes irresistible. In terms of this book, we could see individuals choices about how much and what kind of domestic work as the outcome of previous experiences or 'frames' and/or the interaction of different frames between partners. Chapter four will examine the relationship between attitudes or 'frameworks' as we have come to talk about them and the behaviour of individuals and chapter six will examine more closely the relationship of frames to work and life history. With these conceptual changes, we can find a way to combine the cultural insights of sociologists into the importance of systems of meaning with the scarcity based, cost benefit analysis of the more empirically applicable rational choice and social exchange theory. In this way we can begin to analyse patterns of behaviour as probabilistically structured by a number of interacting factors, rather than determined by cultural values and economic imperatives.

Some Empirical Propositions

What propositions can we raise from the theoretical discussion we have had in this chapter? First of all, according to the NHE theoretical model of the way that households allocate labour time to paid and unpaid work, we should see a relationship between the paid work contributions of the partners and their unpaid work time contributions. Where one partner contributes a higher level of their time to paid work than the other partner, there should be a reciprocal increases in the other partners domestic work time. Time use should also be affected by the relative costs of the partners time in terms of foregone earnings in the labour market and this effect should become more pronounced the larger the difference between the partners incomes (and thus the marginal cost of another period of time spent in paid work). It may be that the NHE model is a sufficient as well as necessary model of the processes that underlie the division of domestic labour, but if not (as I suspect), we should see partners attitudes having a definite effect on the division of unpaid work. Simplistically, we should see more 'traditional' attitudes on behalf of the partners leading to the woman doing a greater proportion of the domestic work, but where the woman has untraditional attitudes these will not be as good predictors of actual practices as the man's attitudes. Using our discrimination model of 'framing' we should see men's' attitudes toward unpaid work as good predictors of their take up of domestic work and thus to a certain extent the woman's attitudes should be effective through the man's attitudes, since the decision to change behaviour would be the man's, but this may be prompted by the woman's influence. It is likely that the partners' attitudes in the present will bear the mark of their past experiences. Thus, partners' that come from households where the mother had a paid job and/or where domestic labour was divided in more untraditional patterns will tend to exhibit more untraditional attitudes. In the same way, women who have worked in the labour market will have more untraditional attitudes than those that have not and we should see this feed into their attitudes on, and behaviour in the domestic division of labour. If attitudes are linked strongly to the woman's proportion of the domestic division of labour, then we should also see relations between her proportion of domestic work, her attitudes and her satisfaction with unpaid work. Thus, attitudes will act either as buffers between high proportions of domestic work and dissatisfaction or precipitates between more average proportions and dissatisfaction. That is to say, her proportion of domestic work will be refracted through her 'frame' through which she sees men and women's proper work roles.

This chapter has described a theoretical approach to the study of the domestic division of labour that should allow us to provide better explanations for the patterns in the data that will become evident in the next chapter. Rather than attempting to create a theory that can explain everything, but cannot generate specific predictions of its own, we have developed a 'theory of the middle range' that has generated specific hypotheses that we can now go on to examine empirically.

Notes

[1] This is not to say that Pahl was not aware of the potential conflicts that could occur within households over the domestic division of labour (see Pahl and Pahl 1971); just that, like others in this period, his concern was with the overall 'household strategy' in use (which implicitly included debate within the household).

[2] Moreover, domestic work is seen as being a source of disutility, and thus partners who have greater power will compel those with less power to undertake these tasks, or in the language of the theory, will 'buy out of it'. Ferree (1976, 1980) has shown that this is an unjustified assumption (she found that many people do housework quite willingly and get satisfaction from it).

[3] This approach is very similar to that adopted by Pahl (1984) in the UK. Unfortunately, Pahl never attempted to spell out the theory underlying his study explicitly.

[4] I will return to this point later in connection with the lack of institutional and normative effects in the division of housework in the new home economics.

[5] New assumptions for SEU theory have transformed it into 'prospect theory' (Kahneman and Tversky 1979) and 'discrimination and framing theory' (Lindenberg 1989).

2 Measuring the Household Division of Labour

The data used in this book come from the Social Change in Economic Life survey. The SCELI survey was funded by the Economic and Social Research Council (ESRC) and was carried out in two phases, the first in 1986 and the second a year later. Its major objectives were to study the nature and determinants of employer labour force policies, the character of and direction of change in worker experiences of employment and the labour market, the changing dynamics of household relations and the impact of changes in the employment structure on social integration and social stratification in the community. The research was carried out in six urban labour markets selected to provide contrasting labour market conditions: Aberdeen, Coventry, Kirkcaldy, Northampton, Rochdale and Swindon. The data used in this book to analyse the domestic division of labour were collected as part of the second wave of SCELI interviews conducted in 1987. At the end of the interview, the members of the household were asked if they would keep a diary of their time use for the following week. In this chapter, I will outline the problems associated with measuring and using this type of data, and describe the structure of the data from the SCELI survey.

If we want to analyse the balance of activities between household members, we need to obtain measures of their time use, and/or the allocation of household tasks. Past research has usually used either task or time as the metric of measurement, but as Berk (1985) has shown, the type of measure used has important consequences for our understanding of, and explanations for the dynamics involved in the division of household labour. In gathering evidence on time use, the standard approach has been to ask respondents to estimate the amount of time they devote to a number of broadly defined categories of household activities (e.g. Szalzai *et al* 1972; Meissner *et al* 1975; Walker and Woods 1976; Robinson 1977), whereas in collecting evidence on task allocation, respondents are asked list who does what task and (though not always) how often they do it (e.g. Blood and Wolfe 1960; Bahr 1974; Oakley 1974; Berk and Berk 1978). However, it was not until Berk's studies of household labour (1978, 1985) that the issue of what was measured was examined in detail. The crucial question is: how do household members make sense of the activities which we generally call domestic, or housework work? I will return to the more fundamental question of what respondents regard as 'housework' shortly but, for the moment, assuming household members, both individually, and as a group have some notion of what domestic work is, how do they make sense of their own and others contributions? It is useful at this point to quote Berk (1985, p40) at length on the difference between these two metrics

....[T]hrough the metric of the task, households may first establish the degree to which they will invest in household labour and then may exercise the mechanisms by which they may ordinarily apportion that labor. In other words, through the unit of the task, household members determine what has to be done and who will do it. However, when the mix of household tasks is "added up" to reflect overall effort, the implications that tasks carry for expenditures of time may become crucial. Based on a sense of time costs, for example, some members of a household may decide to undertake some tasks less frequently because they simply take "too much time". Moreover, household

members may allocate tasks to one another, but some members may never undertake particular tasks requiring time that they are unable or unwilling to give.

Berk makes it clear that there may be both 'rule of thumb' and more rationalised, cognitive processes at work that may only be describable using the different metrics of task and time. Thus, we could view *'time'* spent doing domestic work (whatever we, or the respondents come to define it as) as an abstracted category of 'input' that respondents are aware of, but, the *task* may remain the conceptual unit through which the work is originally defined and allocated (Berk 1985, p40).

Irrespective of the metric used, the usual research procedure used to obtain the data is to ask respondents to make an estimate of their time spent doing a particular activity in a certain period and/or whether they perform a task, and if so, how often. Although respondents may know quite accurately which tasks they do, the same may not be true of the number of times that they do it a week, and is certainly not true of the time they spend doing it. As Gershuny (1992, p5) has stated

> *We have (in general) no reason to know the quanta of time we devote to particular activities. Such knowledge is (in general) of no practical use in daily life. With some very specific exceptions, neither we ourselves nor anyone else needs to know the total hours devoted to particular purposes over a given period. Nor would it be easy for us to maintain such running total estimates of time use. For precisely which categories of activity would we maintain the totals? Over which sort of period? .... Simply: time allocation is not a natural category of self-knowledge.*

There is obviously a strong risk in using this type of respondent estimated methodology that the resultant data will be distorted, if only because it is not a natural category of self-knowledge. Another factor that may lead to such distortion has been outlined by Arlie Hochschild in her book *The Second Shift* (1990). Hochschild spent a year with ten families in the United States examining the ways in which they organised their domestic labour and found an effect that she labelled 'the family myth'. 'The myth' was a systematic misrepresentation of household practices by and to the family members themselves, which allowed arguments about who does or should do what to be disguised from the protagonists. Hochschild derived the concept of the family myth from the work of the psychotherapist Antonio Ferreira (1967) who saw it as a reaction to the cognitive dissonance felt by individuals who were using practices contrary to their own attitudes. As such, it is debatable whether such myths would be successful in stanching conflict between partners if their myths shielded a difference of attitude as to how they should organise their lives (important for the chapters to come), but it would have an effect on the reported division of labour in the household. The effect of the 'family myth' and the more general inaccuracy of time and task frequency estimates casts doubt on the validity of past research which has used these methods (e.g. Szalzai *et al* 1972; Meissner *et al* 1975; Walker and Woods 1976; Robinson 1977). An alternative method that has been used before (e.g. Pleck 1985; Berk 1985) and which is used in this book is to get respondents to keep a diary of their activities for a set period. Diaries would seem to offer a more 'natural' way to get access to the quantity of time people spend on particular activities because they offer a structure within which respondents can log their time use. Although diaries have been used before to obtain data on the domestic division of labour, the SCELI data set is unusual in that it has diaries from both the male and female respondents of the household for a full week. Thus, Berk (1985) had data from wives for a 24 hour period, but not for husbands and

Pleck (1985) had data from both respondents, but only for four 24 hour periods (one Saturday, one Sunday and at most two week days) spaced over a year. These methodological compromises meant that Berk was forced to rely upon husbands estimates of the number of times that they performed certain household tasks whilst Pleck had to construct a 'synthetic week' from the days sampled (the sample was made up of 136 'couples' which formed under one half of the total sample used, the rest being derived from another sample that asked respondents to estimate their household time). Diaries do however generate a particular form of systematic bias (Gershuny 1994). From the diaries returned as part of the SCELI survey, it is clear that most respondents with jobs class all time spent at the workplace as 'time at work' in their diaries. They tend not to log the tea and coffee breaks or lunch breaks that they have during the day, whereas those recording unpaid work in the home do. This leads to a systematic overestimation of the time devoted to paid work as opposed to unpaid work. As women tend to do more unpaid and part time work (and the number of rest breaks is proportional to the hours of paid work), the data will have a tendency to underestimate women's total work time relative to men's.

A more fundamental question that affects any research into the balance of activities within the home is: what do respondents actually regard as domestic work? The previous discussion on the difference in metrics of task and time suggested that respondents conceptualised their own and their partners efforts, primarily through the allocation of tasks. But do we distinguish 'housework' tasks from 'non-housework tasks'? When, for instance does shopping for oneself or the household as a housework task become 'non-work', or playing with the children become 'leisure' instead of 'childcare'? This problem is all the more troubling because it has immediate theoretical implications. As stated in chapter one, the new home economic approach of Schutz (1974) and Becker (1981) holds that work and leisure are inextricably combined in all human activities and thus it is impossible to differentiate between 'productive' and 'leisure' activities[1]. Chapter 1 also argued that such a theory assumes that there are no inequalities in the allocation of work or the distribution of resources which is patently not so. Defining what housework is, is therefore extremely important if we are to explain why these inequalities occur.

There are three main answers which have appeared in the literature, the first two theoretical and the third more empirical. John Robinson (1977) has put forward a typology for dividing household labour from leisure which uses both the social context in which activities are carried out and the intrapsychic states (i.e. how they feel about doing the activity) of those doing them. Robinson gathered retrospective data on time use and asked respondents to specify how pleasant they found each activity. This measure alone was not sufficient to differentiate domestic work from leisure because

> ....certain parts of what we include under homemaking are found to be extremely pleasurable and rewarding.....

Thus, Robinson used a theoretical device of whether he thought that a specific task was 'obligatory' or not as the final arbiter of his definition. An activity was 'obligatory' if, even though enjoyed at the time of doing it, it still 'had to be done'. The problem is that different people have different ideas about 'what has to be done' to ensure the smooth running of a home (as anyone who has flat-shared will testify to), therefore what this definition actually reverts back to is John Robinson's own feelings about how he would like to run his home.

Following Becker's research, many economists became uneasy with the lack of distinction between productive and leisure activities and began arguing for a distinction based upon the principle of 'surrogate-impossibility'. In the work of Gronau (1977), 'productive' domestic work is different from 'leisure' if there are 'market substitutes' (or surrogates) available. A similar, though better-stated principle is offered by Hawrylyshyn (1977)

> An economic activity of an individual is one which may be done by a third person
> (generally hired at a market price) without affecting the utility value returned to the
> individual.

Domestic Work becomes 'work', according to this principle, if in paying someone else to do it the individual loses the utility of doing the task themselves. Although this definition seems quite tractable in empirical research, it does imply that we need to know quite a lot about the internal states of the individuals involved if we are to be sure that they would invoke a market substitute if available. That being said, it is probably quite safe to assume that most day to day domestic tasks are of the 'market-substitutable' kind, and that only certain tasks such as playing with children and some domestic travel would be performed for their intrinsic psychic rewards.

Another, more empirical answer has been suggested by Gershuny (1992). Although his answer does have more than a whiff of tautology about it, Gershuny maintains that a definition of 'work' can be empirically derived by correlating different definitions (and thus totals) of work types for both partners with each other, and seeing which set covaries best. Thus, if we generate total minutes per week of paid work plus some 'core' domestic tasks for both the men and women in the sample, and then vary the tasks involved whilst performing the same statistical exercise, we will find the proper definition of work in the collection of tasks which covaries most highly between the partners. Gershuny freely admits that this type of definition assumes that partners practice what he calls an 'adaptive-partnership' (i.e. they respond to each others changing circumstances), which happened to be one of the theories he was to test when he had constructed a definition of 'work', but maintains that the procedure is more secure than using the 'surrogate-impossibility' principle alone.

Both these answers to the problem of defining what domestic work actually is have their drawbacks, but the market-substitution principle (or surrogate-impossibility principle) does seem to be the option with the fewest drawbacks, whilst being the easiest to operationalise. In the next section, I will describe the choices made in analysing the diary data derived from the SCELI survey.

The SCELI Diary Data

At the end of the second wave of interviewing in 1987, the primary respondent, or primary couple were asked to fill out a time use diary for seven days. A sample page from one of the diaries can be found in appendix (a). Each twelve-hour day was divided into fifteen-minute intervals, starting from 4am, within which diarists were asked to fill out their main activity, plus any other activities, who they were with and where they were (for the main activity). Diaries were distributed to both of the main respondents interviewed in the 1987 sample of households (the Household and Community survey or HCS) and to any other persons living as part of the household.

Unfortunately, due to the low and rather uneven return of these other diaries, I have chosen to use only those from the main respondents. For analysis, the variables derived from the individual diaries were combined to produce a multilevel data set of individuals, 'couples' and households with which the distribution and allocation of household work could be analysed.

Although, as was noted earlier, diary data are singularly suited to measuring the amounts of time that households devote to particular activities, they are costly to collect and suffer from low response rates. Thus, from the 1800 SCELI households (1200 'couples'), we obtain 520 couples (43%) who both returned diaries. In this book, I have taken the difficult decision to reduce the number of couples still further by only selecting those couples where both diaries contain no missing data at all, reducing the number of couples used in the main text to 387 (32%). Although worrying, this loss of data has been examined by Gershuny (1990), and shown to not produce substantial behavioural biases in the sample.

The Measurement of Task and Time

The diary data from the SCELI survey allows us to construct measures of both task and time use for both respondents in the sample of 387 households. In filling out their diaries, respondents had total freedom to describe their activities as they liked, but to transform these entries into usable data, the diaries had to be coded into groups of activities. The code frame to do this was constructed by Jay Gershuny and can be found in appendix B. After selecting those activities to be regarded as domestic work (of which more in a moment), it is a simple matter to perform a count of the number of 15 minute periods that an individual devotes to a particular activity and transform these into measures of time use.

In the last section, it was stated that the diaries allowed respondents to list activities, other than their main activity for each 15 minute period. Although there were never more than three entries in this supplementary activity column, their use is problematic. In this book I am interested, for the most part, only in the total time devoted to a particular activity, or group of activities, thus I have constructed two measures of time: the first is the total of the first, and thus main activity alone, and the second the total of all four possible activities.

Deriving a measure of the number and frequency of domestic work tasks performed is more complex than measuring the total time allotted to categories of activities. First and foremost we need to develop a concept of 'domestic work' - this is the subject of the next section. But, assuming we do have a definition, the problem then is how to divide the flow of activities (including the main and supplementary activities) into discrete 'tasks' that can be used empirically. My answer is to divide (using the categories in the next section) the four possible activities into four separate 'vectors' or strings of variables, starting from 4am on the Sunday diary to 3.45am on the following Saturday's diary (7 * 96=672 variables per vector) and then scan each vector for every variable (15 minute period) categorised as a domestic work task. If the variable was succeeded by another variables with the same code, the task continued into that next period, if not, the task ended and was logged as a single task. This method generated a number which represented the number of discrete tasks performed. A problem with this method is that it does not differentiate between a single, or small number of tasks being performed frequently, and a large number of tasks being

29

performed less frequently. To get round this, I used a similar methodology to count the number of different tasks being performed by each of the partners (irrespective of the number of times it was performed).

Table 2.1   Household and Community Survey (UK1987) Time Budget Coding Frames Devised By Jay Gershuny, University of Bath

Household Work Activity List

1. Food preparation
2. Baking, freezing foods, making jams, pickles, preserves, drying herbs
3. Washing up, putting away dishes
4. Making a cup of tea, coffee, etc.
5. Set table
6. Washing clothes, hanging washing out to dry, bringing it in
7. Ironing clothes
8. Making, changing beds
9. Dusting, hoovering, vacuum cleaning, general tidying
10. Outdoor cleaning
11. Other manual domestic work
12. Housework elsewhere unspecified
13. Putting shopping away
14. Repair, upkeep of clothes
15. Heat and water supply upkeep
16. DIY, decorating, household repairs
17. Vehicle maintenance, car washing etc.
18. Home paperwork (not computer)
19. Pet care, care of houseplants

20. (Other) tasks in and around the home, Unspecified
21. Tasks – unspecified
22. Feeding and food preparation for dependent adults

23. Washing, toilet needs of dependent Adults

24. Shopping for others
25. Fetching/carrying for others
26. Other care of adults
27. Doing housework for someone else (unpaid)
28. Care of adults –unspecified

29. Services for animals (e.g. animals to vet
30. Fetching, picking up, dropping off
31. Home paperwork on computer
32. Gardening
33. Everyday shopping, shopping Unspecified
34. Shopping for durable goods
35. Services for upkeep of possessions
36. Money services
37. Attending jumble sales, bazaars etc.
38. Video rental or return
39. Other service organisations or use (e.g. travel agents)
40. Accompanying adult or child (e.g. to doctor)
41. Shopping/services (travel to or from)
42. Care of others (travel)
43. Posting a letter
44. Knitting, sewing, dressmaking

Childcare

45. Feeding and food preparation for babies and children
46. Washing, changing babies and children
47. Putting children and babies to bed or getting them up
48. Other care of babies
49. Helping children with homework

50. Other care of children
51. Care of children and babies - unspecified

Using the two measures of task allocation, we can analyse whether this metric, as Berk holds, is the primary dimension along which domestic work is divided. On this basis we can then go on to see how the more 'abstract' measure of time use is allocated between households with partners in different occupational situations.

Conceptualising and Measuring 'Domestic Work'

Although, in practice, members of households must have some criterion according to which they define what 'domestic work' is, they would probably still not be able to define this to a researcher explicitly. In the absence of this information, the researcher has to apply some principle or method to derive a list of activities that can be measured and used for analysis. Most promising of the three already examined was the principle of 'surrogate impossibility', or 'market-substitutability'. Applying this, I have culled 44 activities from the list of 183 activities listed in the coding frame in appendix (b) as domestic work tasks. To this list I have added another 7 activities that I have classed as childcare making a full list of 51 activities (see table 2.1) that will be used in the forthcoming analyses.

Some Characteristics of the Sample

In this section I want provide a broad overview of the sample that I am using for analysis in the next three chapters. As well as giving outline statistics for certain characteristics of the sample of 387 households in this part of the book, I will also take a first look at the six measures I have already described as household labour (i.e. the main and subsidiary activity measures for the totals of time use and task allocation and the total number of different tasks).

To reiterate, the sample is of 387 households, but each case has variables for both spouses. Thus, I will provide descriptive statistics for the household as a whole and for each of the spouses. I use 'spouses' here and not 'partners' because the diary data sample is made up of married couples alone. As such, the sample is not representative of UK households as a whole (if a sample of 387 households could ever be representative of a country of 58 million people), a fact underlined also by the absence from the sample of any households from ethnic minorities. Nevertheless, the data set is of a high quality and is larger than those used in many other studies of this subject, though it too bears the marks of methodological compromise.

Table 2.2 presents a list of descriptive statistics for the sample of households and table 2.3 for the sample of husbands and wives. Looking first at the tenure characteristics of the sample, we see that over 75% of the sample own their own home. This figure is above the national average of 64% (Social Trends 1992) and that of the SCELI survey as a whole (56%). Such a figure may be partly explained by the class characteristics of the sub-sample.

In the SCELI sample as a whole, 24% of respondents are from the 'service class' (Goldthorpe 1980), whereas table 2.3 shows that in the sub-sample I am using this rises to 27% among the women and 37% among the men. If we use a dominance principle (Goldthorpe 1983) to derive a household class measure, 43% of households are from the service class.

Table 2.2 Some Household Characteristics of the Sample (N=387)

'Travel to work' Area	%	Highest Educational Qualification of the 'Head of Household'	%
Aberdeen	22.7	None	34.4
Coventry	10.3	Vocational	8.3
Kirkcaldy	19.6	O Level	25.8
Northampton	11.1	A Level	6.5
Rochdale	15.5	Non-Uni Higher Education	11.9
Swindon	20.7	University Higher Education	13.2

Housing Tenure	%	% with Children of Age:	%
Owner Occupier	75.2	None	31
Council Tenant	22	0 - 2 Years	18.9
Private Rent & Other	2.8	3 - 5 Years	15.8
		6 - 10 Years	19.4
		11 - 15 years	23
		16 - 20 Years	18.9
		21 Years Plus	7.8

Table 2.3 Some Characteristics of the Sample of Partners (N=387)

Wife		Husband	
Employment Status	%	**Employment Status**	%
Full Time	27.7	Full Time	87
Part Time	33.2	Part Time	0
Full Time Housewife	33.9	Full Time Housewife	7.3
Unemployed	5.2	Unemployed	5.7
Present Social Class (EGP)	%	**Present Social Class (EGP)**	%
Service	26.6	Service	37
Routine Non-Manual	25.3	Routine Non-Manual	8
Petty Bourgeoisie	2.8	Petty Bourgeoisie	8
Lower Tech. & Sup.	3.4	Lower Tech. & Sup.	8.3
Retail & Private Service	9.6	Retail & Private Service	0.8
Skilled Manual	10.3	Skilled Manual	17.1
Unskilled Manual	22	Unskilled Manual	20.9

	Mean	Std Dev.		Mean	Std Dev.
Age	39.3	10.6	Age	41.6	11.2
Earnings Per Month	£173.34	£196.65	Earnings Per Month	£544.15	£386.35

Since service class households are more likely than any other to own their home, it is not surprising that such a high proportion of service class households will lead to a high level of home ownership. Apart from being 'top-heavy' in structure, the class characteristics of the sample are fairly unremarkable.

Table 2.4 Descriptive Statistics of Partners' Work Time (N=387)

Wife's Work TIME (Minutes Per Day)
(MAIN ACTIVITY ONLY)

	Mean	Std Dev.	Minimum	Maximum
Unpaid	283.43	100.71	30	557.14
Unpaid + Childcare	325.68	125.56	30	720
Paid (all)	131.32	137.62	0	561.43
Paid (Employed Only)	203.93	117.19	0	525

Wife's Work TIME (Minutes Per Day)
(ALL ACTIVITIES)

	Mean	Std Dev.	Minimum	Maximum
Unpaid	350.91	123.1	51.45	805.71
Unpaid + Childcare	413.02	163.76	51.43	1030.71
Paid (all)	133.01	163.86	0	829.29
Paid (Employed Only)	206.19	118.74	0	525

Husband's Work TIME (Minutes Per Day)
(MAIN ACTIVITY ONLY)

	Mean	Std Dev.	Minimum	Maximum
Unpaid	143.59	94.91	2.14	482.14
Unpaid + Childcare	159.68	103.53	2.14	640.71
Paid	288.34	162.9	0	829.29

Husband's Work TIME (Minutes Per Day)
(ALL ACTIVITIES)

	Mean	Std Dev.	Minimum	Maximum
Unpaid	171.56	108.51	2.14	585.0
Unpaid + Childcare	196.19	125.93	2.14	820.71
Paid	290.69	163.9	0	829.29

Special mention must be made of the measure of highest educational qualification. Although a measure of highest qualification for both partners would be preferable, this was not available in the SCELI data set because only the main respondents in the 1986 survey were asked for their educational qualifications as part of the life history segment (not the partners). Luckily, it has been noted in a wide range of literature (Schultz 1974) that there is a high correlation between the educational qualifications of spouses, thus, in this book, I will use the highest qualification of the respondent as 'the household highest qualification' and thus a proxy for that of the partner.

Table 2.5 Descriptive Statistics of Partners' Work Tasks
(Total Number and Frequency) (N=387)

Wife's Work TASKS (Frequency & Total Per Week)
(MAIN ACTIVITY ONLY)

	Mean	Std Dev.	Minimum	Maximum
Unpaid	55.41	22.28	7	139
Unpaid + Childcare	65.87	32.01	7	200

Wife's Work TASKS (Frequency & Total Per Week)
(ALL ACTIVITIES)

	Mean	Std Dev.	Minimum	Maximum
Unpaid	69.84	30.68	10	187
Unpaid + Childcare	84.36	44.22	10	258

Husband's Work TASKS (Frequency & Total Per Week)
(MAIN ACTIVITY ONLY)

	Mean	Std Dev.	Minimum	Maximum
Unpaid	25.1	16.88	1	116
Unpaid + Childcare	28.55	19.75	1	130

Husband's Work TASKS (Frequency & Total Per Week)
(ALL ACTIVITIES)

	Mean	Std Dev.	Minimum	Maximum
Unpaid	31.7	21.46	1	142
Unpaid + Childcare	36.56	25.89	1	163

Household Members Market and Household Labour

Table 2.4 presents the mean, standard deviation, minimum and maximum values for the total time male and female partners spend on unpaid domestic work and paid work per week. Similarly, table 2.5 displays the same information for measures based upon the total number of tasks multiplied by the frequency with which they are carried out each week and table 2.6, the total number of different tasks performed each week.

Table 2.6 Descriptive Statistics of Partners' Work Tasks
(Total Number)

Wife's Work TASKS (Total Per Week)
(MAIN ACTIVITY ONLY)

	Mean	Std Dev.	Minimum	Maximum
Unpaid	11.93	3.25	3	24
Unpaid + Childcare	13.83	4.2	3	30

Wife's Work TASKS (Total Per Week)
(ALL ACTIVITIES)

	Mean	Std Dev.	Minimum	Maximum
Unpaid	13.12	3.6	4	25
Unpaid + Childcare	15.3	4.66	4	31

Husband's Work TASKS (Total Per Week)
(MAIN ACTIVITY ONLY)

	Mean	Std Dev.	Minimum	Maximum
Unpaid	8.03	3.25	1	19
Unpaid + Childcare	9.16	4.02	1	26

Husband's Work TASKS (Total Per Week)
(ALL ACTIVITIES)

	Mean	Std Dev.	Minimum	Maximum
Unpaid	9.07	3.69	1	22
Unpaid + Childcare	10.4	4.6	1	27

As already explained, all the variables can be split according to whether they include childcare time, and/or whether they are derived from the one or four activity measures (i.e. one main activity and four subsidiary activities).

Before discussing the individual measures themselves, it is first necessary to look at the difference between the one and four activity measures. Just as the difference between the metrics of time and task can change one's perception of the dynamics of the household, so too could the number of activities counted when assessing work time and task. It could be for instance, be that men's domestic work is as intensive as women's, if we take the second, third and fourth activities into account along with the first (and primary). Table 2.7 lists the female partner's proportion of the three metrics (time/number different tasks and frequency/number of different tasks) and presents their characteristics when only the primary activity is counted, or all four possible. What is immediately obvious that there is very little difference between the one and four activity measures for any of the metrics. The four activity measures do have smaller standard deviations and higher minimum values, but the difference is negligible.

Table 2.7 Mean Wife's Proportion of Domestic Work Time/Tasks for Selected Variables (N=387)

Variable (All Exclude Childcare)	Mean %	Std .Dev.	Minimum	Maximum
Wife's % of Total H/W Time - Main Activity	68	16	7	99
Wife's % of Total H/W Time, - All Activities	68	15	12	99
Wife's % of Total H/W Tasks (No. & Frequency) - Main Activity	69	16	9	98
Wife's % of Total H/W Tasks (No. & Frequency) - All Activities	69	16	11	98
Wife's % of Total H/W Tasks, - Main Activity	60	11	22	94
Wife's % of Total H/W Tasks - All Activities	60	11	27	94

On the basis of these results it seems sensible to use the one activity (main activity) measure alone in the coming chapters. Since the only real difference is in the standard deviations of the variables, it would be slightly more revealing statistically, to use the single activity measure.

Husband's and Wife's Market Work Time

Going back to table 2.4, we can see that wives devote, on average, 131 minutes per day to paid work (main activity measure) which is about 15 hours per week (all of the diary measures were divided by 7 to give daily totals). This relatively small figure is the result of including all wives, thus table 2.4 also presents summary statistics for the 235 employed wives alone. With only employed wives included, the average number of minutes per day spent in market work rises to 204 or about 24 hours per week, but the standard deviations are large, suggesting that there is much variation in the amount of time wives spend in market work.

Since 87% of all the men in the SCELI diary sub-sample are employed full time, I have presented the summary statistics for the sample as a whole. As such, we can see that men spend an average of 288 minutes in paid work per day, or 34 hours per week. It is immediately obvious that husbands devote more of their time to market work than wives, but as I will go onto show, it is easy to show where wives spend their time.

Husband's and Wives' Domestic Work Time

Table 2.4 also presents the measures of domestic work time. If we concentrate on the measures using just the main activity, it is clear that on average wives spend far more time doing domestic work than their husbands, wives devoting 283 minutes per day to domestic work (326 with childcare) and husbands 144 minutes (160 with childcare). From these figures we can see that the wife does 68% of the domestic work on average. But, how is this average effected by the occupational status of the wife? Table 2.8 shows that if the wife is employed full time, her proportion of the domestic work falls to 62%, otherwise it increases (part time women perform 69%, full time housewives 70% and unemployed women 71%). Although interesting, such figures can be misleading. It is easy to assume that this decrease in the women's proportion of housework is the result of the husband increasing the amount of time he spends in domestic work, taking on the housework tasks that his wife can no longer perform.

Table 2.8   Partner's Total Domestic Time in Minutes Per Day, Excluding Childcare

| | Wife's Employment Status | | | |
	Full Time	Part Time	FT Carer	Unemp.
Wife	206	298	327	308
Husband	139	142	150	140
Wife's % of Total H/W Time	62%	69%	70%	71%
(N=387)	107	128	131	21

In fact, as table 2.8 shows, the relationship is quite the reverse. The husbands of women employed full time actually spend less time doing domestic work than those of full time carers. The husband's proportional increase comes from the wife's decreasing minutes spent in domestic work. As the third line in table 2.8 shows, although the total amount of time that the husband spends on domestic work falls, the more his wife works, this is more than compensated for by the decrease in the wife's domestic work time, thus increasing the husband's proportion of domestic time. It seems clear then that even in couples where both partners work full time, the wife does considerably more domestic work than the husband. However, it is important to remember that these statistics are aggregate and thus conceal differences between couples. For instance, even if we look at the husbands of women who work full time, the standard deviation for a measure of their total domestic work per day is 93 minutes with a mean value of only 139 minutes (excluding childcare). This shows the extent of variation in the sample of husbands (there is considerably less variation amongst wives. For example, amongst full time employed women there is a standard deviation of 80 minutes but on a mean of 206 minutes per day).

Husband's and Wives' Domestic Work Tasks

The picture that was just presented of partner's domestic work time is also fairly representative of the pattern of partner's domestic work tasks. Table 2.9 shows that the husband's number of different tasks and the frequency at which he does them remain almost the same, irrespective of his wife's occupational status, whereas the wife's task number and frequency falls the more market work she does. Although, in the measures of time that we have just looked at, those households where the wife worked full time spent less time in total, doing domestic work than households with wives in other occupational statuses, it was not clear whether this decrease in time was due to certain tasks not being done, or just having less time spent on them. If we look at table 2.9, it is clear neither hypothesis is true. There is only a difference of two tasks between the different types of households (i.e. two different tasks from table 2.1; P=.113), but a great deal more difference in the frequency with which these tasks are done (P<.001). Thus, it seems as if households that are devoting more time to paid work in the market still do the same number of different tasks, they just do them less often. Looking at table 2.9 though, it is not both partners who do the tasks less often, but the wife. Thus, in households where the wife works full time, she has a task frequency score of 42 against that of the full time housewife of 63.

Table 2.9   Partner's Total Domestic Tasks, Excluding Childcare

	Full Time	Part Time	FT Carer	Unemp.
	Female Partner's Employment Status			
Wife's Total No. & Frequency	42	58	63	61
Husband's Total No. & Frequency	25	25	26	20
Husband's % of Household Total	37%	29%	28%	25%
Wife's Total No. of Tasks	11	12	12	13
Husband's Total No. of Tasks	8	8	8	7
Husband's % of Household Total	41%	40%	40%	34%
N=387	107	128	131	21

In summary, the different measures of task and time follow similar patterns, in that the husband's contribution of domestic labour remains fairly static, irrespective of the occupational status of the wife and the wife's decreases the more paid work she is engaged in. But, as has already been noted, these findings are derived from aggregate, and moreover, single instance data which cannot represent changes that occur over time. It may be that husbands of full time employed women do not do more domestic work than those of full time housewives, but we cannot conclude from this that the men are not responding to the needs of the household as it changes from one status to another. Since we only have information from one point in time, such dynamic conclusions are not sustainable using these descriptive techniques. In later chapters we can get a better grip on these questions using other methods.

Notes

1 Households utilise market goods and services in combination with their own time to produce 'outputs'. Thus in the household economy, 'productive' domestic work outputs are not differentiated from 'non-productive' leisure outputs such as watching a video. They both combine a market commodity with income from market work and the partners available time.

3 A Preliminary Model of Partners' Time Contributions to Household Labour

In chapter one, I examined three theories which offered a framework within which to understand the dynamics of the household. Each lent itself to the creation of substantive hypotheses that could be tested with empirical data, but at the end of that chapter I suggested that, although flawed, the new home economic theory (NHE) was the best of the three because it conceptualised domestic work as a productive activity and specified the actual process through which everyday life is accomplished and work distributed in the household. This point is extremely important; whilst exchange theory and dependency theory do specify how domestic work will be allocated, this allocation is seen to be, in large part, the indirect effect of other processes such as the production of personal power or forms of dependency. Although I do not dispute that the household division of labour may in part be affected by the relative resources and power of the parties involved, we should still not be swayed from seeing domestic work as a productive activity that is organised by households so as to maximise the material resources available. As later chapters of this book will show, 'maximisation' can take on many forms depending on the past experiences, present circumstances, and therefore the rationality of the person concerned. Moreover (and as I will show), the person's 'power' over others may be a consideration whilst doing domestic tasks, but we still need to assume that people are, first and foremost, trying to do domestic work rather than producing power or dependency. As such, it seems better to use the assumption that households attempt to maximise in a specific (i.e. new home economic) fashion (as a heuristic device), and then invoke other hypotheses to explain why such maximisation might not occur, rather than assume from the outset that households are not primarily trying to produce their means of existence.

In this chapter, I want to present a selection of models derived from the NHE theory of such as Becker and Schutz to see if they can explain the division of domestic work in a sample of households drawn from the SCELI survey. As was stated above, we need to examine whether the theory's assumption of maximisation is adequate in empirical practice before going on to augment the basic theory with the more sociologically oriented hypotheses as outlined in chapter one. I must stress that this chapter is not a thoroughgoing 'test' of the NHE theory of the household. What I intend to do is to derive certain 'ideal-typical' predictions from the theory and then examine if and how the empirical findings diverge from these predictions. At the risk of pre-empting the findings of the chapter, I will show, using graphical models, that the base theory plus certain additions does not approximate the observed patterns closely enough to stand unaided. After this, I will then use a more thorough statistical model to back up these findings. Becker has stressed that only households 'at the margin' will truly maximise in the manner in which he has suggested, but we should still expect that if the theory has any substance in reality then it should at least approximate the observed patterns.

Defining a Model

Before presenting an empirical analysis of the utility of the NHE theory, we first need to establish the grounds upon which we can assess it. The central tenet of the NHE theory is that households will seek to find the best configuration of inputs (in terms of time and resources), given opportunity costs and productivity in their search for the greatest possible 'well-being'. It is important to remember that the 'greatest possible well-being' does not equal the 'greatest possible income' since the sources of well-being are household commodities, or combinations of market goods and services and household member's efforts. Put simply, the theory requires that in an optimal household, the ratio of the partners' (or all of the members of the household) marginal productivity within the household equals the ratio of their real, or foregone wages in paid work. Thus, if one partner is paid more per hour than the other it makes sense for this person to devote more time to the paid sphere and less time to unpaid domestic work, if on balance the marginal productivity of another hour of their time in paid work is greater than the marginal product of another in unpaid work (a ratio which is decreased if their partner is more productive at domestic work). Becker (1981, p17) takes this to mean that if members of efficient households 'have different comparative advantages, no more than one member would allocate time to both the market and household sectors', with the outcome that one member of the household will become a market specialist.

As explained in chapter one, the theory ultimately relies upon biology to explain why women have a comparative advantage in domestic work, and thus why men tend to be the market specialists. This argument has been given short shrift by most researchers, but even accepting that this is the male partner's role (i.e. following the assumptions of the theory), we should still expect to see some variation amongst women in the extent to which they invest in paid work time (and also amongst men). If so, this gives us a premise upon which to structure an assessment of the theory[1]. Given that the amount of time that the husband will spend on unpaid work is in part determined by the productivity of the wife in the paid sphere, we should see a relationship between the wife's paid work time (since there should be a high correlation between productivity in employment, investment in employment and time spent in employment), the husband's paid work time and the amount of time that he spends on domestic labour (Brines 1993). In essence, if depicted graphically, the relationship should look something like figure 3.1.

In figure 3.1, the four curved lines represent four levels of paid work time amongst husbands (still upholding the assumption that the husband is the market specialist), the lines moving upward from left to right from the point where the wife is a specialist in domestic work. Because the wife is seen to be a specialist in domestic work, there is relatively little difference (though there will be some difference) at this point between the amount of time that husbands of different paid work investments spend doing domestic work. The movement upward represents the predicted increase in the amount of domestic work that the husband does, as the wife does more paid work and his time becomes an efficient substitute for the wife's. The curve of the lines depicts the assumption that the husband's domestic work time yields increasing returns to scale the more his time, within the household, can substitute for his wife's. The rate of this substitution (and thus the curve) depends upon the husband's level of paid work time. For example, if the husband devotes relatively high amounts of time (and investment) in paid work, his productivity means that the point at which the wife's paid

41

work becomes an efficient substitute for his comes relatively later (and thus the line rises less steeply) than a husband who devotes less time to paid work.

Figure 3.1 Husband's Predicted Domestic Work Time

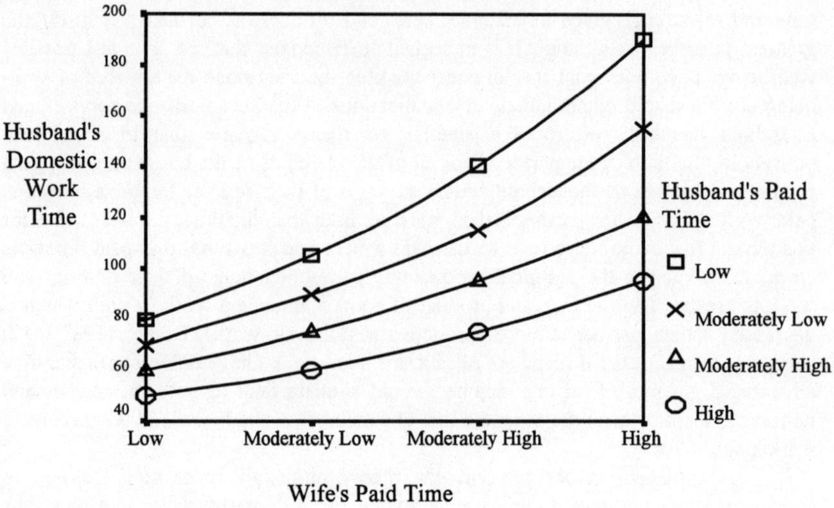

Wife's Paid Time

Defining an Empirical Model

The aim in this section is to construct a set of empirical models that match the restrictive assumptions laid out in the last. The advantage of the NHE theory of the household is its simplicity and the way in which it allows us to move from very parsimonious theoretical beginnings to complex outcomes through the addition of more subtle factors in the model. In this section I will present a 'conservative' examination of the theory using empirical data from the SCELI surveys so as to assess the limits of the theory. If at the end of this chapter there still seem to be important divergences between the predictions of the theory and the empirical evidence produced, then we can go ahead and examine the utility of the more sociologically oriented explanations for the empirical patterns that were outlined in chapter one. If, on the other hand, the theory seems to have some power in explaining the patterns that emerge, we will have to think seriously about incorporating its assumptions.

The first assumption we need to incorporate was proposed by Becker (1981). It holds that in an ideal-typical model of the household, the husband will always be the primary earner because of the comparative advantage that women have in domestic work. Thus, although he acknowledges that some couples will not conform to this economic imperative, he maintains that they are the exception (which is true) and that over time they will tend to move toward the norm of male primary market investor (which is hypothetical). This is a fairly strong assumption, thus whilst disagreeing with it in principle, it is necessary for the benefit of our 'conservative' analysis that the assumption be included. To do so I have included only those couples where the husband's income is equal to or greater than the wife's. Unfortunately, this reduces the sample of households from 387 to 345, but it is necessary if we are to examine the theory on its own ground.

Second, I have divided the wives' and husbands' paid time into quartiles so that the effect of greater investment on behalf of the wife in market work time on the time that the husband spends on domestic work is measured relative to other wives and husbands respectively. The first quartile for wives is thus that of the unemployed or non-employed wife. The differentiation is meaningless to the model initially because it assumes that demand factors force the potential wage up or down relative to the population of female workers as a whole. Each wife thus makes the decision to enter employment because of endogenous household factors (i.e. her relative productivity in the paid sphere as compared to her husband) in the light of the overall level of wages. To avoid complicating the analysis, I have not included childcare time in the models to be presented and have used, as stated in chapter two, a measure of domestic work based upon the main activity for each 15 minute period, rather than the four that were available. All of the analyses presented here were repeated using measures including childcare time, but its inclusion made no significant difference to the findings. Figure 3.2 depicts the mean observed minutes of domestic work that husband's do, per day, relative to their own paid work time and that of their wife.

Figure 3.2 Husband's Observed Domestic Work Time
(Primary Earner Husbands Only)

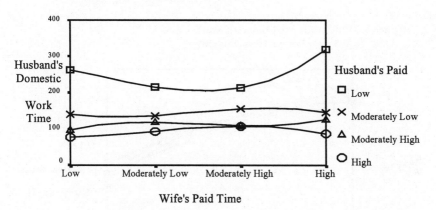

If we compare figures 3.2 and 3.1, it is clear that there is some relationship between the ideal-typical prediction from the theory and the empirical patterns observed. The level of the husband's domestic work time by his paid time quartile is ordered in the way predicted along the vertical axis with the lowest paid time quartile doing the most domestic work and so on. Moreover, the lines stay separated as we move from the left to the right and the wife does increasing amounts of paid work. But, the lines do not rise as expected as the wife does more paid work. Apart from the lowest quartile of husband's paid work, the lines stay fairly flat around the 80 to 120 minutes per day mark (1.3 to 2 hours per day), irrespective of the wife's paid work time. The line for the lowest quartile of man's paid time is interesting in the way that it

43

initially falls and then increases between the moderately high and high wife's paid time quartiles. Looking back to chapter two, the initial fall could well be the lower amount of domestic work carried out by men of full time wives compared to those with part time wives. The highest paid work quartile for wives' is defined as paid work over 231 minutes per day (all time measures are divided over 7 days), or approximately 27 hours per week. Part time work is defined in this book, and more generally, as under 30 hours per week. That the husband's level of domestic work time then increases was not evident from chapter two, though it does begin to approximate the predictions of the NHE theory. On the other hand, the fairly flat response of husbands from the other paid time quartiles to the increase in wives paid time does not seem to match the predictions of the theory.

If we look at the wife's level of domestic work time by both the husband's and her own paid work time, we should get a picture, if the predictions of the theory are true, that is something of a mirror image of figure 3.1, although the lines should be stacked in the opposite order. Figure 3.3 shows that there is some support, as in figure 3.2 for the theory. As predicted, the lines are ordered on the vertical axis with the wives of husbands in the highest paid work quartile at the top and the lowest quartile at the bottom. Apart from the second quartile, the lines also slope downward as the wife does more paid work, except for the second highest husband's quartile which rises first. Although all the lines start from higher up as predicted, there is not the same range as in figure 3.2, which indicates that the amount of domestic work that wives do is not overtly differentiated by the amount of paid work time that their husbands do.

Figure 3.3 Wife's Observed Domestic Work Time
(Primary Earner Husbands Only)

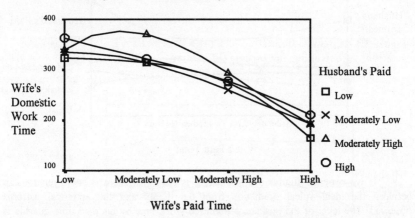

Wife's Paid Time

Looking at the evidence presented so far, it appears that the NHE theory gets some, though limited support in application. As predicted by the theory, it does seem that husbands are differentiated in the amount of domestic work that they do, according to their investment in paid work time. For wives, the amount of time spent on domestic work seems to be related to the paid work quartile of their husband, but the differentiation between wives of husbands in different quartiles is not large. These findings strongly suggest that the paid and unpaid work of partners within households are linked and reciprocal. This also means that we must see both the paid and unpaid work of partners as being to some extent endogenously determined. On the other hand, figure 3.2 showed that, although distributed along the vertical axis in the order predicted, the curve of all the quartile lines failed to rise as predicted when wives did more paid work. This departure from the ideal-typical seems to have a clear implication - husbands do not respond to the paid time of their wives by doing more domestic work. If so, and if the theory of maximisation cannot account for this, we will need to supplement it with more sociological hypotheses. However, if we look back to section two of this chapter, there may be other reasons why our analysis has failed to support the theory. So far we have assumed that the productivity of the partners in either the paid or unpaid sphere is integrally tied to their level of investment in each sector in terms of time. Thus, as we move along the horizontal axis and the wife does more paid work, it is assumed that she is more 'productive' because the theory demands that households would not allocate more labour time to this sector unless the marginal productivity of each hour made it worthwhile. In short, there is seen to be a high correlation between the time investments of household members and their relative productivities. But, need this be the case?

It may be that there are other factors that could intervene in this process of maximisation that would tend to militate against the husband doing more domestic work. One such factor is the difference that may exist between the marginal incomes of the partners. If the difference between the incomes of the wife and husband were sufficiently large it would have the effect of moving the point at which the husband would contribute more in domestic time further to the right. Thus, even though the wife was doing far more hours in the paid sphere, it would still not be optimally productive for the husband to divert more of his labour time to domestic work because

Figure 3.4 Husband's Domestic Work (Minutes Per Day)
Controlling for Income Difference
(Primary Earner Husbands Only)

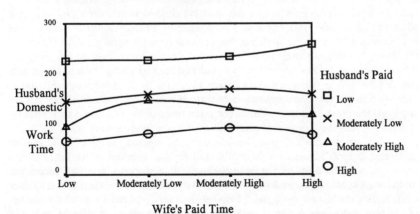

his marginal productivity in paid work was still higher than his wife's.

To analyse whether this is actually the case, we need to control for the effect of any difference in income between the partners on the husband's contribution to domestic work. To do this, I regressed the husband's time spent doing domestic work against a measure of the difference between the incomes of the partners, whilst controlling for the size of the total amount of domestic work done in the household as a whole (i.e. the sum of the husband and wife's time spent doing domestic work) and both partners' paid work quartiles. From this regression we can derive estimates of the husband's contribution to domestic work net of the effect of any difference in income[2]. Figure 3.4 depicts the mean fitted values for the regression. Looking at figure 3.4, it seems that controlling for income difference has several effects. First of all, it is clear that the procedure does not improve the similarity between the observed levels of husband's domestic work time, and those predicted by the theory. As in figure 3.2, the three highest quartiles of husband's paid work time stay fairly flat as the wife's paid time increases, but here, the same is true of the line for the lowest paid work quartile for husbands which remains flat (though from a higher intercept) sloping upward only slightly from the wife's fourth paid work quartile. What do these findings tell us? It is clear that the difference in the incomes of husbands and wives cannot account for the lack of change in husband's domestic work time as wives do more paid time. Yet, income did seem to be exerting some effect on the mean level of domestic work done by the lowest paid work quartile husbands. We should expect that without the effect of income difference, men would, *ceteris paribus*, do more domestic work (remembering that in all the households here the husband's income is greater than the wife's). In fact, the opposite seems to be the case since the slope of this line does not rise as depicted in figure 3.2. One explanation may be that the larger income of the fourth quartile wives of first quartile husbands actually exerted a positive effect on the domestic work of their husbands and thus when we control for income difference we lose this effect. That said, these results are only indicators of any effect, since we are not controlling here for the standard error of the sample as we will do at the end of the chapter.

A second factor that Becker (1981) has stated may have an effect on the husband's level of investment in domestic work time is the number of children that are present in the household. As expected, the rationale as to why this is so leans heavily upon the assumption of the biological advantage of women in doing domestic tasks. To reiterate, Becker holds (p98) that when there are children in the house, the biological advantage of the wife in nursing leads to it being more efficient for her to combine this nursing with other domestic work which happens to be in the same place. According to the theory, even if we exclude childcare work (as we have done so far) from the models, the quartile lines may not rise as predicted because young children are present and this has led to the wife's comparative advantage in domestic work increasing. There is also the subsidiary rationale here that the greater the number of children (of any age), the greater the commitment (or preference) of the household to producing children and thus the greater the specialisation by sex in different work roles.

We can examine both these hypotheses in the same way as the effect of income difference. Figures 3.5 and 3.6 depict the now familiar quartiles of the husband and wives paid work time against the mean husband's domestic work time, but controlling for the number of children under five in the household (figure 3.6) and the total number of children in the household (figure 3.5). As with figure 3.4, controlling for the number of children under five in the household or the total number of children does not increase the similarity of our empirical measures to the ideal-typical model of the NHE theory. In fact, both figures are almost identical and together add weight to the finding of figure 3.2 that husband's of wives who are working do not increase their time doing domestic work.

Figure 3.5 Husband's Domestic Work Time Controlling for
Number of Children (Primary Earner
Husbands Only)

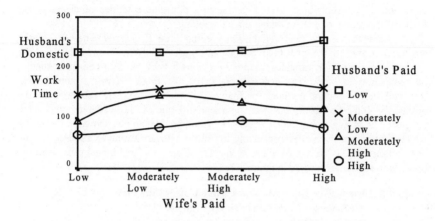

Apart from the difference of income between partners, number of children and number of children under five, Becker (1981) has also intimated that 'commodity substitution' may have an effect on the amount of domestic work that the husband

Figure 3.6 Husband's Domestic Work Time Controlling for
Number of Children Under 5 in the Household
(Primary Earner Husbands Only)

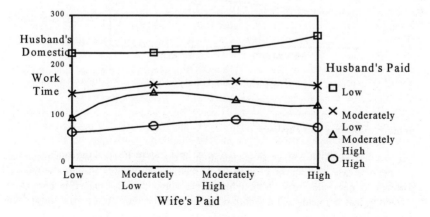

does. Thus, as the wife does more paid work, the household may 'buy in' the labour that was once supplied by the wife in the form of paid domestic help or the help of an unpaid relative. The household could also invest in technology to replace the labour power of the female partner. Most households already contain a selection of 'consumer durables' such as microwaves that might be seen as time saving devices, thus we cannot know whether these contribute toward the type of time use that households practice (although we do have a list of consumer durables that the household contains). However, the SCELI survey did contain questions on the use in households of paid domestic labour, or of domestic labour supplied from outside the household. These questions ask whether help is used in the core domestic activities of cleaning and hoovering, washing clothes, washing-up and cooking.

As with the previous variables, these did little to improve the 'fit' of the empirical model to the predicted picture of figure 3.1. When controlling for the commodity substitution variables, as in the previous figures, the four lines representing husband's unpaid work remained essentially flat. To finish off this section I have followed the procedure outlined for figures 3.4 to 3.6 to create estimates of the husband's domestic work, but this time entering all of the variables that were suggested as having a controlling effect. The resulting depiction is shown in figure 3.7 which shows that, even after controlling for all the relevant variables discussed in the last section, there is no improvement in the 'fit' of our graphical model relative to the predicted picture represented in figure 3.1.

**Figure 3.7 Husband's Domestic Work Time Controlling for
All Relevant Variables (Primary Earner
Husbands Only)**

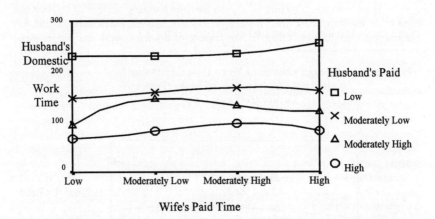

Some Preliminary Conclusions

The last section has presented an examination of the NHE thesis which suggests that the theory is not adequate as an explanation for how households allocate the time of partners to domestic work. Although analyses show that the theory is correct in predicting that husbands will do more domestic work, if they do less paid work (and thus have a lower marginal productivity in paid work), it is clear that men do not respond to their wives labour market time. Thus, although in figure 3.2, men in the lower paid work quartiles do more domestic work than men in the higher quartiles, each quartile line remains flat, even controlling for other factors, suggesting that husbands do not respond to increases in their partners paid work time (i.e. the lines do not rise from left to right as predicted in figure 3.1).

At this point such findings have to be taken as being preliminary since the models that have been presented so far do not permit us to reject the theory outright. The models have displayed the mean levels of husband's domestic work, without reference to the variation within each quartile. Each line may have a large standard error associated with it. Thus, it could be that our graphs happen to give us a poor grasp of the 'real' situation and that the NHE thesis is a good explanation for the patterns in the SCELI data set. Therefore, the next section presents a statistical analysis of the 'ideal-type' model which takes into account the variation in the sample and the standard errors associated with the predicted domestic work time of husbands.

Testing the New Home Economic Model of the Household

To test the NHE model more stringently we need to control for the factors that could make the graphical analyses misleading. To repeat, although the models presented so far give us a picture of the relationship between the spouses' paid work time and the domestic work time of the husband, the relationship is only depicted through the mean values of the husbands domestic labour time without reference to a standard error. Without a confidence interval around these means we cannot be sure that the predictions of the NHE are not met. A further and real test would be one that examined whether the assumption of the NHE thesis that male partners will respond to the paid time of their wives by doing more domestic work, is a better 'fit' for our data than a theory that did not make this assumption.

One way of doing this is to construct two statistical models that can be tested against each other: one that represents the NHE thesis and a more general model which does not assume a specific relationship between husband and wife's paid and unpaid work time. Whereas the NHE thesis includes specific assumptions about the nature of the relationship between the partners' paid work time and the husband's domestic work time, the more general model of the graphical analyses simply asserts that there is some interaction and leaves the nature of this relationship unspecified. If we find that the model that represents the NHE is not significantly different from the general model, or it is a significantly better fit, we have good evidence that our graphical analyses have been misleading us and that the assumptions of the NHE may indeed be true. If on the other hand the NHE model is a significantly worse fit than our general model we have evidence against the NHE thesis.

To do this I constructed two OLS regression models[3], listed below as model A and model B. Looking first at model A, we can see that the equation states the dependence of the husband's domestic work upon the partners' paid work time (βx and βz),the interaction of these two variables (βxz) and the marginal productivity of the husband's paid work time (βx^2). Thus βx^2 represents the assumption in the NHE model that increases in the female partner's paid work productivity will bring about an increase in the male partner's domestic work time. Amongst the following terms, a represents the total household time spent doing domestic work (husband's plus wives' time), b, the income difference between the partners incomes per hour, c, the number of children in the household and d whether help from outside the home is used (commodity substitution variable).

Model A

$$\hat{y}_{xz} = \alpha + \beta x + \beta z + \beta xz + \beta x^2 + \beta a + \beta b + \beta c + \beta d$$

In model B, only the term for the general interaction between the partners' paid work time (in categorical form) and the control variables are present. Thus the model includes no assumptions about the nature of the relationship between the husband's domestic time and the partner's paid time, i.e. there is no assumption that the man's minutes of domestic work will increase with an increase in his partner's paid work and vice versa. Instead, the model simply predicts that there will be some interaction between the partners paid and unpaid work.

Model B

$$\hat{y}_{xz} = \alpha + \beta x + \beta z + \beta xz + \beta a + \beta b + \beta c + \beta d$$

Table 3.1 An OLS Model of the Predictions of the New Home Economic Theory on the Male Partner's Minutes Per Day of Domestic Work (Model A)

Variable	B	S.E B	Significance
βx (Wife's Paid Time)	-7.81	14.17	N.S
βz (Husband's Paid Time)	-23.0	5.72	***
βxz (General Interaction)	-2.77	2.06	N.S
βx^2 (Slope)	8.55	2.65	***
Total Household Domestic Work Time	0.48	0.02	***
Difference in Partners' Incomes	-0.17	1.08	N.S
Number of Children	-4.85	2.65	*
Outside Domestic Help Used	-3.78	1.78	*
Constant	-18.82	22.52	N.S

R-Square (Adj)=0.72   N=345   Deviance=687663   Df=326
*=P<0.05 **=P<0.01 ***=P<0.001

Using an f-test we can see whether there is a significant difference between the 'fit' of the two models, and if so whether model A is a better model than B.

Table 3.1 presents the results of model A. As expected from the graphical analysis in the previous section, the wife's paid work time is not significant, whereas the husband's paid time is. We also have significant negative effects for the variables that represent the marginal productivity of the husband's time. This is interesting as the effects are in the direction predicted by the NHE thesis. It may be then that domestic help from outside of the household is brought in to substitute for an increase in the husband's domestic work time as the wife does more paid work. Similarly, an increase

50

in the number of children has a negative influence suggesting that where partners have a 'taste' for children, this decreases the marginal effect of wives paid work time on husbands domestic work time, an effect the NHE theorists would put down to greater domestic productivity on the woman's part (but which, as we will see, relates more to differences in attitudes).

Table 3.2 An OLS Model of the Predictions of a General Theory of the Male Partner's Minutes Per Day of Domestic Work (Model B)

Variable	B	S.E B	Significance
Total Household Domestic Work Time	0.46	0.02	***
Wife's Quartile(2)	28.27	14.16	*
Wife's Quartile(3)	50	12.25	***
Wife's Quartile(4)	72.34	12.33	***
Husband's Quartile(1)	105.1	13.74	***
Husband's Quartile(2)	43.01	11.34	***
Husband's Quartile(3)	20.65	11.47	*
Difference in Partners' Incomes	-0.56	1.03	N.S
Number of Children	-5.01	2.56	*
Outside Domestic Help Used	-4.63	1.7	**
Wife's Quartile(2)*Husband's Quartile(1)	-49.62	26.29	*
Wife's Quartile(2)*Husband's Quartile(2)	-10.52	19.33	N.S
Wife's Quartile(2)*Husband's Quartile(3)	-29.85	20.39	N.S
Wife's Quartile(3)*Husband's Quartile(1)	-38.32	22.28	*
Wife's Quartile(3)*Husband's Quartile(2)	-2.63	16.44	N.S
Wife's Quartile(3)*Husband's Quartile(3)	-21.98	16.59	N.S
Wife's Quartile(4)*Husband's Quartile(1)	46.39	20.01	*
Wife's Quartile(4)*Husband's Quartile(2)	-2.36	16.63	N.S
Wife's Quartile(4)*Husband's Quartile(3)	3.87	16.65	N.S
Constant	-112.1	12.98	***

R-Square (Adj)=0.75 N=345   Deviance=595007 Df=315
*=P<0.05 **=P<0.01 ***=P<0.001

Table 3.2 presents the results of model B. As we would expect, the effect of the control variables remains the same, but what of the relative fit of the two models? The R^2 statistics for the two models show that model B, our general model fits the data better than the NHE model (R^2=0.72 compared to 0.75). More importantly, an f-test upon the results of the models is significant (P<0.001), i.e. model B is a significantly better fit for the data. This strongly suggests that the rest of the analysis in this chapter was correct in indicating that husband's do not do more domestic work when their wives do more paid work.

Conclusions

This chapter set out to assess the extent to which the NHE thesis could be used to construct an empirical model of the household. Theoretically at least, the thesis holds out the possibility that we can understand the way that households actively produce their own outcomes using the resources at their disposal. Translated into an empirical model, the theory does seem correct in its assumption that the amount of time that partners spend in domestic work will be endogenously determined by other work commitments and productivities. Thus, men do more domestic work if they do less paid work, and vice versa. The problem for the theory is that the domestic time contributions of the partners do not seem to be reciprocally related, at least the husband's are not affected by the wife's. Figures 3.2 and 3.3 show that the husband's domestic time contributions do not change, irrespective of any increase in the paid work time of the wife. This variance with the theory remains even after controlling for those variables that could, in the light of the theory be seen as constraining the contributions of the husband. The final models show that in this form, the theory is not supported by the data. There would seem to be other processes occurring which affect the way that partners and more importantly, husbands allocate their time in relation to domestic work. The following chapters go on to attempt to identify these other processes.

Notes

[1] The structure of this assessment of the new home economic theory owes a great deal to the work of Julie Brines (1993) who makes the theoretical underpinnings of the approach clear and uses a similar graphical analysis. The 'ideal typical' profile in figure 3.1 is derived directly from Brines (1993) article. Unlike Brines though, I have chosen to directly test the new home economic theory using a statistical model at the end of this chapter.

[2] The measure of income used here is the difference between the hourly rates of the male and female partners (wife's rate - husband's). Becker's theory states that the marginal productivity of the next hour of paid work is important in determining whether labour will be allocated to this sector. The predicted affect should be that as the difference between incomes approaches zero, the husband should perform more domestic work (since the marginal cost of his time in doing domestic work, *ceteris paribus*, now equals that of his wife).

[3] I am very grateful to David Firth for his advice on the structure of these OLS models.

4 Establishing the Pattern of Attitudes Toward Men's and Women's Work Roles

The last chapter showed that there is good evidence that the new home economic (NHE) theory of household production is not sufficient to the task of explaining the empirical patterns in the SCELI data set. This finding adds weight to the conclusions of other studies (England and Farkas 1986; Berk 1985; Brines 1993) that have found the NHE theory an insufficient explanation for the patterning of the domestic division of labour. One of the chief problems is that explanation in the NHE thesis is based upon the exchange of pecuniary variables. Once material factors have been accounted for the theory cannot account for differences between individuals. As chapter one showed this is mainly because of the theoretical difficulties inherent in the model, e.g. it subsumes cultural frameworks under the general banner of 'preferences' that are said not to differ substantially for individuals. Thus the theory cannot explain why there should be no response from individuals to changes in the relative productivity of the partners. That men do not seem to increase their contributions to domestic work when their partners do more paid work seems to suggest that there are socially structured choices in operation. Chapter one explored the relationship between the economic model of the new home economists and the more sociologically oriented theory of choice through framing. As was noted, social structure shapes the definition of a choice situation through the work and life history of individuals[1], and I will examine these processes in chapter six. Before going on to do that, we need to find a way of linking individual choice frameworks to social structure. One way to do this is through the attitudes and beliefs that are implicated in these choices. In this chapter I examine the data from SCELI on the general attitudes of women and men towards the position of women both in the workplace and at home. In doing this I hope to uncover the social patterning of these attitudes. This will give us a better grasp of the factors that shape individual 'frameworks' from the social structural level (i.e. macro level phenomena that shape peoples experiences). Clearly, attitudes on the position of women in the workplace and in the home shape the way both men and women think about their responsibilities in the household and what they see as an 'equitable' division of labour. As such, the 'attitudes' expressed in this chapter are the basis upon which we can go on in later chapters to assess the extent to which the organisation of household work is the outcome of intention and negotiation by partners. It also forms the framework in which we can assess the expression of dissatisfaction by partners with their domestic and paid work circumstances.

Before we go onto examine the patterning of attitudes around the work roles of men and women, it seems sensible to first pause and examine the relationship between attitudes and behaviour. I have already suggested that attitudes may hold the key to a proper explanation of the domestic division of labour. But what if attitudes are merely reflections of current practices that give us no more explanation of the behaviour than the behaviour itself? The problem becomes one of inferring causal significance to attitudes (as our only source of information on how people evaluate gender roles) on present behaviour. There are two interrelated types of problems here, one methodological, such as the separation of cohort and life-cycle effects, but also the more theoretical problem of what we understand people to be doing when they express an 'attitude' in a social survey. The methodological problems are mostly tied into the difficulty of establishing causality, but there are also issues concerning the validity of data which connect seamlessly into the more theoretical debates. I will attempt to tackle the problem of causality first.

In this chapter, data on attitudes from the SCELI survey will be used but, as with all data sampled at single point in time, this presents difficulties in separating the effects of generational change in attitudes from those that occur over the life-cycle. Changes in women's employment behaviour since the 1960s mean that there are far more women with young children currently working than was the case when the oldest women in the SCELI sample had young children. With such changes we would expect that there would be differences in the attitudes of the older and younger women about whether women with young children should work. In the same way, the general increase in the number of women entering employment means that younger women may have different expectations for themselves and other women than was true for the older women. This difference in expectation must affect what is seen as possible, and thus desirable. However, it is impossible with single instance cross-sectional data to do more than point to possible dynamics[2].

A more troubling methodological question is that of the validity of attitude data as a source of information about peoples subjective views. In part, this question hangs on the long-running debate about the validity of all survey data to explanations in the social sciences (e.g. Eiser 1980; Marsh 1982; Jowell and Airey 1984; Dex 1988). However, the difficulties of collecting subjective views are not confined to attitude and survey research alone; the measurement of attitudes may be a simplification, but it is a pragmatically justified one. In most cases the extent of simplification is a factor of the care taken to maximise the validity of the data. This may be achieved by introducing supplementary questions as checks and/or refining the attitude questions themselves so that they are fully 'contextualised' and do not ask for the expression of 'beliefs' or 'values' in a vacuum. Both these approaches have been used in the SCELI data set where attitude questions have been constructed either to tap specific attitudinal continua, or are tightly contextualised in the form of what Rossi (1979) has termed 'vignettes' (c.f. Finch 1987). The question of validity also raises the more theoretical problem of how attitudes relate to behaviour. In economics this has not been an explicit problem because of the introduction of the concept of 'revealed preference', though it is interesting to note that this has not eliminated the problem of 'tastes' (Hollis and Nell 1975; Hollis 1989). In sociology and social psychology on the other hand, the issue is still very much a matter for debate. Here, the 'attitude' has ridden a roller-coaster from 'indispensable concept' (Allport 1935) to 'bankrupt concept' (Blumer 1955) and back again. This methodological tension is in part due to the unresolved theoretical question in social research between the study of inner feelings, experiences and intentions, on the one hand, and observable behaviour on the other. In sociology, attitudes have been used as part of the explanation for social action, i.e. why people differ in their behaviour in the context of their structural location in society. Thus, in much research, attitudes are taken as 'given' orientations which are subject to change over time, but are nonetheless stable enough to be studied as autonomous progenitors of action. It is this simplification that has led some with more micro-sociological inclinations such as Blumer (1955) to rail against their use. In social psychology on the other hand, the relationship between attitudes and behaviour has been the subject of intense study in the attempt to predict behaviour. As such there has been a steady accumulation of evidence that addresses the subject of how attitudes relate to behaviour. I want to use this research to get a better understanding of what use attitude measures are to the explanation of how households divide up the necessary tasks of paid and unpaid work. What is it that people are doing when they express an attitude and how does this relate to their behaviour?

Early social psychologists tended to see the relationship between attitudes and behaviour as mechanistic such that attitudes were defined as 'a mental and neural state of readiness' (Allport 1935). In practice this definition tended to rule out many verbal expressions as attitudes since behaviour did not always follow their public airing. For instance, do people who express racist attitudes at a verbal level act toward members of other races in ways that display open hostility or discrimination? The answer seems to be, not necessarily. In a widely cited review, Wicker (1969) concluded that only in a minority of all attitude studies was any close relationship found between verbally expressed attitudes and overt behaviour. One answer to the failure of attitude measures to predict behaviour was to make the concept itself more sophisticated. The 'three-component' view of attitudes (Rosenberg and Hovland 1960) did seem to suggest a better conceptual system for dealing with the 'attitude-behaviour mismatch' problem, but in practice was found to introduce more variables without actually stating the factors which can make the relationship between the different 'components' of a higher or lower order (Eiser 1988). In this sense, simply knowing that an attitude was made up of 'affective' (concerned with feelings, evaluations and emotions), 'cognitive' (concerned with beliefs about whether something is true or false) and 'behavioural' (concerned with intentions and decisions to act) components did not explain any better whether verbal measures of any of the three components could be relied upon as predictors of overt behaviour, though Fazio and Zanna (1981) have suggested that consistency between behaviour and (the affective component of) attitude is likely to be higher for attitudes acquired through direct, personal experience. The missing factor has been proposed by Fishbein and Ajzen (1975) as the 'intention' towards a specific action to be performed to the object or person of the attitude concerned. However, even here, the relationship between attitude and subsequent behaviour is not seen as a direct one. Behaviour is seen as determined by intention, and intention is a joint product of attitude towards the behaviour and what is termed the 'subjective norm'. This is essentially the summation of beliefs about how other people, whose opinions one values, would regard one's performance or non-performance of the behaviour. The essential ingredients of this approach (the 'theory of reasoned action') are, first, a recognition that the relative importance of attitudinal and normative factors in the determination of intention may vary depending on the context, and, second, a tight specification, within the measures of both attitude and subjective norm, of the precise target and context (when and where) of the behaviour in question.

Although the theory of reasoned action has proved successful at predicting behaviour across a range of topic areas (Fishbein 1982; Budd and Spencer 1984, 1985; Pagel and Davidson 1984), does it give us a useful understanding of attitudes and their relationship to behaviour? I tend to think not, for two reasons. First, how specific need attitudes 'toward an object' be? It certainly sounds as if they have to be phrased so narrowly that they look almost the same as the measure of intention that they are supposed to predict. What the theory states in effect is that a general attitude measure of say, agreement with a 'woman's right to work outside the home', will not be a good

55

predictor of behaviour since it does not ask about the individual woman's right to work outside the home, doing a specific sort of work over a finite period of time. If attitudes are so dependent on specific beliefs, is it not simpler to define attitudes as a collection of salient beliefs to individuals? Described like this the theory starts to sound very similar to the economic theory of 'subjective expected utility' (SEU) (Buchanan 1969) described in chapter one, with its assumptions about factual objects in the world rather than socially structured attitudinal stances toward them (a similarity not lost on Fishbein and Ajzen [1975, p 30]). As I showed in chapter one though, this theory has a number of problems that has meant that it has largely been supplanted by alternative theories (Kahneman and Tversky 1984; Lindenberg 1989, p183)[3]. An alternative model of more use may be that of Fazio and Zanna (1981) in which attitude influences behaviour by selectively activating memories which then produce a selective perception of the attitude object. Thus, although attitude is dependent on previous positive or negative experiences, it influences, rather than is influenced by, the 'evaluative beliefs' a person calls to mind when deciding on a course of action. What this means is that, contra Fishbein and Ajzen (1975), people do not decide something is bad or good because of the salient beliefs that they hold, but regard particular beliefs as more or less salient as a consequence of adopting a particular attitude. Whereas Fishbein and Ajzen's individualist theory had called, quite conveniently, for the researcher to determine on any issue, a set of 'modal salient beliefs' (Fishbein and Ajzen 1975) that are likely to be seen as important by one's subjects considered as a whole, Fazio shows, it seems, more sociologically, that people with different attitudes may see different aspects of an issue as salient. Stated like this, Fazio and Zanna's theory bears a strong resemblance to Lindenberg's discrimination model of choice that was laid out in chapter one as it assumes that an 'attitude', or a singular framework (as Lindenberg would say), is the basis upon which aspects of the issue (by which we can read alternatives and their costs) are assessed.

A second reason for rejecting the theory of reasoned action as a general basis on which to analyse the attitude-behaviour relationship concerns the role of previous behaviour. Although, as Fishbein and Ajzen's inclusion of the subjective norm indicates, they do allow for the possibility of behaviour producing feedback (in the form of learning 'social norms' or more accurately, the probabilities of negative social sanction), in other respects their model seems better suited to situations where a person is weighing up the pros and cons of an action for the first time. Yet in reality, the action under consideration will be similar, if not identical to actions performed many times before. This is especially true when we come to analyse the organisation of the domestic division of labour where tasks have to be routinely done, often on a daily basis. Thus, models of the relationship between attitude and behaviour do not simply have to explain 'reasoned action', they also have to explain habit and the effects of previous behaviour on present attitudes. Fazio and Zanna (1981) get round this problem by seeing attitudes, our evaluative frameworks for belief, as the result of previous positive or negative experiences. In essence, this theory is based on the assumption of bounded rationality and the rejection of the (SEU theory) idea that an individual is able to discriminate as many aspects and objects in the choice situation as the researcher finds convenient to assume, but as with Lindenberg's model, Fazio and Zanna show that the 'bounds' to the rationality of the individual[4] are created by the past history of the individual in question. The description of the concepts is different from those we developed in chapter one and the explanatory emphasis is on regulating interaction between persons (rather than choices among objects), but the approach that emerges from the literature of social-psychology seems to point to a theory which states that a person's behaviour will be the outcome of subjective normative beliefs about what others will think of their behaviour, as refracted through the lens of attitudes towards a specific object, event or person(s). However, we are still left with the problem of how experiences interact with attitudes to produce the 'frameworks' through which people restrict their behavioural choices. This is a large question that will be left mostly till chapter seven, for now, it is only necessary to look at the effect of present practices on attitudes. What we are asking in this context is whether attitudes are autonomous verbal expressions of inner feelings toward gender issues and practices as opposed to verbal representations of current behaviour[5]. In one sense it would be strange if attitudes did not reflect behaviour to a certain extent since attitudes now are probably those which had some hand in the construction of present behaviour. But the question asks more than this - are attitudes just rationalisations and justifications of present practices? The theory we have arrived at in this chapter, as in the first, states that attitudes have a conceptually distinct role in shaping a persons behaviour (rather than being a reflection of those practices). But, although attitudes are separate and causal, it is clear that their aetiology is tied to a personal and social history in which past attitudes and practices have combined to shape those that we see in the present.

Like most of the work on attitudes in sociology and social psychology, here I have looked at attitudes as the causal antecedents of action. Yet there is considerable evidence which points in the opposite direction, suggesting that people may actually change their attitudes to bring them more into line with the behavioural decisions that they may have already made. The best example of this is Festinger's (1957) 'Theory of Cognitive Dissonance'. According to Festinger, any decision that people have to make between different courses of action can give rise to tension or 'dissonance', the magnitude of which increases with the difficulty of the decision. The tension will remain after the decision has been taken if doubts remain as to its efficacy and thus the person will be motivated to engage in various kinds of cognitive restructuring to remove the feeling of uncertainty. It is important when using this theory to put it in a social context, by which I mean that tension can be the result of angst about whether a choice will have the outcomes one desires, but it can also be the result of angst about how others will see this choice - i.e., how people will define you afterwards. Many choices about the division of labour in the household are mundane examples of everyday choices about necessary tasks, but there are more important choices such as leaving, or the non-choice of losing a job that have consequences for how people see themselves, especially in relation to others. The theory that has been outlined in this chapter holds that attitudes are the evaluative residues of good and bad experiences that act to structure salient beliefs about objects, people or events around the person. These 'frames' must, in the dureé of events be adjusted or even abandoned altogether in favour of a frame less inconsistent with present circumstances. Attitude change is most probably dependent upon the strength of the original attitude, which again is the topic for a later chapter. As argued above then, we can see attitudes as autonomous orientations to certain types of social action or cognitive choices that are conceptually separate from, but which nonetheless interact with present practices to produce behaviour. This interaction may operate along the 'as if' lines presented in chapter one in Lindenberg's discrimination model. Thus, attitudes will operate as orientations to social action as long as they allow the person to discriminate among alternatives that are presented to them. As other factors rise in importance to match the primary factor (e.g. as the dissonance between present practices [done for whatever reason] and the existing framework increases), the choice probability of the frame moves toward non-discrimination and the frame itself is re-evaluated and possibly replaced with another if the person can no longer discriminate between the alternatives that they face. The rest of this chapter looks at the patterning of men's and women's attitudes toward paid and unpaid work roles.

The Pattern of Gender Attitudes

Unlike some other large-scale surveys such as the *Women and Employment Survey* (Martin and Roberts 1984) or *the Family and Working Lives Survey* (1994), the data from the SCELI survey does not have many attitude questions about women and work. What is valuable about the SCELI data is the range of data sources that it contains, thus the small number of attitude questions that we do have can be related to work and life-history and diary data, as well as to the more standard data on individual and household circumstances. That said, the survey still contains three types of attitude questions that, as the last section mentioned, are well constructed and provide a good picture of attitudes toward women's work and domestic commitments, as well as gender roles in the household. Again, unlike the WES Survey, SCELI contains attitude data for a cross-section of both men and women, not just women and their partners. This allows us far more scope to look at the general pattern of attitudes amongst both sexes. The data analysis in this chapter is divided up into three sections. The first section begins with a descriptive overview of women's answers to a set of questions that asked women to agree or disagree with specific statements about women and work. Having offered a descriptive analysis of this data, the questions are then transformed into a scale which is analysed within a multivariate regression model of women's attitudes which provides a structural picture of their social patterning. These questions and the scale that is derived from them are fairly abstract in nature, thus the last part of this first section analyses a set of 'vignette' (Rossi 1979; Finch 1987) type questions which use a contextualised scenario as the basis upon which to elicit evaluative responses about how men and women should act in specific circumstances. As the proceeding section showed, one criticism that has been made of attitude data is that it is a ramified source of data that cannot tap the complex nature of feelings toward social objects or their connection to people's intentions. The 'vignette' technique tries to get around these problems by using short stories about people in specified circumstances, to whose situation the interviewee is invited to respond. It is a method which, in other words, acknowledges that meanings are social and that morality may be situationally specific. Another advantage is that this technique is non-directive, thus rather than simply giving a respondent a fixed set of choices which may, or may not actually express their beliefs, the answers are left open ended and then coded *post-facto*.

The second section uses the results of questions which ask who should be primarily responsible for certain household tasks to look at the relationship between partners' attitudes toward gender roles. The main aim in this section is to see what the pattern of attitudes is between partners, i.e. do their attitudes reflect each others? The reason for this emphasis will emerge later in the book when we come to look at the processes of negotiation between partners over domestic work. The last section examines men's attitudes (as opposed to just looking at husbands) toward the proper work roles of men and women. This section is structured almost identically to the first in that it starts with a descriptive overview of men's answers to a set of questions that asked them to agree or disagree with specific statements about women and work. This is followed by a regression model containing a number of pattern variables before I once again return to the vignette questions to look at some more contextualised data.

Women's Gender Attitudes on Home and Work

This first section examines evidence from SCELI on women's gender role attitudes. To get a general picture of women's attitudes to paid work and the relationship between this and domestic commitment, we can use four questions from the SCELI main survey (N: 6111), most of which have been used before in other surveys (Marsh 1979; Martin and Roberts 1984). These ask respondents to indicate their extent of agreement with a proposition about women and work, allowing them to respond on a five point scale from 'agree strongly' to 'disagree strongly' with the option of choosing 'no strong feelings'. In full, the questions are:

.... how much do you agree or disagree with the following statements?

1. 'Men are more suitable than women for positions of responsibility at work'
2. 'Most women not are ambitious'
3. 'In times of high unemployment married women should stay at home'
4. 'I'm not against women working but Men should still be the main breadwinner in the family'

Before going on to examine whether the individual statements tap an underlying attitude, I will first examine women's responses to each of the propositions. Table 4.1 shows the extent of agreement/disagreement with the four questions and presents us with an ambiguous set of results. A clear majority of women disagree with the first question, only 15% of women agree that men are more suitable for responsibility, as against nearly 78% who disagree. This seems to suggest that women see themselves as at least the equals of men in the paid sphere. But, if we look at the results for the second and third questions, there are sizeable minorities (33 and 30%) who agree with statements that either unambiguously place women in second position in the labour market, or else suggest they are less eager as a group to succeed there. The secondary nature of women's work is emphasised in the results to the fourth question where 53% (28% strongly) of women agree with the statement that 'I'm not against women working, but the man should still be the main breadwinner in the family'.

Overall, we seem to have mixed results. Although it is obvious that a majority of women feel that they have a legitimate position in the workforce and are the equals of men in this domain, there is still strong support for the notion of the male breadwinner with the females work status as secondary. However, these aggregate figures conceal large differences between the attitudes of women in different work statuses. Table 4.2 shows these differences by work status (excluding students due to small number; cursory analysis did show though that students are much more untraditional than any other group).

Table 4.1 Women's Extent of Agreement with General Statements About Women and Work

Attitude Statement	Agree Strongly	Agree Somewhat	No Strong Feelings	Disagree Somewhat	Disagree Strongly	N:
Men are more suitable than women for positions of responsibility at work	5%	10%	7%	23%	55%	*3376*
Most women not are ambitious	4%	29%	7%	35%	26%	*3371*
In times of high unemployment married women should stay at home	10%	21%	8%	29%	33%	*3375*
I'm not against women working but Men should still be the main breadwinner in the family	28%	25%	8%	19%	21%	*3387*

Row Base: 100%

What is apparent from table 4.2 is that full time working women (83%), and unemployed women (84%) are more likely to disagree, and moreover disagree strongly (63% and 65% respectively) with the proposition that men are more suitable for positions of responsibility at work. Defining unemployment amongst women is problematic, and in some ways it is better to think of female 'non-activity' as a continuum from the registered unemployed, who comprise the official tally of the unemployed, to those with no paid work and no intention of ever working again.

Surveys (White 1983) have found the category 'registered unemployed' problematic in itself and it is hard to place women with very different circumstances and intentions into any one place on the continuum. In answer to these problems, Martin and Roberts (1984) used different definitions depending on their aim, thus when dealing with the topic of women's' attitudes they defined the unemployed as non-active women who were waiting to take up a job already obtained, and/or looking for work, and/or prevented from looking for work by temporary sickness or injury.

In this book, women are defined as unemployed if they were claiming unemployment benefit at the time of the survey, or were looking for work in the proceeding four weeks (part of the International Labour Organisation definition, but here does not include availability to start work in next two weeks).

Table 4.2 Women's Extent of Agreement with General Statements About Women and Work by Work Status

Attitude Statement	Employment Status	% Agree Strongly	% Agree Somewhat	% No Strong Feelings	% Disagree Somewhat	% Disagree Strongly	Total	N:
Men are more suitable than women for positions of responsibility at work	Full-Time	3	8	6	21	63	100%	1143
	Part-Time	5	13	9	27	47	100%	802
	Unemployed	3	6	6	19	65	100%	444
	Non-Working	7	13	8	24	48	100%	958
Most women are not ambitious	Full-Time	3	31	6	35	25	100%	1142
	Part-Time	5	29	8	34	23	100%	800
	Unemployed	4	23	7	34	32	100%	440
	Non-Working	3	29	6	36	25	100%	960
In times of high unemployment, married women should stay at home	Full-Time	6	15	7	30	42	100%	1143
	Part-Time	6	22	8	34	30	100%	803
	Unemployed	8	18	8	26	40	100%	444
	Non-Working	18	30	9	25	19	100%	956
I'm not against women working, but men should still be the main breadwinner in the family	Full-Time	19	22	9	21	29	100%	1146
	Part-Time	32	30	8	18	12	100%	806
	Unemployed	23	22	7	19	30	100%	444
	Non-Working	37	27	6	16	14	100%	963

The category does not include those who are on maternity leave, who are defined as working, but does include those who have obtained a job and are waiting to start work. The temporarily ill are classified according by their work status before falling ill. As table 4.2 shows, unemployed women are closer in attitudes to full time working women than they are to non-working women. In fact, unemployed women are less likely than women in all the other categories to believe that women are in general less ambitious than men, although, as in table 4.1, there is still a substantial minority who agree with this statement. Overall, there is very little difference between the groups in answering this question. The third and fourth statements show the ambiguity of women's work roles, though to different extents between the groups. In the statement about married women working during times of high unemployment, as before, full time and unemployed women are more likely than those employed part time or not at all to express strong disagreement, but amongst the former groups there are still large minorities who agree (42% and 45% respectively) and moreover, agree strongly (19% and 23%) that men should be the main breadwinners. The majorities on both the third and fourth statements for those that work full time or are unemployed do show though that, although there are many who see women's work roles as subsidiary compared to the home and family, it nevertheless has an important role.

What emerges from the above findings is a sense of the importance of paid employment to women and a definite belief amongst women of their equality of ability in paid work, moderated by the fact that the woman's paid employment is still seen as secondary to the main (male) breadwinner in the household. Non-working women were far more likely to agree with both the propositions (the third and fourth) about the proper role of women, i.e. that women should leave the labour force in times of high unemployment and that their paid work was secondary to the man's, but even here there are large minorities (44% and 30%) who disagree with these statements. Amongst the findings so far there have been definite patterns of attitudes which seem to be connected to the issue of the relationship between women's paid work and their domestic role. It may be that this pattern is the result of these questions tapping an underlying or latent attitude toward paid/unpaid work. To find out if this is so, women's answers to the propositions were entered into a factor analysis using a principal components method of extraction. The aim of a factor analysis is to reduce the responses to different variables to underlying 'factors', or groupings of responses, simply on the basis of statistical correlation. This has the dual benefit of establishing patterns in the data that may relate to a subsumed or hidden attitude variable, and making the data easier to handle by reducing a number of variables to one or more factors. As I go on to disaggregate the data along other lines than work status, it will become apparent that the latter benefit is important in making presentation and interpretation easier.

In principal components extraction, linear combinations of the observed variables are formed. The first principle component (factor) is the combination that accounts for the largest amount of variance in the sample. The second accounts for the next largest amount of variance and is uncorrelated with the first, and so on. In this way, we can see if the data can be described using one variable, rather than four. Table 4.3 shows the factor scores for the four questions already used for women in the SCELI survey. The results show that all of the statements are correlated with just one factor, but to differing degrees. The first, third and fourth statements are highly correlated with this factor, whilst the second statement has a much lower correlation. From these results it would seem sensible to combine the variables with the high factor loading on the factor in one new variable. The correlation for the first factor seems to suggest that there is an underlying 'latent' variable that connects the first, third and fourth statements. All of these statements ask respondents to express an attitude about the proper role of women in the workforce. But, the lower correlation of the first (men more suitable for positions of responsibility at work) compared to the other two suggests that the latent variable is an attitude toward the 'male breadwinner role' and that it is this that explains much of the variance between the statements. Whereas the third and fourth statements ask respondents to express an attitude about the primary responsibilities of women, the first is more concerned with their abilities relative to men. Obviously, the first statement is still asking about the 'proper' role of women, but it is doing so more indirectly, and thus has a lower factor loading. A factor score of .6 and above is often taken as an acceptable loading on the latent variable (Nunnally 1978, p336). If we drop the second question we can use the other three as a composite measure of the underlying attitude toward the importance of the male breadwinner role (the four statements attain an alpha of .59, but this rises to .64 if we exclude the second statement).

Table 4.3 Women's Factor Scores for Four General Statements About Women and Work

Attitude Statement	Factor 1
Men are more suitable than women for positions of responsibility at work	0.70
Most women are not ambitious	0.48
In times of high unemployment, married women should stay at home	0.73
I'm not against women working but man should still be the main breadwinner in the family	0.76

To construct this overall attitude measure, the factor scores of each statement are used to standardise the different contribution of each statement to the overall measures and the different numbers and distribution of statements (i.e. if strong disagreement is given a score of one and strong agreement five, this score is 'standardised' by its factor score and the product added to the products from the other questions). What this means in effect is that the measure is relative since although we can compare subgroups of the sample on a scale of high and low, we cannot know whether the women in the sample as a whole are high or low on this measure (Ware 1994, Jenkinson and Layte 1997). Before I go on to model this attitude measure in a multivariate framework, it's useful to look at some simple descriptive statistics of the measure. To do this, I have divided the continuous scale into three groups with low and high scores defined as being more than 0.5 standard deviations from the mean, and medium scores being within 0.5 deviations plus or minus from the mean[6]. I have defined low scores as being 'untraditional' and high scores as 'traditional' since strong disagreement or agreement with all the statements is a measure of rejection or acceptance of the attitude toward the male breadwinner. Table 4.4 shows the distribution of traditional and untraditional attitudes by work status for women respondents in the SCELI survey.

Table 4.4 Women's Level of Traditional Attitudes to the Male Breadwinner Role by Work Status

Level of Traditional Attitudes to Women and Work	Full Time	Part Time	Unemp.	Full Time Housewife	Non Working	All Women
Traditional	21	37	26	50	47	33
Medium	34	39	34	27	37	34
Non-Traditional	45	24	40	23	16	33
Total	100%	100%	100%	100%	100%	100%
N:	*1180*	*797*	*433*	*853*	*74*	*3337*

As in tables 4.1 and 4.2, full time working women and unemployed women are more likely than women who work part time, are full time housewives or are non-working to be untraditional in their attitudes. The composite measure of the woman's attitude towards the male breadwinner role confirms the finding from the individual questions, that there are marked differences in attitudes between groups of different work statuses. As the first section of this chapter showed, attitudes may act as a framework through which choices are made in the present, but these attitudes are themselves the result of past work and life experiences. This means that the differences that we see between woman who work full time, part time or as full time domestic workers are a result of the different paths that these people have followed. This does not necessarily mean that the path has been followed by choice. As Gershuny and Marsh (1994) have shown, individuals can accumulate employment characteristics that make it easier/harder for them to get other types of work in later periods. Thus, the longer a woman spends doing part time work, or being unemployed the greater the chance that she will be unemployed or work part time in the future. This effect (as predicted by the labour market segmentation theory of Doeringer and Piore 1971, and Piore 1980) has also been found empirically by Tam (1997) using data from the SCELI survey. In this situation, it is likely that the indirect effect of this accumulation of employment characteristics would be to frame a woman's attitudes toward more traditional gender role structures since her experiences would be increasingly in this direction. The effect of work history on gender role attitudes will be examined more closely in chapter six of this book. For the moment, it is necessary to examine other variables that may structure the 'frameworks', or attitudes of women toward the male breadwinner role. If we are to separate out effects however, we will need to examine the effects of different variables whilst holding others constant. To do this, the following analysis uses a multiple regression model of attitudes toward the male breadwinner role.

Specifying a Model of Women's Attitudes to the Male Breadwinner Role

Primary among these other variables is a woman's age. As I stated in the introduction to this chapter, research has shown (Dex 1988) that there have been large changes in the distribution of women's attitudes toward gender roles since the 1950s, just as there has been a large increase in the number of women who participate in paid employment. It is likely that younger women will have more untraditional attitudes than older generations of women since they have grown up with women working in the labour market and will thus have different expectations for themselves and others. Age is added as a three category variable, i.e. those aged 20-29, 30-44 and 45-60.

The last forty years have also seen a large increase in the educational attainments of women. Research (Goldin 1990) has shown that this change is reciprocally linked to the increase in the number of women working. Goldin shows how 'demand side' factors (such as the increased demand for labour, especially in occupations more accepted as female) were predominant in attracting women into employment up to 1960. The huge increase after 1960 can though, be more readily attributed to such 'supply side' factors as the effect of women born after 1950 taking advantage of their increased educational credentials and the weakening norms against women working, to secure better paid employment. This 'weakening' of normative constraints could also be interpreted as the strengthening of women's attitudes in favour of them having a paid work role, as well as a domestic one. Educational attainment is entered into the model as a six level variable starting from vocational qualifications through to university degree and higher.

Class may be a complicating factor when assessing the impact of educational attainment since women from higher social classes are more likely to have greater numbers of qualifications by the time they exit from the educational system. But, there could also be a direct effect of class upon attitudes. Bott (1957) has shown how, in Britain in the 1950s at least, being from the working class increases the chance of partners having more traditional attitudes since they are more likely to live closer to kin who reinforce more traditional belief systems about the proper roles of men and women. To test whether there is a class effect, a five level variable representing a collapsed ten class Goldthorpe (1980) scheme is used[7]. This class schema is based on an aggregation of the 36 category Hope-Goldthorpe (1974) scale which is a synthetic measure of the 'general desirability' of an occupation. In the aggregated scheme though, categories have been brought together whose members appear to share broadly similar market and work situations. 'Market situation' refers to the sources and levels of income, degree of economic security and chances of economic advancement, whilst 'work situation' refers to respondents position within the systems of authority and control governing the processes of production in which they are engaged (Goldthorpe 1980). The 'similarity' of respondents' market and work situations in Goldthorpe's scheme is based upon statistical evidence of differential mobility regimes in British society at the macro level (market) and monographic evidence of the effects of authority at the micro (work). If one's experience of work and the labour market is one component in the process of attitude formation, a moot question which will be addressed more fully later, then this measure of class should give us an idea of the general effect and its direction and magnitude.

Table 4.5 An OLS Model of the Determinants of Women's Attitudes Toward the Male Breadwinner Role

	Variables	B	SE. B	Significance
Age	45 to 60	*Ref*	-	-
	Age 17 to 29	-8.5	0.76	***
	Age 30 to 44	-5.7	0.61	***
Goldthorpe Class	Workng	*Ref*	-	-
	Service	-4.03	0.83	***
	Routine Non-Manual	-2.31	0.65	***
	Petty Bourgeois	1.64	1.58	N.S.
	Lower Technician/ Supervisor	-1.48	1.42	N.S.
Highest Qualification	None	*Ref*	-	-
	Vocational	-2.15	1.1	*
	'O' Levels	-1.93	0.67	**
	'A' Level	-4.1	1.01	***
	Non-University Higher	-3.2	1.01	**
	University Higher	-7.6	1.1	***
Employment Status	FT Housewife	*Ref*	-	-
	Full-Time	-7.7	0.68	***
	Part-Time	-3.8	0.72	***
	Unemployed	-7.1	0.86	***
	Sick/Permanently Disabled/Retired	-2.7	1.8	N.S.
Child 15+	in the Household	1.3	0.62	*
Ethnicity	European	*Ref*	-	-
	Asian	4.36	1.7	**
	West Indian	-1.8	3.6	N.S.
Constant		50.23	0.71	***

*=P<0.05 **=P<0.01 ***=P<0.001 R^2 (adj.)=0.18

To control for life-cycle effects, three dummy variables are used which represent the age of the youngest child. The three categories which make up the variable are: having a youngest child aged less than five, having children between five and fifteen years of age and lastly, the youngest child being over fifteen. There is also evidence (Witherspoon 1988) that there are differences in attitudes toward questions about the proper role of men and women among people from different ethnic minorities. To control for this, a variable is entered into the model that represents European, Asian (Indian subcontinent) and West Indian ethnic origins.

In building the model, an F-test is used as the arbiter of whether a variable should remain in the model after initial entry. If the variable explained a significant amount of variance (P<0.05) it was kept in the model. To simplify interpretation, the scale that was constructed from the factor analysis was standardised on a scale from 0 to 100. The constant, or reference group for each variable is that group which is assumed to be the most traditional in most instances. Thus, the constant category are women over 45 who have no educational qualifications, who are full time domestic workers from working class households. The exception to this rule is the ethnicity variable, which uses people of European origin as the constant, and the life-cycle variables where having no child of each category is the comparison group. Table 4.5 shows the results of the regression[8].

Except for the variables that represent whether the woman has any children, all of the variables were significant when entered into the model. The age variable was significant overall ($P<0.001$) and both of the younger age groups had significant negative effects on the dependent variable, e.g., being in the younger age groups made the women more untraditional compared to the oldest age group. Moreover, the effect of being in the youngest age group was larger than being in the middle age group. The variable that represents the woman's class was also extremely significant ($P<0.001$). Here though, only the categories for the two highest classes were significant, but there was a clear gradation in the effect; being in the service class has a greater negative effect (i.e. untraditional) than being in the routine non-manual category. As suspected, the variable that represents the woman's educational attainment was very significant on entry into the model ($P<0.001$). All of the categories of the model were significant, but as with the preceding variables, there is an effect gradient to the beta coefficients. Thus, the negative effect of having 'A' Levels is greater than having either vocational or 'O' Level type qualifications. Having a degree level qualification or higher has the largest negative effect on the scale score. As in the tables already presented, the woman's employment status has a significant effect ($P<0.001$), even controlling for class, age and educational effects. As expected, being a full time worker has a negative effect on the scale, as does being unemployed. Moreover, because the effect of the categories is compared to that of the full time domestic worker, even the category of the part time worker has a negative effect on the attitude scale. The variables that represented the presence and age of children in the household had no significant effect, except for that which represented the presence of a child over fifteen years of age. This variable was significant ($P<0.05$), but had a positive effect on the attitude scale, meaning that being in this category (i.e. having a child over 15 in the household) was linked with being more traditional. This could be interpreted as an indirect age affect has women with a child over fifteen would be in the middle age group at least, but it must be remembered that the woman's age is already controlled for in the model. In this situation it is difficult to interpret the finding.

Lastly, although the variable that represents ethnicity was significant ($P<0.05$), only the category that represents the women being Asian was significant. In essence then, the regression model confirms the previous patterns of gender attitudes that have already been outlined in this chapter. In terms of attitudes toward the role of the male breadwinner we can see that having a full time job, and more surprisingly, being unemployed, makes one more likely to express more untraditional attitudes. On the other hand, being a part time worker, or non-active in terms of paid work seems to be associated with more traditional attitudes. What the regression model has shown is that educational qualifications, class position and age also have significant effects, even when controlling for other relevant variables.

The Vignette Questions

As a general model we have a good picture of the patterning of women's attitudes toward the male breadwinner role. As the first section of this chapter outlined, the relationship between attitudes and behaviour is complex and there tends to be a higher correlation between them if attitude questions are tightly contextualised around a specific situation. One way to create this contextualisation is through the use of 'vignette' questions (Rossi 1979; Finch 1987). The method seems to have originated in a chance remark from the methodologist Paul Lazarsfeld to his research student Peter Rossi (Rossi 1979, p 178) when Rossi was looking for a way to study the underlying principles of the social status judgements that people made of one another and involved using 'thumbnail' sketches of a fictitious family with certain status characteristics. By systematically varying the combinations of the characteristics, Lazarsfeld thought that Rossi would be able to discern how such characteristics fitted together to form an overall status judgement. The method has been used in a number of both British and American surveys, but in rather different ways. The common element amongst all is the use of a hypothetical situation, but this may be long and complex, or simple and short. Vignettes way be used individually, or in batteries of questions which plot a change in circumstances for particular people over a set period. The latter approach has the benefit of supplying a history that respondents can use to further contextualise their choices. The main point is that the vignette is suited to the study of any problem in which evaluations are to be made by persons concerning complicated objects. For instance, Cook (1979) used the method to explore the varying levels of public support for different groups of welfare claimants, whilst Finch (1987) used the technique to investigate normative beliefs about obligations between relatives to provide practical, or material support for each other.

In the SCELI questionnaire for Swindon, vignette questions were used to look at attitudes amongst respondents toward critical decisions that a married couple may have to take. All of the vignettes sketched a situation where a couple were in equally good jobs, but stated different scenarios in which the male or female partner would have to make an important decision which would effect the other partner.

The vignettes used in SCELI are not as detailed as some of those used by Finch (1989, 1993) in that they do not introduce names and facts about the fictitious couple beyond that they have 'equally good jobs' (a vague statement which covers financial as well as subjective satisfaction components), but they nonetheless provide a less abstract way of gaining information about respondents attitudes toward the importance of husband's and wive's roles in the household. Table 4.6 shows the responses to the following question by the woman's work status:

Imagine a married couple who have two equally good jobs. The husband gets offered a still better job, but it means leaving the district. What, in your opinion is the right thing for the wife to do?

The options available to respondents as answers cover what we could call the 'importance continuum' of the wives' employment, i.e. the relative importance that a wife attaches to her own work vis-à-vis that of her husband. If women see their husband's employment as primary, it seems logical that they will see the option of the wife giving up her own job and taking any job in the new area as the best response. Looking at the responses according to the above logic, the results are hard to interpret, given the other findings in this section. Full time working women are slightly more likely than either part time or non-working women to see the woman leaving her job and getting any other job in the new district as the best choice, but the difference is

Table 4.6 Women's Projected Response to a Change in Circumstances of a Married Couple (Husband Gets Better Job)

Situational Response Question	Work Status	Encourage her husband to take the job in the new place and begin looking there for any job she can do	Ask her husband not to accept before she can be sure of finding as good a job there as she has now	Suggest her husband gives the job a try while she keeps her present job and they'll be together at weekends	Tell her husband that taking the job will endanger their marriage	Total	N
Imagine a married couple who have two equally good jobs. The husband gets offered a still better paid job, but it means leaving the district. What in your opinion is the right thing for the wife to do?	Full Time	67	12	21	0	100%	161
	Part Time	66	13	21	0	100%	117
	Unemp.	58	12	28	2	100%	57
	Non working	67	14	18	1	100%	141
	All Women	66	13	21	0	100%	477

*NB. Due to the small number of retired/permanently sick women in the Swindon Sample these have been combined with full time domestic workers.

negligible. Unemployed women are the most unlikely to see this as the best option, and instead are more likely to answer that the partners should be together at the weekend. Although this result would seem to point in the same direction as previous results, over half the unemployed women still see the 'take any job' option as best. The very similarity of proportions in all the options points to a quite generally held belief that the wives employment is secondary to the husbands. Could it be that the Swindon women are more traditional according to our other measures and thus appear more traditional, or at least homogenous in answering the vignette question?

Table 4.7 Swindon Women's Level of Traditional Attitudes to the Male Breadwinner Role by Work Status

Level of Traditional Attitudes to Women and Work	Full Time	Part Time	Unemp.	Full Time Housewife	Non Working	All Women
Traditional	17	39	23	52	63	33
Medium	40	35	30	22	13	32
Non-Traditional	43	26	48	26	25	34
Total	100%	100%	100%	100%	100%	100%
N:	197	134	61	156	8	556

As a comparison of Table 4.7 and the previous table 4.4 shows, the answer is no (P=0.72), the Swindon women are not significantly more traditional according to our factored measures than the SCELI women in general. How then do we account for the difference? The aim of the vignette question is to get a better grasp of how people would respond in real situations, especially critical decision situations. Therefore, it may be that, although women have more or less traditional attitudes to the male breadwinner role depending on their work status, most see a set of 'real' circumstances in the vignette question which makes their answer seem more traditional. 'Real' here could mean in relation to one's partner or in terms of how these women perceive others may view their decision, should they have to make it. Although the review of Fishbein and Azjen (1979) in the first section of this chapter was critical of their stipulation that questions about attitudes had to be tightly connected to the specific situations, it is still important that we remember the possible divergence that can appear between answers to a specific question and those to one of a more general nature. We can link this tendency back to our theory of 'frames' that was outlined in the first chapter. If an abstract question is asked about a choice that has to be made, it is likely that a general framework, say of 'gender equity' will be given prominence. But, if the question is set in a more detailed fashion, other more subjective and practical issues may gain prominence and perhaps lead to the abandonment of the frame. Evidence for this frameworking effect may be apparent in the different responses of women of different work statuses: unemployed women for instance seem less inclined to choose the two options which advise leaving a job at all and are more likely to choose the 'be together at weekends' option, as they are to see the move as endangering their marriage. Table 4.9 shows the results for the same question, except this time the wife gets the better paid job and the husband has to make the decision:

Imagine a couple who have two equally good jobs. The wife gets offered a still better paid job, but it means leaving the district. What in your opinion is the right thing for the husband to do?

What is immediately striking is the change across all the work statuses to the option that the husband ask his wife not to accept until he can get an equally good job in the new district. As before, this indicates the dominance of the male breadwinner role over that of female paid work, even where both have equal jobs. As before though, unemployed women are less likely to choose this option, or that which has the husband looking for any job in the new district, and instead are more likely to choose the 'together at weekends' option. The answers of unemployed women in both tables point to the value which they attach to any job which either partner may have, although they are still more likely, like all the other groups to put the males paid work position first. This attitude comes across strongly in the greater numbers (9% for the unemployed) who see the wife taking the new job as a definite threat to the marriage.

Taking tables 4.6 and 4.8 together, there seems to be some affinity between full time women workers and the non-working. Previous results have shown these two groups to be very different in their attitudes, and yet in these two tables, both groups favour either male or female partners making the move to any job, if their partner should get a better job, although to a much lesser extent if the male has to make the move.

We seem to have a much more uniform set of results from the vignette questions in terms of the responses from women in different work status' than were obtained from either the analysis of the individual attitude questions, or the standardised scale of attitudes. The more contextualised vignette questions may have underlined the fact that, even for those who expressed untraditional general attitudes, when given a set of specific circumstances, they still conform to what they deem to be the expected role. This result supports Fishbein's and Ajzen (1975) finding that subjective expectations of the reaction of others are important factors in the relationship between attitudes and behaviour. For the present, we need to look at the patterns of gender attitudes between partners in the SCELI sample of households. If the woman's attitudes are one possible determinant of the division of labour in the household, then the male partner's attitudes could be another. Before going on to look at men's attitudes overall therefore, the next section looks at the pattern of partner's attitudes together.

The Pattern of Partners' Gender Attitudes

Unfortunately, neither the general attitude questions, nor the vignette questions were put to both partners in the households under study. As part of the main questionnaire carried out in 1986 these were put solely to one respondent in the household.

Table 4.8 Women's Projected Response to a Change in Circumstances of a Married Couple (Wife Gets Better Job)

Situational Response Question	Work Status	Encourage his wife to take the job in the new place and begin looking there for any job he can do	Ask his wife not to accept before he can be sure of finding as good a job there as he has now	Suggest his wife gives the job a try while he keeps his present job and they'll be together at weekends	Tell his wife that taking the job will endanger their marriage	Total	N
Imagine a married couple who have two equally good jobs. The wife gets offered a still better paid job, but it means leaving the district. What in your opinion is the right thing for the husband to do?	Full Time	24	52	22	3	100%	161
	Part Time	16	57	24	3	100%	117
	Unemp.	19	44	28	9	100%	57
	Non working	23	57	14	6	100%	141
	All Women	22	54	21	3	100%	477

*NB. Due to the small number of retired/permanently sick women in the Swindon Sample these have been combined with full time domestic workers.

The Household and Community Survey self completion questionnaire did, however, contain a set of questions on which partner should be ultimately responsible for a number of specific tasks in the household. A self-completion questionnaire was given to both partners who were asked to fill them out separately in the presence of the interviewer.

This precaution should mean that the results are not greatly affected by the influence of partners upon one another, though the extent to which this was true in practice is unknown. The questions used applied to three categories of work in the household: housework, the provision of an adequate family income and the care of children. As such, the questions apply to three key areas of household labour, namely, paid work, unpaid work and the care of children. Our previous measures of attitudes have all been derived from questions about the suitability, or 'rightness' of the different genders to these different tasks in the household, but did so in different ways. The first set of general attitude questions asked for quite abstract attitudes about women and paid work, whilst the second or 'vignettes' about the predominance of one gender's 'role' over the other's in a specific, though hypothetical situation. The difference in results between these two measures of gender attitudes was large, quite possibly because of the different levels of abstraction asked for in each. If so, the next set of questions may prove useful since they are more specific than our two previous measures. These questions ask respondents to think about who should be ultimately responsible for specific tasks in the household, in their *own context* at the time they were interviewed. In the next chapter we will be examining how these attitudes are related to practices in the household and whether partners' perceptions of the type and quantity of domestic work that they do is patterned in particular ways. Meanwhile, in this section we will set the scene for the next chapter with an analysis of the patterns of partners' attitudes toward specific domestic tasks.

The results for the questions on the three areas of responsibility are shown in table 4.9. This is a complex table: the columns represent the male and female partners, according to the female partner's work status, and the rows, the proportions answering that the male, female, or both equally should be responsible for the different tasks. Couples are excluded from this analysis if they answered that neither were responsible for any of the tasks because of paid help. This last group were a small proportion of the sample (for instance, childcare was the household task most performed by paid help but the proportions involved never exceeded 3.8%) and thus do not affect the representativeness of the results. Looking at the far right hand column for all partners first, it is clear that in aggregate, the answers from both male and female partners are closely related, though we can nevertheless discern some patterns in the replies. Men are more likely to see the provision of family income as a male task and women are more likely to see it as shared (P=.037), whilst men see the care of children as a task that should be shared, whereas women are more likely to see it as a female task (P=.006).

Table 4.9 also shows that the pattern of attitudes is more complex if we examine the results by the females work status, rather than at the aggregate sample level. Because the sample of the Household and Community Survey is smaller, I have decided to combine the categories of full time domestic worker and non-workers (permanently sick/retired) in this section. At this level of analysis, as expected there are large differences between different employment groups, but there are also differences in the replies of partners within groups.

Table 4.9 Attitudes About Which Partner Should be Responsible for Specific Tasks in the Household by the Female Partner's Employment Status

Attitudes About Which Partner Should Be Responsible For Certain Household Tasks		Female Partner's Employment Status									
		Full Time		Part Time		Unemployed		Non Working		All Partners	
		Male	Female	Male	Female	Male	Female	Male	Female	Male	Female
Ensuring That The Housework Is Done Properly	Male	1	1	1	0	2	0	2	2	2	1
	Female	61	49	69	76	64	75	74	79	68	71
	Both	38	50	30	23	34	25	24	19	30	28
	Base 100% N:	179	179	239	239	96	96	272	272	792	792
Ensuring That The Family Gets An Adequate Income	Male	47	40	62	62	69	69	75	68	64	60
	Female	2	1	1	1	2	1	1	3	1	2
	Both	51	59	37	37	29	30	24	29	35	39
	Base 100% N:	179	179	239	239	96	96	272	272	792	792
Looking After The Children	Male	1	1	0	0	2	0	1	0	1	0
	Female	20	25	32	34	33	43	31	44	29	36
	Both	79	74	68	66	65	57	68	56	70	63
	Base 100% N:	179	179	239	239	96	96	272	272	792	792

Looking first at differences between groups (i.e. avoiding the differences between partners), households where the female works full time are less likely to see responsibility for the housework as being solely a female task than are all the other groups, and thus, are more likely to see it as a shared task. This finding also applies to the question of the care of children where the 'full time' households differ from all the other groups in seeing this as more a shared task than a female one.

Households with an unemployed female partner seem to answer these questions in a totally different fashion than would be expected from our two previous measures of attitudes. They are the same, or even sometimes more gender specific about the roles of partners than either the 'part time' or 'non-working' households. How do we account for the surprising results from the unemployed households? It may be that the answers from these are more akin to those of the part time and non-working households because the question asks who should be ultimately responsible for specific tasks in the respondents *own situation* at the time of the interview. It seems reasonable to assume that those in households where the woman is unemployed would see the woman's position as more amenable to doing the housework tasks, since she has more free time.

Turning to the relationship in patterns between partners within groups, we find that for most there are no significant differences. For the 'full time' households though, there is a significant difference in the answers for partners on the question of who is responsible for the housework. Greater proportions of men see this task as the responsibility of the woman (61%), against 49% of their partner's. Women in these households are much more likely to see this as a shared task (38% as opposed to 50%; P=.01). For the 'non-working' households, there are significant differences between partners for all the questions, except that concerning the housework. Although the majority (68%) of women in this group see the provision of an adequate income to be the task of the male, this is significantly lower than the proportion of men who see this as their task (75%) and the women are more likely to see this as a shared task (P=.048). This difference should not be overemphasised since the result is only just significant at the 95% level and it may be that non-working women (and to a certain extent their partners) see themselves as sharing in the provision of income because of their role in providing unpaid housework which thus frees the man to work for income. There are highly significant differences between partners within this group over the question of who should have responsibility for the children. Men for instance, are more likely than their partners to see the care of children as a shared task (P=.003).

Overall, from these attitude results, it is clear that amongst all groups there is a high level of role specificity attached to all the tasks mentioned. In the full time households, this is less pronounced (both partners see more of the tasks as shared) but still evident, especially in the case of housework where there is a good deal of disagreement between partners. Both partners in a household where the woman works full time are much less likely than partners from other groups to see domestic work as the responsibility of the woman, but the male partners are far closer to men from other groups than the women are to women of other work statuses. This pattern shows that full time women identify less with the domestic role than women who work part time or as full time domestic workers. But, it seems that there is a high probability that their partners do not share this perception. The responses to the question on responsibility for income suggest similar patterns: full time women are more likely to see the provision of income as a shared task than women in other groups, but their partners are significantly less liable to share this attitude and, moreover are much more likely than their partners to see this as a male task.

These findings are quite revealing. they show for instance, that as we move from households where the women is not working to one where she works full time, both partners are more likely to see the responsibility for some tasks as more ambiguous and flexible, but there are still large proportions of men and women in 'full time' households who still see the roles of domestic worker and breadwinner as sex-specific. However, there is some indication in full time households that men are distinctly more traditional than their partners: only in these households do the men judge the housework to be the woman's responsibility to a greater level than do their partners. These findings are interesting in the light of the theoretical discussion in chapter one since it is clear that experience of one's employment status (e.g. full time work) has an effect on the frame of reference that women have of themselves. We can see that full time women are much less likely to give their partners the primary role as breadwinner, but more likely to see this role as shared. This change of framework would make it more likely that their identity as the prime domestic worker would be less feasible as the salience of factors linked to paid work rose. As non-discrimination approaches (see chapter one), issues of distributive equity may arise more frequently and forcefully, since as we can see from these findings, the new framework is not necessarily shared with the male partner. In this situation, the individual production functions of the partners may diverge (since they now include social valuations that do not necessarily map the 'objective' constraints since they are created through past good and bad experiences) with the result that partners may attempt to exert leverage on the other to pursue their interests. The next chapter will examine the extent to which the attitudes of the partners dictate the proportions of domestic work that they do and what relationship this has to their sense of equity. The final chapter will go onto assess what effect such differences may have on feelings of dissatisfaction. For the moment, we still need to look at men's attitudes.

Men's Gender Attitudes on Home and Work

So far, we have seen how women's attitudes are patterned by various structural variables such as work status, age, class, educational qualifications and to a certain extent, life cycle stage. We have also seen how measures of these attitudes rely upon the questions asked, such that the question context and the degree of abstraction from one's own situation has a major impact on the results obtained. The results that have been obtained also show that, methodological problems aside, attitudes are ambiguous and multifaceted entities shaped by the complex reality people face. The introduction of the male partner into the analysis was interesting in that the answers of male and female partners were not significantly different in the majority of cases, even within different female work status categories.

This section will examine the gender attitudes of men using the measures constructed earlier for the female respondents. In this way we can get a better picture of men's attitudes, via the three main types of measurement, and compare the results with those obtained from the female respondents.

Table 4.10 Men's Extent of Agreement with General Statements About Women and Work

Attitude Statement	Agree Strongly	Agree Somewhat	No Strong Feelings	Disagree Somewhat	Disagree Strongly	N:
Men are more suitable than women for positions of responsibility at work	6	14	22	26	31	*2671*
Most women not are ambitious	4	27	12	34	23	*2637*
In times of high unemployment married women should stay at home	13	21	15	30	22	*2666*
I'm not against women working but Men should still be the main breadwinner in the family	23	21	14	22	21	*2682*

Row Base: 100%

As explained in section two of this chapter, the SCELI main survey contained a set of propositions about women and work which were put to all the 'primary' respondents in the households studied. Respondents had five precoded options available in replying to these propositions which ranged from 'disagree strongly through 'no strong feelings' to 'agree strongly'. We have already seen the results from women respondents, those obtained from the men in the sample are contained in table 4.10. What is immediately striking is the higher proportion of men who reply that they have 'no strong feelings' to all the questions, compared with women respondents. This is especially true of the first question (men are more suitable for positions of responsibility at work) where 22% of men choose this option as compared to 7% of women, thus it may be that men understand these questions to be controversial and thus would rather remain neutral. Noncommittal answers aside, there is a significantly different pattern to the men's answers (P<0.001) compared to those of the women, except in the case of question two (Most women are not ambitious; P=.093). The men are less likely to disagree, and moreover, less likely to disagree strongly with the first statement than are women. Instead, men are more likely to agree that 'men are more suitable for responsibility', or remain neutral. This pattern of agreement does not

77

extend to the second question where the men's answers quite closely resemble those of the women in that 57% disagree (women: 61%) with the proposition that most women are not ambitious, but a still significant 31% agree (women: 33%). The difference in answers between men and women to the first question may reflect a view amongst men that they are more suited to important paid work roles, but this hypothesis is tenuous in the light of the replies to the fourth question where men are less likely to agree (44% as opposed to 53%) and slightly more likely to disagree (43% to 40%) than women that men should be the main breadwinner in the household (P<0.001). This is complex since there is no reason why men should not see themselves as better suited to positions of responsibility and still uphold that women can still be the main breadwinner, but it is an interesting result that men in the sample uphold the breadwinner role less than the women. One factor, as mentioned earlier may be that men are aware of the contentiousness of these statements and thus choose the more 'untraditional' line. This hypothesis entails attributing a degree of 'doublethink' to men that I have not attributed to women, which is rather unwarranted. Thus, for the moment and before we have examined the attitude results from the more contextualised questions, we could hold that men are less traditional than women at the level of aggregate data. The ambiguity of this finding is heightened by the results from the third question (in times of high unemployment, married women should stay at home) to which men are less likely to disagree and more likely to reply as having no strong feelings (P<0.001).

As in the results from the women, overall there seems to be a significant degree of ambiguity in the answers of men to these questions. Even though proportionally fewer of the men agree that the male should be the main breadwinner in the household in comparison to the women, a hefty 44% still agree with this statement. The greater number of men who express no strong feelings may account for some of the differential between the sexes. Moreover, men disagree less with the statement that married women should leave the labour force in times of high unemployment. As before, the results are mixed, but we can say that the questions are still current and contentious, if not resolved as the proportions of strongly agree/disagree show.

To get a better picture of men's attitudes according to this measure, we must break down these aggregate statistics. The last section showed how men's attitudes toward the division of certain household tasks differed by the work status of their partner, thus table 4.11 shows men's extent of agreement with the attitude questions about women and work by their partner's work status. Unlike the results for women when examined by work status, the results for the men (by partner's work status) are surprisingly uniform. We do not, for instance find the division between the unemployed/full time workers occurring as clearly in these results as in those for the women in the SCELI sample. Looking closely, there are differences between groups on different questions, but not across the questions as was apparent for the women. In the first question, partners of unemployed women are significantly more likely to disagree, and less likely to agree with the statement that men are more suitable for positions of responsibility, but this position, on what we took before to be a statement about the inherent differences between men and women, does not recur in the second proposition which states that most women are not ambitious. Here, all the groups mostly disagree, but all have large minorities who agree.

Table 4.11 Men's Extent of Agreement with General Statements About Women and Work by Work Status

Attitude Statement	Employment Status (Partner)	% Agree Strongly	% Agree Somewhat	% No Strong Feelings	% Disagree Somewhat	% Disagree Strongly	Total	N:
Men are more suitable than women for positions of responsibility at work	Full-Time	6	15	18	24	38	100%	581
	Part-Time	5	16	24	27	28	100%	561
	Unemployed	5	5	20	30	41	100%	61
	Full Time Carer	9	14	22	27	29	100%	629
	Non-Working	6	16	25	22	31	100%	32
Most women are not Ambitious	Full-Time	4	31	11	34	20	100%	576
	Part-Time	5	29	12	34	21	100%	560
	Unemployed	0	30	10	20	40	100%	60
	Full Time Carer	6	27	11	36	21	100%	631
	Non-Working	6	34	9	16	34	100%	32
In times of high unemployment, married women should stay at Home	Full-Time	8	13	11	35	33	100%	580
	Part-Time	10	22	15	34	20	100%	563
	Unemployed	15	15	15	23	33	100%	61
	Full Time Carer	20	25	12	26	16	100%	640
	Non-Working	16	25	25	13	22	100%	32
I'm not against women working, but men should still be the main breadwinner in the family	Full-Time	17	18	12	26	27	100%	583
	Part-Time	25	22	12	23	18	100%	564
	Unemployed	21	15	15	16	33	100%	61
	Full Time Carer	32	23	13	18	15	100%	635
	Non Working	34	16	13	25	13	100%	32

The third and fourth questions reveal some more differences between the groups, but again to a limited degree. Partners of full time workers are both more likely to disagree and less likely to agree that men should be breadwinners than are the other groups and moreover are very much less likely to express 'no strong feelings' on the matter. In all the other questions, these 'full timers' partners have chosen this reply, as have all the other groups to a much greater extent than the women respondents did. Could it be that the experience of having a partner working full time has meant that these issues have been discussed and thought about to a greater extent? If the 'full time' partners are less 'traditional' in their answers than the other groups, the partners of non-workers and full time domestic workers are more traditional. These men are more likely to express agreement with the proposition that men should be breadwinners and less likely to disagree. This same pattern emerges in answers to the third question where the partners of full time workers tend to agree less and disagree more than the other groups with the statement that in times of high unemployment, married women should stay at home. The partners of non-workers on the other hand tend to agree more than the other groups and disagree less.

Overall then, the men's results are less differentiated by the partners' work status than were those for women respondents (using women's own work status), except for the answers to the third and fourth propositions concerning whether women should be the main breadwinner, or should stay in the labour force (if married) during times of high unemployment. Here the partners of the full time employed and those of non-workers did stand out with patterns of attitudes tending in different directions. As with the women respondents, can we see some underlying attitude here? It is clear from the results from the men that they do not differ as greatly in terms of their attitudes as do women when examined in relation to partners work status, except when the issue of the primary work role for women is raised.

Table 4.12 Men's Factor Scores for Four General Statements About Women and Work

Attitude Statement	Factor 1
Men are more suitable than women for positions of responsibility at work	0.74
Most women are not ambitious	0.53
In times of high unemployment, married women should stay at home	0.77
I'm not against women working but man should still be the main breadwinner in the family	0.78

The different patterns for the partners of full time and non-working women suggest the existence of an underlying attitude scale about women's proper work role, or more precisely (as in amongst the women respondents), the extent to which the 'male breadwinner role' is seen as primary. To test whether this is true, a factor analysis, identical to that carried out on the answers for the female respondents, was also applied to the answers from the male SCELI sample. The results are shown in table 4.12. The high factor scores for the first, third and fourth statements show that there is a very significant underlying attitude scale which is highly correlated with these three statements. The second statement does not explain as much variance as the other three, thus as in the previous analysis of the data from the women respondents, all the questions, except for the second are acceptable for use in the construction of an attitude scale toward the primacy of the 'male breadwinner role'.

Table 4.13 Men's Level of Traditional Attitudes to the Male Breadwinner Role by Work Status

Level of Traditional Attitudes to Women and Work	Female Partner's Work Status					
	Full Time	Part Time	Unemp.	Full Time Housewife	Non Working	All Males
Traditional	25	36	28	46	44	35
Medium	31	33	30	28	34	32
Non-Traditional	44	31	43	26	22	34
Total	100%	100%	100%	100%	100%	100%
N:	576	557	61	624	32	1850

Chronbach's alpha statistic shows how the withdrawal of the second question improves the scale, with the alpha increasing from 0.67 to 0.69.

Using this scale, table 4.13 shows the distribution of traditional and untraditional attitudes amongst the SCELI sample of men by their partner's work status. This shows the male partners of full time employed women to be the least traditional and the most untraditional according to this measure, followed by the partners of the unemployed. The partners of full time domestic workers are almost twice as likely as those of full time workers to hold traditional attitudes. Using this measure, it is not possible to compare the men with the women respondents since the standardisation procedure only allows comparisons within the groups to be made (i.e. within sex). Nonetheless, looking at table 4.13, it is still true to say that that, as amongst the male respondents, there is a definite patterning by the female partner's work status. However, as shown by the analysis of women's attitudes, implicit in this patterning of gender attitudes by the female partner's work status are a host of other variables. It may be easier to use a multiple regression model to unravel the main determinants of men's gender attitudes. Using a regression model we can establish what variables are salient and the magnitude of their effect, whilst controlling for all others entered into the model.

Specifying a Model of Men's Attitudes to the Male Breadwinner Role

This model uses the same variables and interactions as used to assess the determinants of women's gender attitudes, *viz.*, the man's work status, age cohort, class (five class Goldthorpe (1980) classification), age of youngest child and educational qualifications (seven level variable). In this model for male respondents, the employment status of the female partner is also added. The reference categories for this model, as in that for women, are those categories that are taken to be the most 'traditional', except for the variables that represent ethnicity and the age of children in the household. Thus, full time male workers who have partners who are domestic workers, but have no educational qualifications and are in the working class are the group to which other categories are compared. West Indian and Asian respondents are compared to European respondents, primarily because this will allow us to look at the effect of one particular category, that of Asian men. The model of women's attitudes showed Asian women to be more traditional than the reference group of European respondents.

Dummy variables are used to represent the presence of a child in the age groups listed, thus the constant for these variables is not having a child of this age (or of having no children at all living in the household). As in the model of women's' attitudes, this model also uses an F-test after the entry of each variable as the arbiter of whether it should be retained. The traditionalism scale was also standardised on a 0 to 100 scale. Table 4.14 shows the results of the regression.

The results from the regression on men's attitudes were extremely similar to those in the female partners' model. Thus, independently, the man's age ($P<0.001$), class ($P<0.001$) and educational level ($P<0.001$) were all strong predictors of his attitudes. But, whereas the woman's work status had a strong affect on her attitudes, here it was the female partner's work status that was important ($P<0.001$), with the male partner's being insignificant ($P=0.76$).

Both of the younger age cohorts where significantly less traditional than the reference category and there is a gradient in the parameter estimate with the youngest grouping having a larger negative effect than the 'middle' age cohort. It is interesting that the petty-bourgeoisie class category had a significant negative effect on traditionalism, whereas it had been insignificant in the female partners' model. This is hard to interpret since the routine non-manual category was not significant (i.e. we are not just seeing the extension of the effect in the women's' model further along the class categories).

The insignificance of the male partner's work status is also of interest. The overwhelming majority of men in the SCELI sample who have jobs work full time, but even if we compare these respondents to men who are unemployed or retired, as chi-sq. statistic shows that there are no significant differences in attitudes ($P=0.82$). On the other hand, there are differential effects for the categories of the female partners' work status. Although all of the categories of the female partners' work status are shown to have a negative effect on traditionalism (compared to the reference category of the full time domestic worker), table 4.14 shows that the having a female partners who works full time or is unemployed has a much larger negative effect on the male partners' degree of traditionalism compared to having a partner who works part time or who has retired or is permanently sick/ill.

Table 4.14 An OLS Model of the Determinants of Men's Attitudes Toward the Male Breadwinner Role

Variables		B	SE. B	Significance
Age	45 to 60	*Ref*		
	Age 17 to 29	-8.9	0.89	***
	Age 30 to 44	-5.1	0.77	***
Goldthorpe Class	Working	*Ref*		
	Service	-2.6	0.87	***
	Routine Non-Manual	-1.3	1.4	N.S.
	Petty Bourgeois	-2.4	1.3	*
	Lower Technician/ Supervisor	-1.8	1.3	N.S.
Highest Qualification	None			
	Vocational Qualification	-1.7	1.1	N.S.
	'O' Levels	-3.5	0.84	***
	'A' Level	-6.1	1.2	***
	Non-University Higher	-4.8	1.2	***
	University Higher	-9.6	1.3	***
Partner's Emp. Status	FT Housewife			
	Full Time	-8.3	0.95	***
	Part Time	-3.7	0.93	***
	Unemployed	-7.6	2.2	***
	Retired/permanently sick	-5	2.9	*
	Single	-3.3	1.1	**
Children in HH	1 or More			
	None	2.1	0.89	*
Ethnicity	European			
	Asian	8.6	1.9	***
	West Indian	1.1	4.6	N.S.
	Constant	54.22	0.9	***

*=P<0.05 **=P<0.01 ***=P<0.001 R^2 (adj.)=0.18   N=2644

Moreover, the effect of the female partner's work status and the male partner's educational qualifications were statistically autonomous - neither acted as a proxy for the other within the models. All of the categories of the male respondents own educational qualifications, apart from that representing the possession of vocational qualifications have a significant negative effect on traditionalism compared to the reference category of men with no qualifications. What is interesting is that there is a definite inverse gradient to the effect: the higher the level of qualification the greater the negative effect on traditionalism.

The variable representing ethnicity was highly significant (P<0.001), but this reduction in the scaled deviance can almost all be attributed to the effect, as expected, of the category of Asian men. This category had a large positive (i.e. increasing traditionalism of attitudes toward the breadwinner role) effect on attitudes compared to the reference category. Although we cannot directly compare the effects of variables between men and women (since the attitude scales are relative to each sex), it is interesting that the parameter estimate for the effect of being an Asian man is almost twice as large as that for being an Asian woman. Finally, if we turn to the effects of the dummy variables that represent the presence of children in the household of different ages, only one has a significant effect and this is the dummy which represents having no children in the household (whereas in the women's' model only the variable representing having a child over fifteen in the house was significant). This is a difficult effect to interpret, but as with the effect in the women's' model, of having older children (i.e., no children in the household would mean your children having grown up and left for a large proportion of those in this category, relative to those who have not had their first birth yet), we could be seeing parents adopting an attitude toward the present or approaching work roles of their children that is more traditional.

Overall then, similar patterns emerge from this model of men's attitudes as emerged from that for women. The men's gender attitudes are strongly associated with the working status of their partners, in the same way that the women's attitudes were associated with their own work status, even when controlling for the man's work status and other variables such as class and educational qualifications. In terms of general gender attitudes and the more specific attitudes toward the male breadwinner role then, there are large differences that seem to be patterned around the working role of the female partner, but are also shaped by his age, educational qualifications and to a limited extent his social class. These are all interesting findings, but are they artefacts of abstract attitude questions that have no analogue in actual behaviour?

The examination of the answers to the vignette questions for the women respondents showed that differences in attitudes between women in different work status' evaporated when the context of the question was outlined more fully and a choice of different responses presented.

Table 4.15 shows the result of the following vignette question for men by their partner's work status:

Imagine a married couple who have two equally good jobs. The husband gets offered a still better job, but it means leaving the district. What, in your opinion is the right thing for the wife to do?

Unfortunately, because these questions were only asked of the SCELI sub-sample for Swindon, the small number of male respondents with unemployed partners means that this group has been excluded from the analysis. Excluding this group though, Table 4.15 shows that there are discernible differences between groups for the Swindon men, much more so than for the Swindon women. Although in all groups, by far the most frequent choice is for the wife to leave her job and get any other job in the new district. On the other hand, the partner's of full time workers are far more likely to say that the wife should ask the husband not to make the move until she has found a job in the new district which is as good as the one she has at the present. If we apply the logic used in the interpretation of the results for this question from the women respondents, it seems that partners of full time workers have a stronger sense of the importance of the woman's job than do the partners of part time or non-working women.

Table 4.15 Men's Projected Response to a Change in Circumstances of a Married Couple (Husband Gets Better Job)

Situational Response Question	Female Partner's Work Status	Encourage her husband to take the job in the new place and begin looking there for any job she can do	Ask her husband not to accept before she can be sure of finding as good a job there as she has now	Suggest her husband gives the job a try while she keeps her present job and they'll be together at weekends	Tell her husband that taking the job will endanger their marriage	Total	N
Imagine a married couple who have two equally good jobs. The husband gets offered a still better paid job, but it means leaving the district. What in your opinion is the right thing for the wife to do?	Full Time	47	36	17	0	100%	83
	Part Time	52	13	29	6	100%	79
	Non working	49	21	26	3	100%	98
	All Men	47	26	23	4	100%	260

*NB. Due to the small number of retired/permanently sick women in the Swindon Sample these have been combined with full time domestic workers.

Since the question was asked as part of the main SCELI survey, and thus only of the main respondent, we cannot compare male and female partner's answers together, but these results point to a greater difference amongst the male respondents than was found for the female respondents. It is interesting that a far higher proportion of the male respondents in all groups, except partners of part time workers, compared to the women respondents, see the husband not making the move until the wife has got as good a job as the best option. Overall though, the majority in all groups see the wife making the move and getting any job as the best outcome to the situation outlined.

If we reverse the situation and this time it is the woman who gets the better paid job, the distribution of answers is more difficult to interpret. Here, the question asked becomes:

Imagine a couple who have two equally good jobs. The wife gets offered a still better paid job, but it means leaving the district. What in your opinion is the right thing for the husband to do?

Table 4.16 shows the results for this question. Whereas the majority of the choices in the previous question where for the option of the wife taking any job in the new district, here the greater proportion of men say that the man should ask his wife not to accept the new position until he has secured a position similar to the one he has at present. As in the women's answers to this question, the men obviously attach more importance, for whatever reason, to the man's job, or his work role in the household. Unlike the answers to the last question though, the partners of full time workers are not distinctively different from those from the partner's of part time or non-workers.
In fact, it is difficult to pick out any patterns from the results at all, apart from the larger proportion of the 'part time' male partners who see the husband getting any job in the new district or partners seeing each other at weekends as the best outcomes.

In essence, what we can take from the results to these two questions is further evidence that amongst both men and women, the man's job is seen as more important than the woman's, although there is evidence that the men are more 'untraditional' in the sense that a greater proportion still say that the best option, if the wife gets the better paid job is for the man to get any job in the new district that he can. This interpretation is problematic in that the question asks respondents to sum up the best option, given all the circumstances and implications that the choice may have. It may be that the sexes choose differently because they see different circumstances, pressures or consequences as salient, thus the women may be more uniform because women believe that the social expectation is for the wife to move, even if it is detrimental to her own career. As in all attitude questions, we have a reflexive relationship between the social knowledge and beliefs of the respondents and their professed attitudes in the face of a contentious question of this sort.

Table 4.16 Men's Projected Response to a Change in Circumstances of a Married Couple (Wife Gets Better Job)

Situational Response Question	Female Partner's Work Status	Encourage his wife to take the job in the new place and begin looking there for any job he can do	Ask his wife not to accept before he can be sure of finding as good a job there as he has now	Suggest his wife gives the job a try while he keeps his present job and they'll be together at weekends	Tell his wife that taking the job will endanger their marriage	Total	N
Imagine a married couple who have two equally good jobs. The wife gets offered a still better paid job, but it means leaving the district. What in your opinion is the right thing for the husband to do?	Full Time	24	54	21	1	100%	83
	Part Time	25	39	30	5	100%	79
	Non working	18	52	22	7	100%	98
	All Men	22	46	27	6	100%	260

*NB. Due to the small number of retired/permanently sick women in the Swindon Sample these have been combined with full time domestic workers.

Conclusions

The first section of this chapter used past and current attitude research to speculate upon the relationship between the expression of attitudes in social research and actual behaviour. This question has obvious importance for all social research that looks for an 'explanation' of behaviour both in the structural circumstances in which people live their lives and the meaning and beliefs with which they imbue it. Attitudes are one of the chief routes through which we can tap these meanings and the evaluations implicit in them, but as shown, their relationship with both current (and past) circumstances and current behaviour is complex. The empirical findings of this chapter testify to this complexity since they have shown that the patterning of gender attitudes can be changed substantially through the use of different questions and measures. Between the three different measures used here though, we have obtained a coherent picture of the main variables that pattern gender attitudes amongst both men and women. Although the effect of the male partner's attitudes on those of the female has to be left until a later chapter, it is clear that there is a reciprocal relationship between the work status of the female partner, her attitudes and those of the male partner. This is good evidence for one of the major themes of this book, i.e. that the household has to be seen as an interactive system in which the aspirations, attitudes and circumstances of both partner's react with and upon each other to produce the behavioural outcome of a substantially inequitable division of household labour. The actual pattern of domestic practices and their relationship to the expressed attitudes of partners is the subject of the next chapter, but for the present it will be useful to sum up the main findings of this chapter.

Amongst the female respondents, it is apparent that paid work has an important place in the lives of many women and that women do not, in general, see themselves as less suited to this role in terms of their own abilities or aspirations. This belief and associated attitudes is complicated by the question of how this possible role combines with household responsibilities and with the primary role of breadwinner given to the male partner. Although women express the belief that they have a legitimate place in paid work, majorities in all work status groups still feel that the male partner should be the main breadwinner in the household. The extent to which women express this belief differs widely between women of different work statuses, thus it is more common amongst part time workers, full time domestic workers and non-working women. Nonetheless, large minorities of full time and unemployed women still express this attitude. The finding that the latter group are more 'untraditional' than either part timers or full time domestic workers is contrary to the findings of past research (Martin and Roberts 1984) and this may be an artefact of different definitions of unemployment between this book and others. But the evidence seems clear that unemployed women, at least according to the measures used here, are a distinctive group with attitudes closer to full time workers than to non-workers.

The importance of the 'breadwinner' question was underlined by the factor analyses for both men and women where unguided statistical correlation pointed to this issue as a salient dimension in gender attitudes. Using the standardised measure of attitudes derived from these scores, the patterning of attitudes by work status became more clearly structured. However, the measure also showed that women's attitudes are strongly related to their birth cohort, class and educational level, although the last two are highly inter-correlated. Women from higher classes with more qualifications are much more likely to express 'untraditional' attitudes.

The relationship of the attitude scale measure to actual behaviour is thrown into doubt by the results of the vignette questions, where the differences by work status seemed to disappear and a much more uniform set of attitudes was found. The explanation for this is likely to be complex, but it may be that women took the strong social expectations on a wife into account when answering this question. Above all, the uniformity of the results showed the strength of the assumption that it is the man's job which comes first in situations of change[9]. The comparison of partners attitudes on who should have primary responsibility for certain household tasks (Table 4.10) was useful in tying together the results of the other two measures since they showed that in the concrete context of households in different work circumstances, the differences by the female partner's work status reasserted themselves. The gendered nature of household tasks such as earning the family income and doing the housework should have meant that these questions too were affected by the weight of social expectations. In fact, there were differences both between groups, and between partners within groups as to who should be ultimately responsible for certain tasks.

For the male respondents, the pattern of gender attitudes is similar to those amongst the females, most notably because the female partner's work status has a significant effect upon the attitudes of the male, *ceteris paribus*. But, there are differences. In the questions put to male partners about who should be primarily responsible for certain household tasks, in general, the men were far more likely to say that tasks should be shared, except in the case of the partner's of full time women workers who saw the housework as a mainly female task. Overall, in answering these questions it seemed as if the women had a much greater sense of the gender specificity of tasks than did the men (especially amongst women full time domestic workers); we may see why this is so in the next chapter. The next chapter will also show the extent to which these attitudes are merely reflections of, or predictors of actual household practices.

Notes

[1] As explained in chapter one, here social structure is defined as the 'rules and resources recursively implicated in the reproduction of social systems. Structure exists only as memory traces, the organic basis of human knowledgability, and instantiated in action.' (Giddens 1984, p377). It does not refer to institutional forms or material systems of exchange.

[2] Martin And Roberts (1984) and Dex (1988) have both analysed this dynamic using data from previous surveys, notably that of Hunt (1968).

[3] The theory seems to have a similar structure to the economic model of 'subjective expected utility' in that it sees attitude as the sum of beliefs about the probability of certain consequences happening as a result of a particular act, each multiplied by how good or bad the individual considers each consequence to be. Yet like SEU theory, how literally is one to take the implication that before anyone can decide whether they approve or disapprove of some action or object, they have to search their memory for a set of salient beliefs, then perform a likelihood-by-evaluation multiplication on all these beliefs, and then summate the products?

[4] It would be more accurate and more in keeping with the arguments of chapter one of this thesis if we referred to attitudinal patterns as giving rise to 'subjective' rationality (Boudon 1989) rather than bounded rationality. The former implies discrimination amongst (cognicent) alternatives, the later a 'blinkered' choice.

[5] The theoretical relationship between behaviour and attitudes is a vexed area and in reality is best tackled empirically (c.f. chapter seven). This point is made strongly by Marshall 1981 in his critique of the 'vocabulary of motive' literature ('Accounting for Deviance': International Journal of Sociology and Social Policy, Vol.1, pp17-45) and Mann 1979 ('Idealism and Materialism in Sociological Theory' in Freiberg: 'Critical Sociology', pp97-119.)

[6] This definition is based upon that used by Martin and Roberts (1984) p172.

[7] The 10 category Goldthorpe class schema is collapsed into 5 categories by combining the higher and lower service classes into a single service category, and pooling all self-employed respondents into a single 'petty bourgeois' group. Finally, lower routine non-manuals (sales and private service workers) are combined with skilled manual, unskilled manual and agricultural workers to form a 'working class' (c.f. Goldthorpe *et al* 1980).

[8] The SCELI data set over-sampled the unemployed so as to collect an adequate number of individuals for analysis. All regressions in this chapter have been weighted to take account of this.

[9] The 'vignette' questions asked were structured so as to test, in the context of both partners having jobs of equal worth, whether there was a gendered type of decision making as to whose job took priority.

5 The Relationship Between Attitudes Toward Gender Roles and Domestic Work Practices

In the last chapter we examined the patterning of men's and women's attitudes towards the work roles that they should fulfil. It was plain from that chapter that attitudes towards the roles that women should fulfil are ambivalent, even contradictory. On the one hand, there was very general support amongst both women and men for the belief that women have a legitimate position in the workplace. On the other, there was still the widespread belief that the male partner should be the main breadwinner within the household. Dex (1988) has examined the changing nature of women's attitudes towards work roles and has shown that women's attitudes towards their economic role in paid employment have become more egalitarian. However, Jowell and Witherspoon (1985) have shown that the same is not true of attitudes towards the domestic division of labour within the home. Attitudes on this subject have changed much less, but are now more varied, which as chapter four has shown, reflects the greater variety of work roles amongst British woman. It was plain from the answers to the questions about responsibility for certain household tasks in the last chapter, that the wife was still seen as having ultimate responsibility for domestic work within the household. What was interesting was that the level of support for these sex specific roles varied between women of different paid work statuses. Full time working women and women defined as unemployed were much more 'untraditional' than were women who were working part time or were full time housewives. Although these differences disappeared when the answers to the 'vignette' questions were examined, they were evident in the answers to the questions about who should ultimately be responsible for certain household tasks. The male partner's attitudes towards domestic work tend to mirror those of their partner, except in households where the woman works full time. In this case, as chapter four showed, the woman's attitudes tend to be more egalitarian. As we have seen though, the division of domestic labour is rarely egalitarian, even in households where the female works full time. Chapter three showed that a purely economic, or material account of the mechanisms of allocation was not a sufficient explanation for the non-response of men to the increased number of paid work hours worked by their female partner, thus could attitudes be the key variable? As was explained in chapter four, attitudes and behaviour are reciprocally linked, thus we would *expect* that those with more untraditional attitudes would divide domestic labour along more egalitarian lines. But chapter four also showed that the link between attitudes, beliefs and behaviour is complex and difficult to tap using quantitative data, thus this chapter seeks only to uncover the patterned relationships that exist between attitudes and household practices.

Examining the effect of attitudes on practices sounds simple, but it is hard to examine empirically. There are three main reasons for this. First of all, people may not be fully aware of the actual division of labour that they practice. Arlie Hochschild (1990) has reported how many of the couples in her qualitative study developed what she called a 'family myth': a set of beliefs or statements about their behaviour that were at odds with their behaviour as Hochschild observed it. This concept is interesting in that the myth represents the attempts of partners to resolve the contradiction between their 'gender strategy' and their lived reality. By 'gender strategy', Hochschild means

> .... a plan of action through which a person tries to solve problems at hand, given the cultural notions of gender at play. To pursue a gender strategy, a man draws on his ideas about manhood and womanhood, beliefs that are forged in early childhood and thus anchored to deep emotions. He makes a connection between how he thinks about his manhood, what he feels about it and what he does. It works the same way for women. (Hochschild 1990, p15)

Hochschild identified two ideal type strategies: the 'traditional', where the woman was seen as the homemaker and the man as the breadwinner, and the 'egalitarian' where both partners identify with both the breadwinner and domestic, or homemaker roles. While most of the partners that she interviewed tended to be 'transitional' in that they were somewhere between the two ideal types, some voiced egalitarian attitudes and claimed to share domestic work equally whilst actually maintaining a 'traditional' pattern of work responsibilities. Others had the opposite gender strategy in that they espoused very traditional attitudes, but the husband did a large proportion of the domestic work. The nature of the 'family myth' is rather problematic, as are all claims by sociologists that respondents are suffering from false consciousness of their true situation. In reality, people rarely know, with certain exceptions, how much time they spend doing specific activities. If paid by the hour, we would tend to keep a log of how many hours we have worked but, as Gershuny et al (1994, p157) have remarked, in general we have no reason to know the quanta of time we devote to particular activities. It could be then that in the absence of good information about their time use, some couples' perceptions of how domestic work is divided up may be shaped more by their attitudes towards the proper roles that men and women should fulfil than by the 'reality' that the sociologist might observe.

Secondly, even if attitudes are found to be congruent with behaviour, how do we know what is causal upon what? It may be that households who hold 'untraditional' attitudes organise and accomplish their domestic work in a different manner to other, more 'traditional' households. But, as we have seen, the attitudes of both the male and female partners about who should be responsible for certain household tasks are correlated with the work status of the female partner. As outlined in the examination of the literature in chapter one, we would expect that the organisation of household domestic work would be shaped to a large degree by the paid work commitments of the partners. Thus, the partners in a household may have very untraditional attitudes, but if the male partner works a great many hours and earns a large salary and the female partner does a small number of hours for a much smaller salary, we should expect that the female partner will do a great deal more domestic tasks and spend more time doing domestic work than the male partner. To separate these effects we will need to examine the relationship between attitudes and behaviour within a multivariate framework where we can control for the effects that material constraints may have. By doing this, we can see, controlling for other relevant variables whether attitudes still have a net, and thus autonomous (at least conceptually) effect.

Mention of the relative effects of different variables brings me to the third and final problem of the attitude/practices relationship. Although we can discern whether attitudes have an autonomous effect net of other factors, we have to keep in mind the fact that attitudes may differ between partners and that one partner's attitudes could be far more powerful in shaping practices than those of the other. By concentrating on how the woman's attitudes lead her to do more, or less of the unpaid work, we could ignore the possibility that she may have to do more because the man refuses to. This has been a constant theme of much of the qualitative work in this area and forms one of the central interests of this book. In Arlie Hochschild's (1990) study 'the Second Shift', the man's refusal to do housework, or ineffectiveness in doing it led some of the women in her study to take on those tasks against their own beliefs that the man should be doing his fair share, and to develop a 'family myth' about how unpaid work was actually carried out. But, Hochschild's study, like many that have looked at negotiation between partners is qualitative and cannot tell us how widespread the processes she describes are. Thus in this chapter we will investigate whether and to what degree the woman's attachment to the domestic role, as expressed in the attitude measures in the SCELI data set, lead her to performing a greater proportion of the domestic work. Yet, at the same time, we need to examine the effect of the male partner's attitudes on practices since, as just explained, the male partner must agree to take on the tasks that the woman no longer does. Even if the woman has untraditional attitudes, the male partners attitudes and practices are still important in determining whether the division of labour will be egalitarian. If the above logic is correct, where partners do not have the same attitudes, especially where the man has more untraditional attitudes than the woman, we should expect to see the man's attitudes having a greater effect on what actually gets done.

The first section of this chapter will examine whether Hochschild's notion of the 'family myth' gains empirical support from the SCELI data set. The second section will begin the process of analysing the differential effect of partners' attitudes on practices through data from the SCELI survey on whether respondents feel that their domestic work contributions are fair, and if not, why this is so. If past qualitative research and the above logic are correct, we should see some influence of men's refusal to do domestic work and ineffectiveness at it in their own and their partner's responses. Only later in the book will we get to examine, via the qualitative studies of the area, whether the patterns that emerge here are often related to conflict between the partners and the exercise of differential power resources. The last section of this chapter will model the simultaneous effect of both partners' attitudes whilst controlling for material factors that might act as a constraint upon the structure of domestic work practices. Here again, we should expect that after controlling for other factors, the man's attitudes will have a more powerful effect in structuring the proportion of domestic work that the partners do individually. First of all, we turn to an examination of Hochschild's concept of the 'family myth'.

The Family Myth

One of the great strengths of the SCELI survey for a study such as this is the combination of both self-report and diary information on the domestic division of labour that it contains, both types of data being collected as part of the second wave of interviews (the Household and Community Survey) in 1987.

As part of the household questionnaire, husbands and wives were asked independently about whom usually do certain household tasks. Answers were precoded into a five point scale (running 'female entirely', 'female mainly', 'both equally' etc.)

which, although quite crude, does give us the chance to compare the answers of both partners with each other. At the end of the interview both partners were asked to fill out a diary of their activities for a week, thus giving us a source of data with which to compare their self-estimates from the questionnaire (see chapter two).

These two types of data give us the opportunity to examine the relationship between the family myth (in the form of partners' estimates of the woman's proportion of domestic work) and the actual division of domestic labour in the household (the diary data). There are however, two different interpretations of the family myth that we can examine here[1]. On the one hand, there is the 'weak' version of the family myth, that partners' estimates of their practices and their actual practices will differ and that the gap between them can be explained via their attitudes and/or the information they have about such a non-natural category of knowledge. On the other, there is the 'strong' interpretation, that the family myth results from the conflict that occurs when one partners' attitudes toward the proper work roles of men and women are contradicted by their own practices. In this interpretation, the 'myth' can also be the coping mechanism that partners use to damp down conflict between themselves over the way domestic work should be divided.

Table 5.1 Mean Woman's Number of Minutes Per Day and Proportion of 'Core' Domestic Work from Male and Female Self-Estimates and Diary Sample

Activity	Male Estimates	Female Estimates	Male Mean Mins Per Day	Female Mean Mins Per Day	Diary Data Mean Female Contribution
Cooking	77	81	14.38	56.05	80
N	1195	1202	385	385	385
Washing Up	66	70	8.22	24.44	75
N	1181	1177	368	368	368
Cleaning & Hoovering	76	81	5	26.29	84
N	1183	1185	308	308	308
Clothes Washing	87	90	1.48	27.38	95
N	1187	1197	367	367	367
Painting & Decorating	34	37	12.93	4.7	27
N	1162	1152	158	158	158
Gardening	41	45	24.99	10.88	31
N	1142	1125	387	387	387
Car Maintenance	21	23	7.97	0.98	11
N	1042	1034	173	173	173

The latter interpretation is much harder to examine using quantitative evidence than the former since it requires us to have such rich, detailed information on the relationship between the partners and how this is affected by their attitudes and their domestic work practices. As such, my analysis in this section will be, almost exclusively, of the former interpretation, though I will return at the end to a rudimentary test of the latter interpretation.

As explained above, when answering the question in the Household and Community Survey (HCS) respondents will not have a very clear idea of how much domestic work they and their partner actually do. As such, their estimates should be strongly affected by the family myth, if Hochschild's finding has any weight. On the other hand, the diary evidence should not be overly affected by the myth, as it relates to a non-natural category of self-knowledge, unless respondents have kept up a sustained attempt to mislead the researchers about their time use. Table 5.1 shows the aggregate means for three measures of household domestic work in seven categories from the HCS. After the column on the left that lists the seven categories of domestic work, the next two list the mean self-estimates of the proportion of domestic work that the woman does, first from the man and then the woman in the relationship[2]. The next two columns list the mean minutes per day that men and women do, as derived from the diary data. The last column shows the mean proportion of domestic work of women as derived from the diary data.

What is immediately striking about these aggregate figures is the closeness of the self-estimates from men and women to the woman's proportion of domestic work time as derived from the SCELI diary sample. It is also apparent that the women's self-estimates are closer to the diary derived mean values than those of the men. It must be remembered though that these are mean values from aggregate data and do not reflect the true relationship between the self-estimates of each partner and the totals derived from diary data. To get an accurate picture of the relationship between these variables we need to compare the self-estimated scores from each partner in each household with the diary scores for the household as a whole (or at least the partners that we have sampled). To do this I constructed a summary measure of the four domestic tasks that we could take to be the 'core' domestic tasks: cooking, washing-up, cleaning and hoovering and clothes washing. The remaining tasks were excluded because the number of couples that actually do these tasks is much lower than the four core tasks, thus making the analysis less robust. The remaining tasks are also done considerably less often, if done at all, and thus are not good indicators of the day to day household economy of time (Gershuny 1994).

Table 5.2 Spearman Correlation Coefficients of the Partners' Self-Estimates of the Woman's Proportion of Core Domestic Tasks and the Diary Derived Measures of Time

	Female Partner's Self	Estimates Male Partner's Self	Estimates Diary Derived Measure
Female Partner's Self-Estimates	-	0.61(N=354)***	0.32(N=371)*
Male Partner's Self-Estimates	0.61(N=354)***	-	0.34(N=368)*
Diary Derived Measure	0.32(N=371)***	0.34(N=368)***	-

*=P<0.05 **=P<0.01 ***=P<0.001

The summary measure is simply the mean of the measures for the four tasks for the two self-estimates and the diary derived measure. We can then look at the correlation's between the three scores to see if and how, they relate to one another. To reiterate, Hochschild's theory about the household myth holds that we should see a higher correlation between the self-estimates of the partners than between the individual self-estimates and the diary measure. Table 5.2 shows the correlations between the three measures.

From table 5.2 we can see that the correlation between the three measures is not very strong. There is a 0.61 correlation between the self-estimates of the partners and a correlation of 0.32 and 0.34 between the diary measures and the female and male partners' self-estimates respectively. It seems that the partners' estimates are closer to each other than to the diary data.

There is real support here for the argument that the partners generate a consistent (if not necessarily agreed) 'story' of the division of domestic labour that they practice which is substantially different from the story that we get from the diary sample. This finding is strengthened by the finding that over 75% of the partners sampled made estimates of their practices which were within 11% of each other (i.e. one standard deviation plus or minus from the mean difference of the estimates of all the partners sampled). The correlation's between the partners self-estimates and between the diary data and the estimates increases slightly if we use a measure of partners' contributions to domestic work based upon the woman's proportion of the number and frequency with which certain tasks are completed (see chapter two) in the household.

Table 5.3 Spearman Correlation Coefficients of the Partners' Self-Estimates of the Woman's Proportion of Core Domestic Tasks and the Diary Derived Measures of Task

	Female Partner's Self	Estimates Male Partner's Self	Estimates Diary Derived Measure
Female Partner's Self-Estimates	-	0.61(N=354)**	0.37(N=371)**
Male Partner's Self-Estimates	0.61(N=354)**	-	0.34(N=368)**
Diary Derived Measure	0.37(N=371)**	0.34(N=368)**	-

*=P<0.05   **=P<0.01   ***=P<0.001

The questions in the HCS asked 'who usually does...?' which we would expect to relate more closely to a diary based measure that uses the frequency with which a certain task is performed as the metric. Table 5.3 shows that all of the correlation's are of the same order as those in table 5.2, except that the correlation's between the task based measure and the woman's self-estimate is of a slightly higher order.

Is the disjunction or 'myth' between the estimated and actual practices of partners fairly stable, or are there variations? My earlier argument was that we could see the myth as the outcome of peoples limited information about a non-natural category of self-knowledge, i.e. exactly how much time they spend doing specific tasks, coupled with gender attitudes that will shape their perception of their practices to a certain degree. If this is correct, can we construct a hypothesis to perform a limited test of the theory? One limited hypothesis may be as follows: 'in situations where couples have to assess their time use more carefully and thus discuss the subject to a greater depth, we will see an increase both in the correlation between partners estimates and the diary measures'. Just such a situation would occur when one of the partners in a household works full time in paid work.

Table 5.4 Spearman Correlation Coefficients of the Partners' Self-Estimates of the Woman's Proportion of Core Domestic Tasks and the Diary Derived Measures of Task by Woman's Work Status

	Woman's Work Status	Female Partner's Self Estimates	Male Partner's Self Estimates	Diary Derived Measure
Female Partner's Self Estimates	Full-Time	-	0.77(N=97)***	0.44(N=103)***
	Part-Time	-	0.57(N=118)***	0.23(N=124)***
	F/T Housewife	-	0.4(N=119)***	0.22(N=124)*
	Unemployed	-	0.61(N=19)***	0.58(N=19)***
Male Partner's Self Estimates	Full-Time	0.77(N=97)***	-	0.45(N=100)***
	Part-Time	0.57(N=118)***	-	0.34(N=121)***
	F/T Housewife	0.4(N=119)***	-	0.17(N=126)
	Unemployed	0.61(N=19)***	-	0.82(N=20)***
Diary Derived Measure	Full-Time	0.44(N=103)***	0.45(N=100)***	-
	Part-Time	0.23(N=124)***	0.34(N=121)***	-
	F/T Housewife	0.22(N=124)*	0.17(N=126)	-
	Unemployed	0.58(N=19)***	0.82(N=20)***	-

*=P<0.05 **=P<0.01 ***=P<0.001

To be more specific, if the theory is correct we should see higher correlation's both between partners estimates of the division of domestic tasks and between these estimates and the diary proportions in households where the woman works full time than where she works part time. These same correlation's should also be higher in households where the woman works part time than in those where she is a full time domestic worker. Table 5.4 shows the correlation's between the estimates of partners to each other and to the diary based measure of time, controlling for the work status of the woman. The table shows a very clear difference between all the groups, with the partners with an unemployed female partner having the highest correlation's both between the self-estimates and the estimates and the diary data, followed by the full time employed group. The correlations between the partners' estimates for the unemployed group are almost twice as large as those for households where the female partner is a full time housewife. For the same groups, the correlation for both the man's and woman's estimates and the diary scores are over three times as large.

It does seem then that the concept of the family myth gets a large amount of support from the SCELI data, but it is clearly not solely shaped by the gender attitudes or 'gender strategy' of the partners alone, if at all. The results in table 5.4 show that when time use is more critical, partners tend to agree more closely about how their household practices are divided. This could be because the decreased availability of time leads them to discuss the subject more explicitly, or it could be that they are both just more acutely aware of how they spend their time. Which ever it is, this process also leads to a decrease in the effect of the family myth on how partners perceive their actual practices. This is quite dangerous territory and I would not like to suggest that partners in households where the wife works full time or is unemployed are less led by their attitudes than partners in households where the wife works part time or is a full time housewife. It is more likely that the distribution of domestic work has become much more of an issue for the former groups, leading them to concentrate far more closely on the details of how they arrange their time.

The results for households where the woman is unemployed offer some evidence for this. By definition, these women are claiming unemployment/supplementary benefit or looking for work. Around two thirds have had a job, 55% of which were full time in the recent past and will have established routines of unpaid work in that role (though the numbers here are rather small). When unemployed these routines have to be altered and/or renegotiated with their partners, leading the partners in this group to have a heightened grasp of each other's ideas and their actual work distribution. This is the subject of the next chapter where we will examine the effect of past work and life history on attitudes and practices in the present. For the present, it is clear that partners' beliefs about the division of labour that they practice and their actual behaviour are loosely tied and depend in large part upon the paid work role of the female partner.

Do attitudes contribute at all to the nature of the family myth? Moreover, can we find evidence in favour of the 'strong' interpretation outlined earlier, i.e., that the myth is the result of the contradiction between partners' practices and their attitudes? The evidence so far points to the woman's paid work status as being a very important variable in defining the extent to which partners both come to see each others contributions and their position overall. Yet Hochschild holds that a persons 'gender strategy' is a defining factor in the family myth. We can construct an approximate test of Hochschild's theory by using some of the attitude variables in the SCELI data set and combining these with the questionnaire self-estimates and the diary data[3]. To isolate the family myth and allow us to look at the affects of other variables, I constructed two simple ordinary least squares regression models. The dependant variable in each is the female partner's proportion of household core domestic work as found in the diary data minus either the male or the female partner's self-estimated proportion of core tasks (depending on whether it is the man's or woman's model). If Hochschild is correct in her claim that partners form some kind of agreed 'myth' about their domestic work practices when actual practices diverge from the woman's attitudes about gender roles, we should find that when a woman has untraditional attitudes, but also performs a high proportion of domestic work this should lead to an increase in the gap between the measure from the diary data and the partners' estimates of their practices.

The HCS questionnaire of the SCELI survey included questions, answered independently by both partners, which asked who should be ultimately responsible for certain household areas. Two of the areas surveyed were domestic work and responsibility for earning an adequate income, where respondents were asked whether the man, woman or both should be ultimately responsible. We can use the question that asks about primary responsibility for domestic work to represent partners' attitudes on this subject. Although there are three possible responses to the attitudinal questions, here I have combined the 'untraditional' responses into one category and the 'traditional' responses into another. This means that on the question that asks who should have primary responsibility for domestic work, the answer 'female' is taken to be 'traditional' and the answers 'male' or 'both' are taken as 'untraditional'. On the other attitude question (primary responsibility for income), this is reversed, thus the traditional category is now 'man responsible'. This type of response is very crude and obviously peoples attitudes are more complex than this, but here we are looking to see if attitudes have any affect on the man's or woman's estimate of the woman's proportion of domestic labour. As chapters two and three showed, the partners' work statuses have a large affect on the woman's proportion of domestic work. Therefore, I have controlled for these two variables within this small model so that we can get a clearer idea of the affect of attitudes. To aid interpretation, I have divided the variable representing the woman's proportion of the core domestic tasks from the SCELI diary data into a three level variable. The three categories were constructed by cutting the original continuous variable at two points half a standard deviation above and below the mean. We can thus refer to the woman's proportion of the diary based totals as being of a high, medium or low nature. The base or reference category of the predictor variables are those which are taken to be the 'most traditional' - i.e. women who are full time housewives and men who are full time workers, and the category of traditional attitudes (i.e. the woman should be primarily responsible for domestic work, men should be primarily responsible for income). However, to aid interpretation, the reference category for the variable that represents the proportion of domestic work according to the diary data is the lowest category (woman's proportion smallest). As each of the variables was entered into the model, the decision whether to retain it or not was dictated by an F-test of the variance explained ($P<.05$).

Tables 5.5 and 5.6 give the results for the regressions on the woman's and man's estimates respectively. I will describe the outcomes of the equations together since the results in both reflect upon the other. Both of the variables controlling for the partners' work statuses were insignificant predictors on entry into the models, whereas that representing the woman's proportion of the diary measure of domestic labour was very significant ($P<0.001$ in both models). In the same way, the variable representing the woman's attitudes toward domestic work were very significant ($P<0.001$) in both models, but the man's attitudes toward domestic labour were only significant predictors in the woman's model ($P<0.01$). This is an interesting development since it could be that the woman is increasing her estimate of the amount of domestic work that her partner does if he has untraditional attitudes, controlling for his proportion of core unpaid work.

Table 5.5 An OLS Model of the Difference Between Woman's Diary Proportion and Her Self-Estimate of Her Proportion of the Domestic Division of Labour (The 'Family Myth')

Variable		B	S.E of B	Significance
Main Terms:				
Woman's Emp. Status	FT Housewife			
	Full Time	3.7	2.2	*
	Part Time	0.8	2	N.S.
	Unemployed	-2.2	3.4	N.S.
	Retired	7.5	7.9	N.S.
Man's Emp. Status	Full Time			
	Part Time	0	Aliased	N.S.
	Unemployed	11.3	3.1	N.S.
Full Time Housewife		3.1	3.9	N.S.
	Retired	10	6.9	N.S.
Woman's (Diary) % HW	Low			
	Medium	26.8	2.6	***
	High	35.9	2.7	***
Woman's Beliefs About Responsibility For Domestic Work Untraditional		15	3.6	***
Man's Beliefs About Responsibility For Domestic Work Untraditional		3.4	1.8	*
Interactions:				
Woman's (Diary) % HW HW Attitudes	Medium +Untraditional	-10.4	4.4	**
Woman's (Diary) % HW HW Attitudes	High +Untraditional	-8.9	4.9	*
N=387 R^2 (Adj.)=0.29	Constant:	-29.31	2.7	***

*=P<0.05 **=P<0.01 ***=P<0.001

This adds a twist to the idea of the 'family myth' because here, men with untraditional attitudes are estimated by their partners as having a higher contribution to domestic work than they really do (i.e. the positive coefficient means that the gap between the diary based woman's proportion of domestic work and her estimated proportion becomes more positive, that is, she will underestimate her proportion. Remember that the dependant variable is the diary proportion minus the estimated proportion thus if the woman's contribution is under-estimated, the dependant variable will be positive). However, this test of the 'family myth' rests specifically on whether the gap between the partners' estimates and the diary data increases when the man's real contribution is low, but the woman's attitudes are untraditional. To test for this relationship an interaction variable was entered into the model of the woman's proportion of core domestic tasks (diary measure) and her attitudes. This variable was very significant upon entry into both models (P<0.001).

Table 5.6 An OLS Model of the Difference Between Woman's Diary Proportion and Her Partner's Self-Estimate of Her Proportion of the Domestic Division of Labour (The 'Family Myth')

Variable		B	S.E of B	Significance
Main Terms:				
Woman's Emp. Status	FT Housewife	*Ref*		
	Full Time	3.3	2.2	N.S.
	Part Time	0.3	2	N.S.
	Unemployed	0.8	3.4	N.S.
	Retired	15.6	8	*
Man's Emp. Status	Full Time	*Ref*		
	Part Time	0	Aliased	N.S.
	Unemployed	3.5	3.1	N.S.
	Full Time Housewife	8.2	3.9	*
	Retired	4.6	7	N.S.
Woman's (Diary) % HW	Low	*Ref*		
	Medium	27.8	2.6	***
	High	36	2.7	***
Woman's Beliefs About Responsibility For Domestic Work Untraditional		18	3.6	***
Man's Beliefs About Responsibility For Domestic Work Untraditional		1.7	1.8	N.S.
Interactions:				
Woman's (Diary) % HW HW Attitudes	Medium +Untraditional	-13.8	4.4	***
Woman's (Diary) % HW HW Attitudes	High +Untraditional	-16.1	4.9	***
N=387 R² (Adj.)=0.29	Constant:	-25.4	2.7	***

*=P<0.05   **=P<0.01   ***=P<0.001

Examination of the final models in tables 5.5 and 5.6 reveals some extremely interesting results, not all linked directly to the family myth. For instance, in the woman's model, the significance of the category of the woman working full time and the positive effect (i.e. the woman being in this category increases the gap between her estimate and the proportion from the diary evidence) suggests that these women over estimate their proportion of domestic work. Could it be that these women feel that they are doing less domestic work than they should be and are thus increasing the amount they estimate they do, or do they just feel that they do more than they do because they are so busy?

In both the men's and the women's models, if the woman's proportion of domestic work is medium or high (compared to the reference category of 'low'), this increases the estimate of the man's proportion of domestic work. Moreover, there is a slope to the effect with the 'high' category having a larger affect than the 'medium' category in both models. If the woman's attitudes are untraditional this also has a positive affect on the dependant variable. Both these effects offer some evidence in support of the family myth, but more important than the effect of the diary and attitude variables on their own is the effect of the interaction between these variables in the models. In both, if the woman's proportion of unpaid work, according to the diary measure, is medium or high and her attitudes are untraditional, there is a large negative affect on the partners' estimates. Thus, even though having untraditional attitudes and the woman doing the highest proportion of domestic work individually increase the partners' estimates of the male partner's contribution, these characteristics together have a negative affect, i.e., they decrease the partners' estimates of the male partner's contributions. This could mean that when these characteristics appear together the partners are more aware of the structure of their practices. Put another way, it may be that if the woman has untraditional attitudes there is a tendency for the partners to play down her proportion of domestic work. Similarly, the partners may tend to underestimate the woman's contribution when she does a high proportion of the domestic work (controlling for her work status), but when the two occur together, the contradictory nature of the situation concentrates their attention upon their practices and this pushes down their estimates of the male partners contributions. If so, this evidence does not support the 'strong' interpretation of Hochschild's thesis, although the significance and the direction of the effect of the variables individually does support the weaker thesis.

This section has shown that, overall, the partners' paid work status has a significant effect upon the weaker interpretation of the family myth, but so do the attitudes of the partners. The effect of attitudes on the family myth was large and significant in both the men and the women's models. What was more interesting was the lack of effect, or small effect of the man's attitudes compared to the woman's on estimates. It was clear that the female partners attitudes have a direct affect on the man's estimates of his contributions, if not on the actual practices. When supplemented with the findings from tables 5.2 to 5.4, the models suggest that partners have a shared notion of their domestic work practices which bears some resemblance to the 'real' story from the diary data, but which is also shaped both by the problems of getting accurate information on such a non-natural category of knowledge and their own gender role attitudes toward domestic work roles. However, the affect of attitudes on the family myth is not wholly as Hochschild suggests, since we found no interaction between attitudes and actual practices in estimates when we should have expected that one would be present if the theory is correct.

Having explored the concept of the family myth and it's relationship to partners' attitudes in this section, it is clear that, even though the relationship between partners' estimates and the diary measures was loose this did not hide the fact that most partners are well aware of the generally large difference between the contributions of the male partner and those of the female partner. If partners are aware that there are large differences in their contributions to domestic work, are these seen as unfair or inequitable? If not, this is good evidence that beliefs about the proper domestic work roles of men and women have some effect in shaping the domestic work practices of the partners. The next section looks at whether respondents see their current situation as equitable and offers some of the respondents own definitions of why it may not be.

As chapter one pointed out, much of the literature on the domestic division of labour since the mid-1960s has examined the equity or inequity of household arrangements within a changing labour market. Inequity of work, power and opportunity was a major theme of Oakley's (1974) *Housework* and the central theme of Meissner *et al's* (1975) *No Exit for Wives*. 'Equity' was also the basis from which those researchers such as John Scanzoni (1970, 1972, 1979) working in what can generally be termed the 'social exchange' school, began their analyses. Whereas the feminist authors such as Meissner and Oakley used the concept (and lack) of equity as a spur to social and political action, the social exchange theorists used it as a building block for their theories about how the individual experience of having to perform domestic labour translated into the sociological patterns that we see in the statistics presented both here and in chapter two. To be a little less abstract, they assumed that 'reciprocity' between partners was just one example of what other theorists have termed the 'general norm of reciprocity' (Gouldner, 1960). The concept has a long history in sociology. Gouldner (1960) traces it through Lévi Strauss and Georg Simmel to social exchange theorists like George Homans, Thaibut & Kelley and Peter Blau. Between partners, such a norm led the wife to take on the brunt of the domestic work in the household, in exchange for the economic role of the husband. When the wife works full time in paid employment, the exchange is sustained by the 'generalised norm' of gender based work roles. This approach has manifold problems, but Scanzoni *did* see that the increased paid work of women could lead to stresses appearing between the twin norms of reciprocity and gender roles.

We have already seen the critiques of exchange theory and 'norm' based analysis, but there is a problem here in that we know from the last section that partners do weigh up their contributions to the total amount of domestic work accomplished in the household, but they may still have attitudes and beliefs that legitimise any large differences that exist. This point has been put forward by Thompson (1991) and studied empirically by Blair and Johnson (1992). The latter used the 1988 US. National Survey of Families and Households to test whether the division of labour within families was linked to wives perceptions of how equitable it was. They found that the amount of time that the husband spent doing domestic work was positively correlated with the wife's perception of fairness, but only amongst households where the woman was employed and the woman had untraditional attitudes toward gender roles. Wilkie, Ratcliff and Ferree (1992) show how the partners' attitudes can lead to a situation where inequalities in the division of tasks are represented in negotiation such that 'fairness' is most often seen as wives doing more household work than their husbands.

'Equity' is problematic and we cannot assume that differences in contributions inevitably lead to a sense of inequity. Hakim (1996) has criticised sociological studies that seek to attribute women's relatively high satisfaction with, and predominance in, poorly paid manual work to either the ideology of domesticity or the imposition of discrimination. Whilst I do not totally agree with the conclusions she draws about the choices that women make, it is still clear that some women may not find their 'objectively' one sided situation as inequitable. Nonetheless, we should expect that as women do more paid work, the contradiction between the 'twin norms' mentioned earlier should have the effect of increasing women's perceptions of unfairness, if their contributions to domestic work remain at the same level. The same may also be true of their male partners; what is interesting are the reasons why men and women feel their contributions remain inequitable. This section looks at the evidence from the SCELI survey on how partners perceive the equity or fairness of their contributions and why they may do more or less than their fair share.

In each of the six areas surveyed by the SCELI, a proportion of the questions asked were designed by the researchers in that area and asked in that area alone. Through this method, the survey team hoped to get better access to the historically and contextually specific situations of the different areas. The main surveys for Rochdale, Coventry and Aberdeen (carried out in 1986) included questions on whether respondents felt 'their share of the housework' to be fair and if not, why they thought this was so. Since the main survey did not ask the partner any questions we do not have information on how they felt about the household situation, nevertheless the questions do offer a valuable source of information on how respondents of both sexes view the equity of their division of unpaid labour. Unfortunately, the survey team for Coventry did not include questions on the reasons why respondents may find the division of labour within their household fair or unfair, therefore I have taken the decision to restrict the analysis in this section to respondents in Rochdale and Aberdeen.

Table 5.7 Male Partners' Beliefs About the Fairness of Their Share of Domestic Work by the Work Status of Their Partner

		% Believe Their Share Is Fair	% Believe Do More Fair Share	% Believe Do Less Than Fair Share
All Men	N=609	56.7	2.5	40.9
Partner Works Full Time	N=198	55.6	3.5	40.9
Partner Works Part Time	N=174	51.7	1.1	47.1
Partner Is Full Time Housewife	N=221	60.6	2.7	36.7
Partner Is Unemployed	N=16	68.8	-	31.3

The combined responses of men and women in both Rochdale and Aberdeen can be seen in tables 5.7 and 5.8. Looking at tables 5.7 and 5.8 together, a slight majority of both men and women see their current division of labour as fair. As expected, the majority of men in table 5.7 who do not see their practices as fair believe that they do less than their fair share, whereas the women in table 5.8 who do not see their practices as fair tend to believe that they do more than their fair share. Yet from the evidence presented in this book on the large difference that exists in the contributions of partners to domestic work, it seems something of a contradiction that the majority of both men and women believe that their division is fair.

For instance, the SCELI diary sample shows that the man does 50% or more of the domestic work (in terms of time spent including what might be termed 'male' tasks such as DIY and car maintenance) in less than 12% of households (N=387). This imbalance is not just confined to the diary sample.

Table 5.8 Female Partners' Beliefs About the Fairness of Their Share of Domestic Work by Their Work Status

		% Believe Their Share Is Fair	% Believe Do More Fair Share	% Believe Do Less Than Fair Share
All Women	N=831	56.8	41.2	2
Full Time	N=264	53.4	44.3	2.3
Part Time	N=264	57.2	41.3	1.5
Full Time Housewife	N=258	59.7	38.8	1.6
Unemployed	N=45	57.8	35.6	6.7

The diary sample was collected a year after this data from Rochdale and Aberdeen, but even if we look at self-estimates taken from men and women in Rochdale at the time of the 1986 (main) survey we see a similar picture[4]. Over 72% of men in the Rochdale sample (N=438) report that they do not do any of what might be called the 'core domestic' tasks (cooking, shopping, cleaning and vacuuming and washing clothes). Only 10% of men report doing one or more of these tasks. Women in Rochdale report a very similar contribution from their partners with 93% (N=567) reporting that their partners do not do any of the core tasks mentioned above. If the aggregate figures report that the majority of both men and women are happy with this large difference in the contributions of partners, is there any difference between the partners in households where the female partner works in paid work and those where she does not? Our hypothesis outlined earlier was that the 'tension' between the fulfilment of the domestic role and the need for equity would lead to a fall in the proportion of women (and perhaps men) who see their practices as fair as the woman does more paid work. Tables 5.7 and 5.8 show that this is not so. There is very little difference in the answers from women working full time, part time or as a full time housewife, a conclusion confirmed via a chi-square calculation (P=0.075). The same is also true of men whose partners work differential amounts of time in paid work (P=0.46).

From these findings, we need to take seriously the hypothesis that attitudes and beliefs about the proper division of labour between male and female partners in the household are strong influences on practices since a majority of female partners see their proportion of domestic work as fair, even though few will share this work equally with their partner. Tables 5.7 and 5.8 do show though that almost half the samples of men and women did not see their contributions as fair - the women believing their contribution to be more than fair and the men less. Luckily, the area specific surveys for Rochdale and Aberdeen also included questions on why respondents felt their contribution to be unfair. We can use these to shed some light upon the respondent's beliefs as to why their practices are shaped as they are.

Explaining Inequity

Respondents in Aberdeen and Rochdale who stated that their contribution to domestic tasks was unfair were asked to select the reasons why they thought this was so. This is invaluable data, but unfortunately, it has several methodological problems. First of all, the small number of unemployed women respondents and partners makes it difficult to comment upon these cases (especially when they are divided by work status), thus for the rest of this section I will omit these cases from the analysis. Their exclusion is unfortunate, but not too serious given the fact that there is a larger number of full time housewives in the sample. Secondly, the area specific surveys for Aberdeen and Rochdale

Table 5.9 Rochdale Men: Reasons Why Do Less Than Fair Share of Domestic Work by Their Partner's Work Status

Reason	Partner's Work Status		% Citing Reason
No Time Because of Paid Work	All	N=125	53.6
/Spouse Is At Home	Full Time	N=45	40
/Spouse Doesn't Work	Part Time	N=38	71.1
	FT Housewife	N=38	50
We Have An Arrangement	All	N=125	14.4
/Partner Does Domestic Work	Full Time	N=45	28.9
/I Do HH Maintenance,	Part Time	N=38	10.5
Gardening Etc.	FT Housewife	N=38	2.6
Not a Man's Work	All	N=125	17.6
/Wife's Responsibility	Full Time	N=45	13.3
/Other Traditional Reasons	Part Time	N=38	10.5
	FT Housewife	N=38	28.9
Preference/I Don't Like Doing	All	N=125	11.2
Domestic Work	Full Time	N=45	15.6
/I'm Lazy/Inefficient	Part Time	N=38	7.9
/Spouse Is Good At It	FT Housewife	N=38	10.5

coded the respondents answers as to why they did more or less of the domestic work in different ways, therefore the responses have been divided into different tables by area.

Since only 2.5% of men believed that they did more domestic work than was fair, table 5.9 shows the proportions of those men in Rochdale who stated that they do less than their fair share who cited various reasons why this was so. Table 5.9 shows that the different work commitments and available time of partners is by far the most cited reason that men in Rochdale give for doing less than their fair share of domestic work. This ties in with the findings of chapter three of this book that showed that the amount of time that men spend doing paid work is strongly related to the amount of time that they spend doing unpaid domestic tasks. The dominance of this reason adds an extra complexity to the problem of equity and fairness since, in aggregate, these men obviously feel that the amount of domestic work that their partners are doing is unfair and not the justifiable result of a division of labour between a breadwinner and domestic worker. The proportion of men whose partners work full time that cite this as the reason for the unfairness is significantly ($P=0.017$) lower than that of the other groups, which does suggest that these men do not see their work commitments as a justifiable reason to the same degree as those whose partners are part time paid workers, or do not work at all. This does seem understandable, but it does not fit well with the very large, and again significantly different proportions of men whose partners work part time or do not work at all who cite this reason. One reason may be that the partners of women who work part time view the limited commitment of their wives to the paid sphere as a good reason why they should do less domestic work (i.e. they are more acutely aware of the reciprocity of the situation), whereas those partners of full time housewives see 'traditional' reasons (29% cite this reason compared to 10% of the partners of part time workers and 13% of partners of full timers) as more important (the difference is just insignificant at $P=0.071$). This would tie up with the analysis of chapter three which showed that the male partners of full time housewives, like their partners were much more likely to have more traditional attitudes.

Whereas the partners of women that work full time are less likely than those of full time housewives to cite traditional reasons as to why they do less unpaid work, they are much more likely to state that they do less because of arrangements between them and their partners ($P<0.01$). This suggests that the hypothesis stated in the last section (that as women do more paid work the division of unpaid tasks becomes a more acute and thus more discussed 'problem' that needs to be assessed more carefully and not consigned to previous methods of organisation) has some weight to it. Unfortunately, this view of how domestic work is organised does not seem to be shared by those female partners who work full time. Table 5.10 shows that women in Rochdale who work full time are more likely, but not significantly ($P=0.11$) more likely than those that work part time or are full time housewives to cite arrangements between themselves and their partner as the chief reason why they do more of the domestic work.

For women in Rochdale, as with the men, the chief reason cited is the work commitments of the partners ($P=0.028$). Again, like the men though, women who work full time are the least likely to cite this reason, compared to both part time workers and full time housewives, probably for the same reason. Instead, full time women are much more likely than the male partners of full time women to cite traditional reasons as to why they do not do their fair share of domestic work. This is an interesting finding that runs contrary to the hypothesis of greater acuity of time to households where the woman works full time and also to the findings of chapter three. Could it be that these women are attributing their greater proportion of domestic work to their partner's traditionalism? Some evidence in this direction is the statistically insignificant but large proportion of full time working women (as well as part time and full time housewives) who attribute their greater proportion of unpaid work either to their partners inefficiency/preference or their own abilities in this domain.

Table 5.10 Rochdale Women: Reasons Why Do More Than Fair Share of Domestic Work by Their Work Status

Reason	Partner's Work Status		% Citing Reason
Employment Reasons	All	N=151	41.7
/Spouse Is At Work	Full Time	N=59	30.5
/I Don't Work	Part Time	N=42	57.1
/I'm At Home During The Day	FT Housewife	N=46	43.5
We Have An Arrangement	All	N=151	8.6
/I Do Domestic Work	Full Time	N=59	13.6
Partner Does HH.	Part Time	N=42	2.4
Maintenance, Gardening Etc	FT Housewife	N=46	6.5
	All	N=151	24.5
Not a Man's Work	Full Time	N=59	28.8
/Wife's Responsibility	Part Time	N=42	16.7
/Other Traditional Reasons	FT Housewife	N=46	26.1
Preference/Spouse Doesn't	All	N=151	27.8
Like Doing Domestic Work	Full Time	N=59	30.5
/Spouse Is Lazy, Inefficient	Part Time	N=42	23.8
/I'm Good At It	FT Housewife	N=46	28.3

If true, this finding would support the position of many feminist writers on the domestic division of labour who hold that women's inequitable share of unpaid work is more the result of the man's intransigence in the face of a greater need for his efforts than it is the result of women's attachment to the domestic role. Such intransigence could manifest itself in incompetent attempts to do domestic work that result in the woman taking on those tasks, or in a flat refusal to do them. More evidence will presented on this question later in the book, but for the present, the coding system of the questions in the Aberdeen specific question do offer some information, as presented in tables 5.11 and 5.12.

As in the Rochdale sample, the Aberdeen men cite the reason that their partner has more time, or is around as the greatest reason why they do less than their fair share. But, over a third of the partners of women who work full and part time state that their partners are more efficient as a reason. A quite substantial 17% of the male partners of full time workers and 14% of the partners of full time housewives also cite their laziness as a reason. Like the Aberdeen men, table 5.12 shows the Aberdeen women to be most conscious of the absence of their partner as the chief reason why they do more than their fair share and this is given added weight by the differences between the different work statuses (P=0.025) - again confirming that time limitations and work commitments are major determinants of the division of domestic labour.

Table 5.11 Aberdeen Men: Reasons Why Do Less Than Fair Share of Domestic Work by Their Partner's Work Status

Reason	Partner's Work Status		% Citing Reason
	All	N=123	13.8
Am Lazy	Full Time	N=36	16.7
	Part Time	N=44	9.1
	FT Housewife	N=42	14.3
	All	N=123	13
I'm Too Tired	Full Time	N=36	8.3
	Part Time	N=44	11.4
	FT Housewife	N=42	16.7
	All	N=123	26.8
Partner Is Around	Full Time	N=36	19.4
	Part Time	N=44	27.3
	FT Housewife	N=42	33.3
	All	N=123	3.3
Partner Is Interested	Full Time	N=36	2.8
	Part Time	N=44	4.5
	FT Housewife	N=42	2.4
	All	N=123	35.8
Partner Is Efficient	Full Time	N=36	33.3
	Part Time	N=44	43.2
	FT Housewife	N=42	31
	All	N=123	11.8
Partner Should Do It	Full Time	N=36	8.3
	Part Time	N=44	9.1
	FT Housewife	N=42	16.7

But like the Rochdale women, a large proportion of those in Aberdeen, of all work statuses, also cite the lack of interest of their partners as a reason. Most interestingly, full time women workers in Aberdeen are much more likely than those that work part time or not at all (P=0.017) to cite the inefficiency of their partner as a reason. Again, could it be that those women that work full time have tried to get their partners to do some of the household domestic tasks and found the results wanting, thus drawing them back into doing them? As in with the Rochdale data however, this type of quantitative data does not tell us whether these women simply expect their male partners to not be able to do these tasks because of their beliefs about the proper roles of the sexes, or whether they have tried to get them to do them and failed, or simply picked them back up themselves when the results were too poor to withstand.

Table 5.12 Aberdeen Women: Reasons Why Do More Than Fair Share of Domestic Work by Their Work Status

Reason	Partner's Work Status		% Citing Reason
	All	N=188	23.9
Like To Be Busy	Full Time	N=58	22.4
	Part Time	N=67	26.9
	FT Housewife	N=51	19.6
	All	N=188	19.1
Partner Works Too Hard	Full Time	N=58	13.8
	Part Time	N=67	20.9
	FT Housewife	N=51	21.6
	All	N=188	28.2
Partner Is Not Around	Full Time	N=58	15.5
	Part Time	N=67	32.8
	FT Housewife	N=51	37.3
	All	N=188	21.8
Partner Is Not Interested	Full Time	N=58	25.9
	Part Time	N=67	17.9
	FT Housewife	N=51	27.5
	All	N=188	12.2
Partner Is Inefficient	Full Time	N=58	22.4
	Part Time	N=67	6
	FT Housewife	N=51	9.8
	All	N=188	5.3
Partner Should Not Do It	Full Time	N=58	1.7
	Part Time	N=67	6
	FT Housewife	N=51	7.8

The lack of 'traditional' reason (i.e. the answer - 'partner should not do it') responses tends to militate against the first explanation.

In conclusion, this section of the chapter has shown that we cannot simply take the generally high proportion of the domestic work that female partners do as indicative of a failure of men to take on those tasks. Even if women are justifying the status quo within their households by stating that they are satisfied with the division of labour as it stands to a certain degree, we cannot explain 50% being satisfied with the fairness of their arrangements in this way. Obviously, some women see the division of labour between themselves and their spouses as legitimate. As predicted in the opening part of this chapter, partners in those households where the woman works full time, and to a certain extent part time, are more likely to see specific arrangements as the reason why tasks are divided up. This reason was stated less by female partners, but was strongly suggested by the answers from male respondents. In the same way, although male partners tended to stress time and work related reasons as to why they did less housework, there was much evidence that women saw the ineffectiveness, or disinterestedness of their partners as a major reason why they did more domestic work. The large proportions of full time female respondents in the Rochdale sample who cited 'traditional' reasons was added evidence of this, though as explained, the interpretation of such results from quantitative data is difficult. Does male disinterestedness and ineffectiveness act as a drag upon the adoption of more equitable practices? That is to say, do men's attitudes shape the domestic work practices of the household more than the woman's? The next section of this chapter will examine the relationship between partners' attitudes and their practices.

Attitudes and Practices

It is clear from the first two sections of this chapter that attitudes toward the proper work roles that partners should fulfil have some influence on how partners see their own practices. Section one showed that after controlling for the real amounts of domestic work that partners accomplished, attitudes toward who should be responsible for certain household tasks had some, though unquantified effect on the self-estimates that partners made of their own and their partners contributions. If correct, this evidence adds more weight to the argument that I was making in chapter three that we cannot solely see households as utility (and thus time and material) maximisers[5]. The evidence not only shows that most households have a very general knowledge of how much time they spend doing specific tasks, but this knowledge is intimately bound up with their culturally derived beliefs and attitudes about how much unpaid work they should be doing.

Section two showed that perceptions of fairness and unfairness are not directly attributable to either the real amounts of domestic work that partners do, or the self-estimates that they make about their contributions. In the same way, the work status of the female partner made little difference to whether practices were seen as unfair or not. These findings must mean that there are more processes going on here than partners making 'rational' calculations of time-use that then feed into their perceptions of equity based upon some generalised 'norm of reciprocity'. If attitudes have an effect on self-estimates, they may also have an effect on practices, either directly through the stances of the partners, or through taken-for-granted assumptions that evolve into specific work practices. The last section showed that these 'stances' could be either the reciprocal arrangements of the partners (as the partners of full time women claimed) or the flat refusal/ intransigence and ineffectiveness of one partner in the process of doing domestic tasks as many women (and men) in the last section claimed. These categories are almost certainly not discreet and there is bound to be some overlap in the way that the processes occur, but it is clear that they do occur. This section will focus more closely on the relationship between attitudes and practices using data from the SCELI survey.

Chapter four showed that both abstract attitudes about the proper work roles of women and more direct attitudes on who should do specific tasks in a heterosexual household are highly correlated with the work status of the female partner. This presents us with a tricky analytical problem. Indirectly, the evidence seems clear that attitudes are implicated in the processes through which the division of domestic tasks occurs, but it is difficult to separate these effects from the material circumstances of respondents' lives. These 'circumstances' are themselves, at least to some degree the outcome of the interaction of attitudes and experiences that respondents have 'lived' prior to the SCELI study at which point the general situation of each household was ossified at a particular moment in time (at least metaphorically). How then do we separate these factors so as to get a clearer picture of the processes that have occurred? the next chapter will examine the interaction of attitudes and practices over time, but for the moment we can make certain assumptions that will help us unpack the complex picture within the data.

Strictly speaking, we need longitudinal data on the domestic practices and attitudes of the partners if we are to answer this question. More realistically, we can endeavour to construct models of the determinants of the division of domestic tasks and time between the partners as found at the time of interview. We already know that paid work practices are significant determinants of domestic practices, but, if in the context of these multivariate models the attitude variables turn out to be significant predictors of the division of labour within the household, we can be fairly certain that they play some role. We could not be sure of the direction of the causal link involved, although as the theoretical discussion of chapters one and four illustrated, attitudes and paid work practices would tend to be symbiotic determinants of the domestic division of labour. On the other hand, if the attitude variables turn out to be insignificant in the context of the multivariate model, it will be clear that we will have to revise our theoretical model of the processes at work and the interpretations made of previous evidence presented in this chapter.

Adding Attitudes to the Preliminary Model of the Domestic Division of Labour

We have already seen several models of the domestic work practices of partners in the SCELI survey in chapter three. The aim there was to assess whether the new home economic approach to the division of domestic work was sufficient to explain the patterns that we see in the data. In a comparison of a general model and a more specific model tightly derived from the assumptions of the NHE theories, we found that the latter did not explain enough of the variance in the sample to merit much support. This is not to say that the model found no support in application. It was clear from the regression models that partners' contributions to domestic work are reciprocally linked in a way that suggests that there is some *quid quo pro* trade-off between their paid and unpaid work time, but the general conclusion was that there were other factors that shaped partners' contributions other than those of utility maximisation. The results of chapter three mean that, although we found the NHE theory wanting we must still retain the variables used as predictors there in the models to come. This means that we are still working within the theoretical framework of the theory to a certain degree, except that in this chapter we go forward to suggest that culturally shaped attitudes and beliefs are also significant predictors of the division of labour within households.

The theoretical arguments of chapter one showed that it is difficult to include more culturally motivated spurs to action within the parsimonious framework of the NHE theory, and I make no attempt to fuse the two into a formal theory. However, we do have to accept that households are productive and allocative systems that selectively allocate time and energy in certain directions. We also have to accept that the contributions of the partners are reciprocally related (as shown in chapter three), *but* these assumptions do not mean that we have to accept that the allocation of labour is either consensual, or based entirely on the preferences of the 'household head'. Instead, the attitudes of partners will be used as separate variables that could have contradictory effects on the division of labour within the household, or could combine within an 'interaction effect' to produce specific patterns. The key point is that we accept that the model retains the premise of maximisation, but within a more complex set of assumptions about the relationship between the partners. Chapter two showed that the type of measurement that we make of the domestic division of labour makes a difference to the outcomes that we see. Thus, although the number of discrete tasks that a woman does when she works full time in the paid sphere do not vary much compared to those of a women who works part time, the frequency with which these tasks are done is lower. This means that she will spend less time on domestic work than the part time woman will overall. Because of this, we need to look at both these metrics outlined in chapter two: the woman's proportion of domestic work time and number of discrete tasks.

Specifying the Models Both of the models in this section use the woman's proportion of the specific metric (i.e. time, number of tasks) as the dependant variable in a regression equation. Although the OLS regression is very well suited to analysing the relationship between a continuous variable (such as the woman's minutes of domestic work time) and a set of categorical or continuous independent variables, it does encounter a particular problem when faced with a dependant variable which is proportional to the independent predictors of the model. This problem was pointed out by Karl Pearson as long ago as 1897 in a paper on spurious correlation where he showed that errors can be produced when analysts attempt to interpret correlation between ratios whose numerators and denominators contain common parts. He termed this problem that of 'compositional data' (Aitchison 1986, xii). The inherent problem with compositional data is that the proportions of a composition (i.e. the woman's proportion of domestic work) are naturally subject to the unit sum constraint, i.e.:

$$\chi_1 + \ldots + \chi_D = 1$$

This means that if we attempt to model the change in the woman's proportion of domestic work, we are liable to invoke spurious correlation and error within the estimations because the proportion of domestic work is inherently connected to the amount of paid work that both she and her partner do, since there are only 24 hours in a day. The dependent and independent variables are proportions of a greater whole, i.e. the 24-hour day. The problem is particularly acute in this context because all of the measures of time use are derived from the same source - the diary survey that was carried out in 1987. Luckily, Aitchison (1986) suggests that we can avoid these statistical errors by using the natural log of the proportion that is to be the dependent variable. Therefore, all of the models that are presented in this section use the log of the woman's proportion of the domestic labour within the household as the dependant variable. Parameter estimates for the effects of the independent variables are given in this logged form and show the additive effect of the category of interest on the group of reference, or base group.

As in chapter three, we need to control for the amount of time that each partner spends in paid work, in line with the assumption that the household as a whole will allocate unpaid work time in a way that seeks to find the best configuration of 'inputs' in terms of time and resources, given opportunity costs (i.e. wages forgone by not doing more paid work) and productivity. Put simply, this means that we expect some adjustment in the amount of time that the respondents spend doing domestic work according to the amount of time that they spend doing paid work. In the models, paid work time is depicted by a four-category variable for each partner, each category representing a quartile of the continuous measure of paid work time derived from the diary survey. By using quartiles to represent the amount of paid work done by male and female partners, we compare the investments of each to other male and female partners respectively. Paid work time is rarely allocated on a minute by minute, or hour by hour basis as people tend to allot time in discrete 'chunks' (influenced by institutional constraints and the impossibility of constantly rejigging time in relation to other commitments). The structure of the paid work variable goes some way to modelling this problem since we are comparing men against men and women against women, thus depicting the cleavages that occur in the work hours of each sex. Thus, the first paid work time quartile for women depicts those that do no paid work at all and the break between the third and fourth quartiles is between what is commonly taken to be part time and full time work (approximately 30 hours per week).

Secondly, we need to control for the income difference between the partners as this affects their relative productivity in domestic work. If one partner has a job with a higher salary than the other, we should expect that this will have an impact on the way that the partners allocate their time, since the opportunity costs of the higher paid partner doing domestic work rather than paid work are higher than if the lower paid partner were to do it. The measure for income difference was constructed by taking the male partners income from that of the female partner - a calculation that means that as the difference decreases (i.e. becomes non-negative) we should see the effect on proportion of domestic work that the woman does. This is premised on the fact that men's average earnings are higher than women's, with a substantial number of women having no income at all. I have not attempted to construct a shadow wage for those with no income, since this introduces a whole new set of problems connected with the availability of work and runs against the static nature of the models in this section, which simply attempt to see the effect of income difference on the contributions of partners. If the assumption about the effect of income difference is correct, we should see a positive relationship between the income difference between the partners and the woman's proportion of domestic work.

Respondents who are not working may nonetheless be signed on as unemployed and be claiming state benefits (or may be claiming income support for low earnings). Thus two variables are included which depict the effect of added household income either through benefits or savings that are returning an income. This is a household variable (i.e. not tied exclusively to one partner) and it is difficult to predict through the theories outlined so far how this income will affect the woman's proportion of domestic work.

A number of studies (Pahl 1984; Brannen & Moss 1991; Pleck 1985) have shown that men tend to do more domestic work (as opposed to child care work) when there is a young child in the house, thus a dummy variable is used to depict the presence of a child under five in the household. Though small children may increase the partners' domestic work time, the presence of older children may lead to a reduction as they begin to contribute to the overall work burden. To control for this, a set of dichotomous variables are entered into the model that refer to whether help is given by either a male or female child on four different activities - washing-up, cleaning and hoovering, cleaning clothes and cooking. This type of domestic help to partners is one form of a more general effect that must be controlled for, that of commodity substitution. For instance, it could be that the household gets help from a member of the family that lives outside of the household (most usually a mother of one of the partners) or the household 'buys in' the services of someone by employing a domestic help. To control for these effects, two other sets of variables are entered that control for whether a relation from outside the household or a paid person helps with the same core domestic work tasks as outlined above.

Finally, as in the first section of this chapter, the responses to two questions in the HCS survey on who should be responsible for domestic work and the provision of an adequate income for the household are used to depict attitudes about what is seen as the proper division of labour between the partners. As explained in the last section of this chapter, the responses from these questions are entered as dummy variables where the traditional response is taken as the comparison group (i.e. woman should be responsible for the domestic work question and the man should be responsible for the question on income). If attitudes do have any effect on the domestic work practices of the households within the sample, we should see some effect from the variable depicting respondents answers as to who they think should be ultimately responsible for domestic work. A slightly more tenuous connection may exist between the answers to the question as to who should have ultimate responsibility for the provision of an adequate household income and domestic work practices. On the one hand, a belief on behalf of either partner that the man should be responsible for this task would mean that they have some belief in the traditional division of tasks between men and women, and thus could influence them to divide the domestic tasks in a more traditional manner. On the other, a belief in this task being the man's responsibility could just imply that the organisation of income and finance in the household is his task, and say little about the division of the other domestic work tasks that we are interested in here. In all of the models, the base category is that which is taken to be the 'traditional' one, thus the first quartile of women's paid work and the last of men's and the attitude that domestic work should be the female partner's responsibility and income the male's.

A Model of Domestic Work Time

The first of the models in this section is of that of the woman's proportion of total household time spent doing domestic tasks. This measure is the same as that outlined in chapter two and includes what could be termed the 'core domestic tasks' such as cleaning & hoovering, washing up, cooking, washing clothes and shopping as well as the more infrequent tasks such as DIY and car maintenance. As a reference, a base model was constructed from all of the independent predictors listed above (apart from the attitude variables) to which the attitude variables were then entered. Attitude variables were retained in the model if they explained a significant degree of variance in the sample, as measured through an F-test ($P<0.05$). The attitude variables depicting each partner's beliefs about who should ultimately be responsible for domestic work were then entered into the base model first. Our major interest here is the possible direction of, and size of the effect of the attitude variables, but we also need to see whether the attitudes of each partner have a significant effect, controlling for the others. This will help us discern whether the man's or the woman's attitudes have more effect on the division of labour within the household and thus go some way to analysing the hypothesis outlined earlier in this chapter, i.e. that the man's are going to be of prime importance since domestic work is traditionally seen as the women's role, thus needing the man to be proactive in taking tasks from the female partner. In the absence of the will to make a difference, it would be possible for the man to retain a traditional division of labour, irrespective of the woman's attitudes.

In building the model shown in table 5.13, F-tests on the entry of the two attitude variables showed good support for this theory: the variable depicting the woman's attitudes towards who should be responsible for domestic work did not explain a significant amount of variance within the sample (P=0.62), whereas the man's attitude had a very significant effect (P<0.001). It seems then that the man's attitudes towards who should be ultimately responsible for domestic work within the home are much more powerful predictors than those of the woman.

Testing the partners' attitudes about who should be ultimately responsible for the provision of an adequate income in the same way produced a rather negative result. Neither of the spouse attitudes on this variable made any significant difference to the model (woman's attitudes: P=0.97; Man's attitudes: P=0.46). This result may mean that the point made earlier in the discussion of the variables, i.e. that this question is tapping an attitude that does not have much relevance to the division of labour within the household, has some truth to it. The non-significance of these two variables persisted even if the other variables of the base model were removed, showing that no other variable was acting as 'a proxy' for these and thus restricting the amount of variance that could be explained by them. Given their lack of significance, these variables were dropped from the base model.

The significance of the variables in the base model, plus the variables depicting the domestic work attitudes of the male partner are shown in table 5.13. As none of the base model variables representing the household labour of children or the effect of commodity substitution are significant, I have included these (12) variables as one line in the table with the interval over which their parameter estimates range.

Looking at table 5.13, most of the variables have effects in the directions predicted earlier on in this section. The reference category for the amount of time that the man spends in paid work is that of the highest, thus as predicted, each of the other categories in the table have an increasingly negative effect on the woman's proportion of domestic work (i.e. she does a smaller proportion as he does less paid work). In the same way, the more paid work that the woman does, the greater the estimated decrease in the proportion of domestic work time that she does. As in chapter three, it is clear that the amount of time spent in paid work has a large effect on the domestic work contributions of the partners. As in past research, table 5.13 shows that the presence of a young child has a significant negative effect on the proportion of domestic work done by the woman, but none of the other base model variables have a significant effect on the woman's proportion of domestic work apart from a slight positive effect for income from benefits.

To sum up this section, the models show that attitudes do shape the division of domestic labour, but the man's attitudes were by far the stronger predictors of behaviour and unlike the woman's attitude variable, accounted for a significant proportion of the variance in the model.

Table 5.13 An OLS Model of the Woman's Proportion of Domestic Work Time

Variable		B	Sig.
Man's Paid Work Quartile	High	*Ref.*	
	Low	-0.49	***
	Medium Low	-0.17	***
	Medium High	-0.08	*
Woman's Paid Work Quartile	Low	*Ref.*	
	Medium Low	-0.06	N.S
	Medium High	-0.16	***
	High	-0.33	***
Child <5 In Household		-0.08	**
Income Difference (Woman - Man)		0.01	N.S
Income From Benefits		0.0	N.S
Income from Other Sources		0.0	N.S
Children's Labour and Commodity Substitution Variables		-0.08 - 0.18	N.S
Man's Attitude to HW	Traditional	*Ref.*	
	Untraditional	-0.1	***
N=387 R^2(adj.)=0.45	Constant	4.52	***

*=P<0.05   **=P<0.01   ***=P<0.001

These findings give much support to the hypothesis made earlier in this chapter that it is the man's willingness to take on domestic tasks that is most important since the man's attitudes have a much more direct effect on practices compared to the woman's attitudes. The corollary of this is that the man can exercise a large amount of control over his proportion of domestic work either by refusing to do the work, or by being inefficient at them, as shown in the second section of this chapter.

A Model of the Woman's Proportion of the Total Number of Domestic Work Tasks

This second model examines the effect of the partners' attitudes on the woman's proportion of the total number of domestic tasks accomplished. As explained in chapter two, the metric of the number of tasks measures the number of different tasks performed, not the frequency with which they are done. Why use this measure at all if we already know the influence of attitudes on domestic work behaviour from the last model? Again, as chapter two showed, the mean number of different tasks accomplished by women tends to remain the same as she does more paid work, but it appeared that these tasks were done far less often. The differential between the metrics throws in to relief the trade offs being made by the woman (the man's frequency, as with time, also falls, but not at the same rate as the woman's as she does more paid work). As shown in the work of Sarah Berk (1985), the general picture is of women maintaining their 'slice' of the cake of domestic tasks, but attempting to rationalise on the amount of times that these tasks are accomplished in the face of growing paid work commitments. As such, the metric of domestic work that measures the total frequency of tasks will tend to mirror the measure of time use (a model of the frequency of tasks, not included in this chapter, showed this to be approximately true), whereas that of the number of discrete tasks has a different dynamic. The question for this section is what effect do attitudes have on this process? Do traditional attitudes mean that the woman does a greater proportion of tasks, controlling for other factors such as work status? Do the woman's attitudes have more or less effect on her proportion of this metric than they did on the measure of time use? The dependant variable in this model is the log of the woman's proportion of the total number of different tasks done in the household. The independent variables remain the same as in the last model, thus I will not reiterate what I said about these then. As in the last model, apart from the variables in the base model, all others had to explain a significant degree of variance to remain in the model (P<0.05). This is a fairly high hurdle to clear in this context since the degree of variance in the data is much smaller than in the dependant variable of the last model. This is clear from the initial results after entering the main terms for the attitude variables.

As in the last model all of the categories representing the paid work time of the partners where significant, except for the category representing women's second paid work quartile. In the same way, the variable depicting a child under five being present in household was also significant. This matches our expectation, couched upon the findings of others such as Pahl (1984), that the presence of a young child means that the wife can no longer do the range of tasks that she once did and these are forced onto the male partner, or else will not be performed. None of the other base model variables reach significance. In terms of the attitude variables, the picture presented is similar to that in the last model, with the terms for the male partners attitudes reaching significance (P=0.03) as against none of the females (P=0.71).

That the male partner's attitudes are significant within this model shows that they have a fairly strong effect, but as before, both of the variables representing the attitude toward 'breadwinning' are insignificant. As in the last model, the reasons for this are fairly opaque. Table 5.14 shows the significance of each category and the parameter estimates of their effect. As in the model for domestic work time, both of the significant categories for men's paid work reduce the woman's proportion of the number of tasks. In the same way, women in the fourth paid work quartile reduce their proportion and do so to a greater extent than women in the 'medium high category'. These are not as large as in the first model, but quite significant falls nonetheless. Having a child under five in the household reduces the woman's proportion by a small amount. Overall then, we have further confirmation of our hypothesis that it is the readiness of the male partner to take on domestic work tasks that is crucial in determining the female partner's proportion of the domestic division of labour.

Table 5.14 An OLS Model of the Woman's Proportion of Domestic Work Tasks

Variable		Exp. B	Significance
Man's Paid Work Quartile	High	*Ref.*	
	Low	-0.24	***
	Medium Low	-0.08	***
	Medium High	-0.05	*
Woman's Paid Work Quartile	Low	*Ref.*	
	Medium Low	0.01	N.S
	Medium High	-0.06	*
	High	-0.13	***
Child <5 In Household		-0.07	**
Income Difference (Woman - Man)		-0.01	N.S
Income From Benefits		0.0	N.S
Income from Other Sources		0.0	N.S
Children's Labour and Commodity Substitution Variables		-0.04 - 0.17	N.S
Man's Attitude to HW	Traditional	*Ref.*	
	Untraditional	-0.04	*
N:=387 R^2 (Adj.)=0.25	Constant	4.23	***

*=P<0.05   **=P<0.01   ***=P<0.001

However, the findings of the model in table 5.14 show that this readiness takes on certain forms. The parameter estimates for the variables depicting the woman's paid work time in table 5.13 are much larger, almost three times the size of the effects in table 5.14. This suggests that as the woman does more paid work, this does not reduce the women's proportion of *tasks* to the same extent as it reduces her proportion of *time* in the last model. This supports Sarah Berk's (1985, p121) finding that the redistribution that does occur tends to occur on the basis of the amount of *time* spent rather than the number of *tasks* accomplished. The number of different household tasks accomplished may be relatively fixed since one cannot choose to cut back on most areas. However, one can choose to spend less time performing these tasks. For example, each day households (or individuals within households) have an evening meal and under most circumstances one would not do away with this task even when other commitments begin to encroach upon it. Instead, less time is spent making the meal, or a substitute is found in the form of food from outside the household or outside labour to create the meal within. But, these models show that as other commitments, like the woman's paid work time, build up, it is more likely that the male partner will spend more time doing the same tasks as before, rather than taking on new tasks.

Conclusions

This chapter has cast some light onto several important areas. First of all, it has shown that partners' perceptions of their practices are affected by what Hochschild (1990) has termed 'the family myth'. Here though, we have been able to be more specific about the nature of the myth itself and the relationship between the 'myth' and the picture expressed in the diary data. It is clear from the tables that looked at the correlation between the estimates and the diaries broken down by work status, that households where the female partner works full time, or is unemployed, are more acutely aware of their practices. At the same time, if we control for paid work time and the diary totals, it is also clear that these estimates are still affected by what Hochschild called the 'gender strategies' or attitudes and beliefs of the partners. When added to the evidence from the models of the difference between the partners' estimates and the diary data, these findings strongly support the weak interpretation of the family myth, i.e. that partners' estimates of their practices are shaped by the level of knowledge they have of these practices and their attitudes toward them. The models did not however, support the 'strong' interpretation of the myth, i.e. that it is shaped by the conflict that occurs when the partners' have attitudes that are contradicted by their practices. An interaction between the woman's attitudes and her proportion of domestic work showed that when a woman does a high proportion of the domestic work and has untraditional attitudes, this did not increase the gap between the partners' estimates of their practices and that registered in the diary data.

It was also clear that the generally lopsided nature of the division of domestic work tasks does not go unnoticed, yet the second section of this chapter showed that this does not necessarily lead to practices being seen as unfair. The majority of men and women saw their household arrangements as fair, even controlling for the woman's work status. Unfortunately, we could not directly link attitudes to this data, but it was clear that we have to accept, as in the work that has been done on women's satisfaction with low paid, unskilled jobs, that many women see their main role, in some generalised sense, as that of the homemaker. Nonetheless, the reasons that men and women in Aberdeen and Rochdale gave for this inequity were illuminating. Many men and women saw the situation as the result of the man's greater involvement in paid work, but a large proportion of women also cited their partners ineffectiveness and disinterestedness as a major reason why they did more of the domestic work. Thus, even if attitudes do lead some men and women to feel that the woman's proportion of unpaid work is fair in general, there is also evidence here that many women would like to see their partners involved more but find themselves having limited ways of encouraging this.

The last section of the chapter was important in establishing the effect of attitudes on the woman's proportion of domestic work. More specifically, it showed in a multivariate environment that it is the man's attitudes that tend to dictate the women's proportion, rather than her own. This was true in both the models and suggests again that we have to see the processes underlying the distribution of domestic work as suffused with power relations. 'Power' is a difficult concept to examine in empirical studies, but it is clear from the results from this chapter that men can shape practices by withholding their domestic labour. Such a finding supports the qualitative work of feminists researchers such as Meissner *et al* (1975) or Delphy and Leonard (1986) that highlight the conflictual nature of domestic relations. We will see in chapter seven whether the patterns we have examined here result in dissatisfaction on behalf of the female partner and perhaps conflict between her and her partner.

It is clear from the last two models that the amount of paid work that both partners do has a large bearing on their contributions. This reiterates the point made several times before that we have to see the household as a maximising entity, even if a vague and complex one. It is also clear from the findings of this chapter and the last that the partners' attitudes, paid work choices and domestic practices are intimately inter-linked. This suggests that we need to analyse the division of domestic tasks as a long run process that has its roots in the past work and life history of the partners. This is the subject of the next chapter.

Notes

[1] I am very grateful to Liz Fraser for pointing out the different interpretations that could be made of the 'family myth'.

[2] The self-estimates were transferred into quantities by expressing the partner's choice about who did the task ('female entirely', 'female mainly', both equally etc.) into proportions where female entirely equals 100, female mainly equals 75, both equally equals 50 etc.

[3] I am grateful to Duncan Gallie for his helpful suggestions concerning the structure of these models.

[4] The self-estimates of both partners in the HCS survey (1987) show that less than 5% of both male and female partners estimate the man's contribution to core domestic tasks as being 50% or more.

[5] Whilst making this point, I do not want to 'throw the baby out with the bath water'. The results of chapter three also showed that the paid work practice of the partners' was a good predictor of the level of unpaid work that they do. This was true as much for the men as for the women and thus speaks of some form of maximising behaviour occurring, even if only of a loose and often inequitable kind.

6   The Effects of Life and Work History on Gender Attitudes and Domestic Work Practices

Thus far, we have concentrated on what we could call the 'immediate' factors that influence the domestic division of labour, rather than the antecedent factors such as the work history of the partners in the household. It was necessary to examine the patterns of attitudes and economic variables, such as partners' work status in the present, to establish the relevance and explanatory power of the different theories outlined in chapter one of this book and give us a picture of the patterning of these variables, before turning to those that represent life and work history processes. This chapter will first examine the nature of the relationship between attitudes in the present and certain types of experiences that partners may have had over their lives; second, it will examine the relationship between life and work history variables and the domestic practices of partners in the present. The aim is to show empirically, that the theoretical stance adopted in chapter one of this book is an improvement over previous models of household processes. The end point of the chapter will be a set of models that build upon the ground already established in the book by adding work and life history variables to those already examined.

What have we established so far though? Chapter three showed clearly that the work status of partners has a direct influence upon how unpaid work is distributed within the household. What it also showed was that, although male partners tend to do more domestic work the less time they spend doing paid work, we could not detect a significant increase in male contributions to unpaid work in response to an increase in the allocation of time to paid work on behalf of the female partner. The first finding shows that when translated into an empirical model, the theories of the NHE is at least correct in predicting that the amount of time that partners' spend in domestic work will be endogenously determined by other work commitments and their marginal productivity (this belief is strengthened by the fact that the difference in income between the partners had a small, though significant effect). Unfortunately for the NHE thesis, the second finding shows that such factors are a necessary, but not adequate explanation for the patterns that we see emerging in the data from the SCELI data set. All the figures in chapter three showed that we could not account for the lack of response on behalf of the male to changes in the female's paid work time within the terms of the theory.

Together, the findings of chapters four and five went some way toward finding an explanation for this discrepancy. Whilst there are identifiable differences between the attitudes toward the work roles that men and women should fulfil amongst women of different work statuses (and their partners), there is still much support for what is usually termed the 'traditional' division of labour, even amongst women who work as many hours in paid work as their partner. Moreover, chapter five showed that the majority (57%) of women thought that their domestic work practices were 'fair', even women who in full time paid work (53%). These findings confirm those of Dex (1988) and Jowell and Witherspoon (1985) that there is a large variation in attitudes toward the 'proper' division of domestic work time and tasks between couples.

However, what was perhaps most illuminating about chapter five was the differential significance of male and female partners attitudes on their domestic work practices. Even if the female partner has untraditional attitudes, their effect on how things actually get done seems to be negligible. On the other hand, the male partner's attitudes are much more powerful predictors of practices. These statistical patterns seem to indicate, for households where the female has untraditional attitudes at least, that it is the man's unwillingness to take on domestic tasks that leads to problems experienced by the NHE models in chapter three. Chapter Five offered more evidence of this in the form of reasons from female partners as to why their domestic work practices were unfair: many answered that it was the lack of interest and ineffectiveness in domestic work of their partners.

What theoretical picture can we put on these findings? It is clear that, in so far as there are differences between the contributions of male partners who do different amounts of paid work, the economic theory of maximisation holds some empirical water. On the other hand, it is also clear that the respondents in the SCELI survey are cultural as well as economic actors, having beliefs about the proper division of domestic labour that limit the effect of economic imperatives in shaping practices. Contrary to the structural theories outlined in chapter one though, these 'cultural forces' are not homogenous, but vary quite widely across the population surveyed. Within households, there is definite evidence that where there are differences between the attitudes of the man and the woman, the man is more able to make his beliefs count in practice than the woman is. What is beginning to emerge is a picture of households where partners, as *individuals* make choices about their paid and unpaid work contributions along lines that are not always in perfect agreement. This finally puts to rest Becker's theory that households are units with a single utility function, led by a head with the interests of all members at heart. If the assumption seemed unreasonable in chapter one, then there is ample evidence from later chapters that it is simply untrue. The final chapter of this book will outline the effects of the imbalances that may emerge from this situation in more detail.

Process and the Topography of Attitudes

If the cultural landscape of attitudes toward gender roles is not smooth and of the same type, from where do the different features emerge? Chapter four showed that there was likely to be, and indeed seemed to be, a large interaction and correlation between the attitudes of both female and male partners and the female partner's work status in the present. As we have seen, these variables are strongly implicated as determinants of the domestic division of labour, but we have not been able explicitly to disentangle the relationship between them. This is to be expected given the complexity of the relationship, yet we need to assess where the topography of attitudes comes from and the effect of past paid work practices on the present division of domestic labour. Unless we do so, the aim which we set ourselves in the opening chapter of this book will not be fulfilled, i.e. to inject 'process' into models of the division of domestic labour. By process, I mean those factors in a persons past life and work history that have led him or her to order their activities in certain ways and believe certain things about the relationship of men and women to domestic work practices. Arlie Hochschild

(1990) had a limited (and vague) sense of these factors in her concept of the 'gender strategy' as outlined in the previous chapter. For Hochschild, childhood experiences play a large part in shaping the gender strategy that a man or woman will hold. Whilst not disputing this, we also need to view individuals within households as experienced and knowledgeable persons who have learnt to adapt to changes throughout their work lives as well. As this book has shown, attitudes toward domestic work are not always matched by practices because other factors are as important, and because, quite often, actors do not know what their practices are. Attitudes are in this respect general factors in the shaping of domestic work practices and not always direct contributors.

Chapter two showed that the notion of 'domestic work' covers a very large number of individual tasks and operations. These tasks are not always discrete and separable and together form a large corpus of activities that are not easily structured. Juggling these activities whilst performing other necessary activities such as paid work is difficult, and once routinised, not easily changed (Oakley 1974). Although sometimes monotonous to perform, the complex structures that these activities create tend to have a certain inertia to change that can defy even the most ardent reformer. Thus people tend to build up structures of household work organisation that take time to change, even if the original conditions which caused them have long since ceased to be imperatives to that type of structure. As such, we need to examine how the experience of past work statuses effects the type of organisation that individuals and households adopt in the present.

Once routinised, the majority of domestic tasks do not require a great deal of reflection or concentration when being carried out, but this should not disguise from us the importance of this type of action to the outcomes that we see in the data in this book. One of the great problems in sociology is to explain the taken for granted ways of achieving certain ends that people use in everyday life and the assumptions they make about them. Certain rational choice theories assume that persons take a direct interest in and calculate each outcome from their actions (the basis of subjective expected utility theory), but the vastness of this project would mean that most people would cease to act (as outlined in chapter four). Instead, people have assumed ways of dealing with everyday tasks that act as 'frameworks' for their decision making and cut down on the number of choices that must be made at anyone time. In chapter one, I discussed Parsons and Shils' (1956) 'value' theory of choice and criticised the theory for not being able to encompass changes in costs or value in its model of decision making. Yet, if we include habitual action in our models, does it not mean that we will have another restrictive model of choice? Is habit going to replace 'norms' as an overarching structure, which determines behaviour? Fortunately not. If we look back to chapter one, I outlined a discrimination model of choice put forward by Siegwart Lindenberg. This assumes people will maximise, but that people act rationally if they only follow alternative routes when the costs of not doing so are high, or the outcome has a high degree of certainty (and their present 'frame' now offers little discrimination between outcomes). Lindenberg is not alone in putting forward this kind of approach, but his argument is the clearest. A theoretical outline of this approach to understanding certain types of action has also been given by Bourdieu (1990) in his rather elliptical writings on *habitus*

> The conditions associated with a particular class of conditions of existence produce habitus, systems of durable, transposable dispositions, structured structures predisposed to function as structuring structures, that is, as principles which generate

and organise practices and representations that can be objectively adapted to their outcomes without presupposing a conscious aiming at ends or an express mastery of the operations necessary in order to attain them....It is of course never ruled out that the responses of the habitus may be accompanied by a strategic calculation tending to perform in a conscious mode the operation that the habitus performs quite differently, namely an estimation of chances presupposing transformation of the past effect into an expected objective (Bourdieu 1990, p53)

A clearer account of this idea is given by Lindenberg (1989, p175-198) who produces a much more rigorous typology of how choices are made through frameworks, where a framework is

.... a situationally specified goal together with the criteria for judging approximation of the goal. The goal acts like a special pair of glasses with which the situation is seen. The salience of the frame dictates the degree of discrimination of alternatives. Salience in turn, can vary, and it is determined by other goals that are strong enough to exert some influence, but at least at the moment, too weak to displace the frame. (Lindenberg 1989, p195).

Lindenberg's overall theory of frames is complex (c.f. Lindenberg 1985, 1986, 1989) in application, but fairly simple in theory, as chapter one and the above quote indicate. It simply states that a person's perception of alternative choices is bounded, thus they cannot discriminate as many aspects and objects in the choice situation as the researcher feels free to assume (as in subjective expected utility theory). The bounds of perception are fluidly set by the 'frame of reference', not in the form of a pair of blinkers, but in the form of a filter for perception that allows people to discriminate amongst alternatives. Present frames present a much higher degree of discrimination than other background frames, thus only when the present frame no longer allows discrimination of alternatives does the 'salience' of the present frame fall and that of other background frames rise. We can see 'habitus' or 'frameworks' as the outcome of experiences at various stages of peoples lives that shape the persons perception of specific objects (goals), or ranges of objects in their lives and thus lead them to follow certain choice paths or activities that only change when the pressure, or 'salience' of another frame becomes irresistible. In terms of this book, we could see individual's choices about how much and what kind of domestic work as the outcome of previous experiences or 'frames' and/or the interaction of different frames between partners. In essence, we can find a way to combine the cultural insights of sociologists into the importance of systems of meaning, with the scarcity based, cost benefit analysis of the more empirically applicable rational choice and social exchange theory. In this way we can begin to analyse patterns of behaviour as probabilistically structured by a number of interacting factors, rather than determined by cultural values and economic imperatives. On this basis, let's go on to look at some previous work that has been done concerning the domestic division of labour that uses work history analysis.

The Lagged Adaptation Thesis

In chapter one, I mentioned evidence put forward by Gershuny (1994) which shows that as women enter the labour force, their male partners do more of the core domestic work (as well as childcare) and they do less. Gershuny was arguing against the thesis put forward by sociologists such as Meissner *et al* (1975) that the present unequal division of domestic labour would not improve because women were seen as a source of dependant labour whose primary role was in the household. Thus, as Meissner *et al* saw the situation, both men and women are prisoners of a fixed gender ideology that does not permit them to redistribute the present unequal burden of domestic work.

Gershuny's theory is that people's gender ideologies and practices are not fixed, but flexible in the face of changing economic and social circumstances, though the pace of change is to some extent constrained by differential ideologies about the proper division of labour between the sexes, itself a factor of their experiences earlier in life. In a 1993 paper, Gershuny outlines an empirical argument that shows that men do more domestic work after their wives enter the labour force, but only after a period of 20 months. This movement he terms 'lagged adaptation'. He also offered evidence to the effect that the parents division of labour has a large affect on the practices of partners in the present. As in this book, Gershuny's theory is that partners follow patterns, or 'frames' as I have termed them, set down by their parents, but that they also seek equality in work time over a period.

Unfortunately, there were several problems with the analysis of the data that means that much of the findings of his paper are incorrect. For instance, Gershuny shows through multiple-classification analysis (a type of ANOVA) that there is a steady increase in the proportion of total work (both paid and unpaid) that the man does, the longer his wife is in paid employment. As evidence he puts forward a graph which, controlling for the age of the youngest child, shows that if the wife has been in the labour force for up to 20 months in the last decade, the man does roughly 46% of total work. From 21 to 60 months this total rises to 49% and after 60 months to 50% plus. However, although these totals control for the age of the youngest child they do not take into account the fact that the husband's proportion of total work depends upon fluctuations that may look like increases, but are in fact decreases. For instance, if the woman's contribution to domestic work decreases, but the man's stays static, this will increase the man's proportion of total work, but this does not mean that he does any more domestic work. We could also be seeing a change in the paid work time totals between the partners, rather than a change in the domestic work contributions. Finally, all of the proportions are mean scores and thus give us no idea of the spread or variation. With no standard error, it is impossible to say whether the graph is a good representation of the data, or a figment of the mean score[1].

On a more theoretical level, although Gershuny tries to show that there is adaptation, albeit lagged adaptation to the female partners circumstances, he makes no attempt to look at the effects of work history on the present patterns of domestic labour beyond the summary statistics on the woman's employment in the last ten years. It could be for instance that, in those partnerships old enough, periods of work further back than the last ten years may have some effect. In a way, Gershuny is simply extending the present-oriented studies that I have outlined already in this book in that he is looking at the micro-sociological processes through which the present division of labour is arrived at. There is no real attempt to look at the interaction between the partners' formative experiences/work history experiences and their attitudes, and these same determinants and the domestic division of labour. Since attitudes are highly implicated in the production of present work practices, what is really needed is a multivariate model that looks at the formative influences on attitudes and present practices in separate models.

In this section I want to build and examine a model of the male partner's attitudes toward who should have ultimate responsibility for domestic work. We have seen in previous chapters that attitudes toward responsibility are good predictors of actual practices and seem to be significant even when controlling for the work statuses of partners. This implies that attitudes are in some part independent of present work status and operative on the domestic division of labour net of this variable. In this chapter, the aim is to examine whether there are life and work history determinants of attitudes. I have already explained why this is theoretically necessary, i.e. to escape the present-oriented strictures of previous models, but here, as in the last chapter, it is very difficult to establish causal mechanisms using cross-sectional data. Once again, all we can do is test for the independent effects of life and work history variables after controlling for those variables such as present work status that have some effect upon it. If after controlling for these variables there is still a significant affect on the dependant variable, then we can assume with some confidence that what we are observing is a real effect and not the outcome of correlation between variables.

Specifying a Model In essence, a model of men's attitudes is fairly simply constructed. As in chapter five (where they were independent predictors) I will use the responses to the question of whether men think that the ultimate responsibility for domestic work should rest with the woman, the man or be shared as the dependant variable. I will use the variable in a dichotomous form so that the error term is logit, and the outcome is reported in terms of the odds of the man replying in a 'traditional' or 'untraditional' manner. As explained in chapter five, this type of response is very crude and obviously peoples attitudes are more complex than this, but we gain nothing by having the 'untraditional' responses divided into two groups (i.e. men should be responsible, both should be responsible). Though attitudes are much more complex than this variable can express, we have already seen in chapter five how highly related they are to the partners' domestic work time. Traditional responses are those which see the woman as responsible for domestic work, whereas non-traditional responses see it as shared or done by the man.

To control for the present work statuses of the partners, categorical variables are entered, each having five levels: full time, part time, unemployed, full time house worker or non-working. Unemployment was defined as looking for work in the last four weeks and/or claiming unemployment/supplementary benefit on the grounds of unemployment. As in all of the variables that I am presenting in this chapter, the comparison groups for work status are those that would seem to be the most traditional in their responses from previous analyses, thus for women the comparison group is full time housewives and for men, full time workers.

Since attitudes towards gender roles have changed quite substantially over the last half-century (c.f. Dex 1988), we need to have some control within the model for the age of the partners. Age is entered as a three category variable where the categories are 17 to 29, 30 to 50 and 51 to 60 years of age. Chapter three showed that it is the oldest age group that tends to have the most traditional attitudes, therefore these will be used as the reference group. If we are to see the independent effect of life and work history variables on the man's present attitudes, it is important to control for those of the female partner since her attitudes may be correlated with her own work history. Thus, the woman's responses to the same question are entered as a dichotomous predictor with the traditional (i.e. the woman should be responsible) as the comparison group. It is also interesting to see the effect of the man and woman's attitudes toward who should be ultimately responsible for the provision of an adequate income on the dependant variable, therefore I have also entered these as variables to the equation. Unlike the question on domestic work though, here the comparison group is those that see the man as ultimately responsible. Together these variables represent the 'base' model of the man's gender role attitudes.

Life and Work History Variables

The variables of real interest in this model (and the next) are those which represent work and life history. We could say that chronologically, it is the early life experiences that occur first, but I will first outline the work history variables used in the model. Although it would be interesting to see the effect of the man's experiences over his work life, the data show that the majority of men in the sample have worked full time work most of their lives. Unlike women, only a tiny proportion of men had ever worked part time. Moreover, since the surveys were carried out in 1986 and 1987 (update in 1987), the majority of men experiencing prolonged spells of unemployment, had done so within the preceding five to seven years. Such uniformity makes it very difficult to obtain any sensible results, especially when the variable that represents the man's present work status also denotes the recent spell of employment, and possibly unemployment. As such, I made the decision to enter the variables that represent the woman's work history alone as predictors of the man's attitudes. According to the lagged adaptation thesis, it is the woman's experiences of work in the past which could be of prime importance in defining the man's attitudes towards the proper division of labour. By this I mean that, through his partner, the man may have experienced different types of household arrangements that would have required him, and the household as a whole to invent new permutations of paid work and unpaid tasks. In doing so, it could be hypothesised that new 'frameworks' could emerge that would either persuade, or dissuade him of the merits of a type of household arrangement and thus affect his attitudes. The effect could fall both ways, in that it could make his attitudes more traditional if the experience was bad, but also less traditional if it became obvious that this arrangement was a viable alternative. In reality, men may well have been part of other households and thus their experiences there will not be tapped by the work-history variables of their present partner. Since we have no information on this, I will simply enter the variables of the present partner.

It is not at all plain how we should go about constructing variables to represent parts of the woman's work life. Since work history data is made up of a 'vector' or long chain of events, we need theoretical tools to cut up this history and assign certain elements of it significance as predictors of present behaviour or attitudes. Dex (1984) used the work history data from the Women and Employment Survey (1980) to examine the changing patterns of work, but did not attempt to look at the dynamic effect of this history on individuals present situations. To give an example, she did not examine how having periods of the work life in part time work, or in unemployment could shape an individuals present chances of being in employment. Our chief interest is in the dynamic effects of past work and life history, thus Dex's type of analysis would not help us understand the work life processes that have led to present attitudes. A better method would be event history analysis, as advocated by Blossfeld (1995), but unfortunately this type of analysis would require longitudinal, but also time varying information attitudes upon which the model could predict the effects of independent (time dependent) co-variates like work life events. Since we only have data at one time point for the analysis of attitudes it will not be possible to use this method. In the same way, when we come to look at the effects of work and life history variables on domestic work practices, the single instance and moreover continuous dependent variables are unsuitable for hazard analysis. Instead I will use logit models of the odds of holding untraditional attitudes given certain past experiences.

Specifying a Model of Men's Gender Role Attitudes

Since our major interest is in the processes, or events that may have led to the emergence of certain practical 'frameworks' of action, it seems theoretically justifiable to look at the most recent activities to see whether these have an effect on attitudes. To do this I constructed a number of different variables. The first represents the last period of employment and whether this was in either full time or part time work. If it was, the variable has five levels to represent the length of the event, i.e. up to 20 months, 21 to 40, 41 to 60, 61 to 80 and 80 plus months (a sixth is no full or part time work in the last period). These periods are the same as those used by Gershuny (1993) to examine full and part time work in the last decade, but here they refer to the last employment event only (the cleavages reflect the distribution of cases rather than any definite theoretical device). Another, almost identical variable has the same structure but refers to full time work in the last period only.

According to our 'frameworking' theory, it is likely that women who have changed from one work status (such as full time housewife to full time worker for example) have a different frame of reference than those that have remained in full time work from the penultimate to the last work event. To test for this type of effect, two variables were constructed. The first grouped the female partners according to whether their second last activity was as a full time house wife followed by being a full time worker, as compared to a group that had stayed in full time employment over the period. The second variable was identical, except that it grouped women according to whether they had worked part time in the penultimate event. If the woman's recent work history does indeed have an effect on the male partners present attitudes, then there should be a difference between the men whose partners are in the comparison group of women who have remained in full time work and those that have changed from part time or started work.

As in Gershuny's work on the effect on the proportion of total work that the man performs, I constructed a set of variables that looked at different types of employment statuses in the last decade. The ten year cut off allows us to look at the aggregated effect of different work statuses in the recent past, rather than the direct effect of one (the last) work event. As in the last set of variables, these 'decade' variables represented periods of full time plus part time work, or full time work alone. In contrast to the last set, here I constructed two more variables, identical to the last two mentioned except that they included unemployment spells as well. The justification for this is that, as shown in chapter three, women who are unemployed are closer in attitudes to women working full time than to full time housewives. As I suggested then, this may be due to the fact that they are more closely connected to the labour market, and expect to take another job when possible (as in the ILO definition of unemployment). These variables were also put into categorical form in the manner of the last employment duration variables.

The last set of work life variables refers to the proportion of the woman's work life that she has spent in various work statuses. Even when controlling for age in the model, there are still unavoidable ceiling effects for the 'decade' variables just mentioned for the youngest age group in the SCELI sample. These variables avoid this by using the proportion of the work life. As in the previous two subsections, these variables refer to the proportion of the work life spent in part time/full time work, full time alone, part time/full time/unemployment and finally full time/unemployment. To aid interpretation, all these measures were transformed into three way categories based upon percentiles. All of the measures used in the analysis of the effects of work history are listed in table 6.1.

Table 6.1 List of Work History Variables

Variable	Which Period of Work History	Type of Work
WDULAF	Last activity in work history	Full time
WDULAFP	Last activity in work history	Full time + Part time
WFP10GP	Last ten years of work history	Full time + Part time
WF10GP	Last ten years of work history	Full time
WFPU10GP	Last ten years of work history	Full time + Part time+Unemp.
WFU10GP	Last ten years of work history	Full time+Unemp.
WPCARFP	Proportion of whole work history	Full time + Part time
WPCARF	Proportion of whole work history	Full time
WPCARFPU	Proportion of whole work history	Full time + Part time+Unemp.
WPCARFU	Proportion of whole work history	Full time+Unemp.
FTHWTOFT	Penultimate and last activity	Full time to Full time Houseworker v.'s Full time to Full time
PTTOFT	Penultimate and last activity	Full time to Part time v.'s Full time to Full time

The life history variables used in the analysis represented factors connected with the parents of both of the partners. The HCS survey (1986) not only asked both of the partners in the household to estimate their own division of certain core domestic work, it also asked them to try to estimate that of their parents. It could be said that the partners' estimates of their parents division of domestic labour would not be reliable due to memory failings, or the effect of their present attitudes or present practices. The first problem may well be present, but it does not seem from the data that the estimates are closely tied to the partners' self-estimates of their own division of labour (which were related to their attitudes). Table 6.2 lists the correlation coefficients between the partners' own self-estimates and their estimates of their parents division of the core domestic tasks.

Table 6.2 Spearman Correlation Coefficients of Partners' Self-Estimates of the Woman's Proportion of Core Domestic Tasks and Partner's Self-Estimates of Their Mother's Proportion of Core Domestic Tasks

	Female Partner's Self-Estimate	Male Partner's Self-Estimate	Female Partner's Estimates Of Parents	Male Partner's Estimates of Parents
Female Partner's Self-Estimate	-	0.62 (N=1090)***	0.14 (N=974)***	0.1 (N=998)***
Male Partner's Self-Estimate	0.62 (N=1090)***	-	0.07 (N=977)N.S	0.21 (N=1005)***
Female Partner's Estimates Of Parents	0.14 (N=974)***	0.07 (N=977) N.S	-	0.08 (N=928)***
Male Partner's Estimates of Parents	0.1 (N=998)***	0.21 (N=1005)***	0.08 (N=928)***	-

*=P<0.05   **=P<0.01   ***=P<0.001

It is fairly clear that although there is a quite substantial correlation between the estimates of the partners of their own division of domestic tasks, the same is not true of their estimates of their respective parents. The estimates by the men of their own parents practices is the highest at 0.21, but this is a low score in its own right. On this basis, it would seem safe to use the estimates to represent the parents division of labour, and thus the effects of childhood experiences of a how certain domestic tasks should be divided. To aid interpretation, these two variables were made into three level categorical variables based upon whether the continuous score was 0.5 of a standard deviation above or below the mean.

A third variable used to look at early life experiences is one that represents whether the mother was employed during childhood. It could be that having an employed mother when growing up may contribute toward more untraditional attitudes towards women's work roles and thus about the division of domestic labour. The variable to represent this was divided up into six categories: whether the mother worked all of the time during their childhood, most of the time, or some of the time with another three categories to represent whether the mother did not work at all, did not live with the child, or was dead during childhood. On entry into the model, each variable needed to significantly improve the fit of the model to be retained (P<0.05). Only the variables of the base model remained in the equation if they did not reach the required level of significance.

The Model Since chapter three of this book it has become apparent that the work statuses of the partners has a large bearing upon both their time use and their attitudes. But, it is also clear that the woman's work status is more important than the man's work status. Upon entering the work status variables into the logistic regression this pattern was again apparent with the woman's work status being highly significant compared to the man's having very little significance at all in a chi-square test. The direction of the effects was similar to those in chapter three. Men whose partners work full time are two and a half times more likely to hold untraditional attitudes compared to those whose partners are full time housewives, with those partners of unemployed women being nearly twice as likely and those of part timers one and half times as likely.

With the age group variables the pattern of significance is the opposite of the work status variables with the woman's age being insignificant and the man's very significant. What is interesting is that, although the woman's age group is significant if entered alone (due to the high correlation between the partners' ages), it does not reach significance once we have controlled for the man's age. This indicates a strong link between the man's age cohort and his attitudes that has been remarked on elsewhere. The other attitude variables are significant, as expected, except for that which represents the woman's attitudes toward who should be ultimately responsible for the provision of an adequate income. This is in contrast to the man's answer to this question that reaches a high level of significance, as does the woman's answer to the question concerning responsibility for domestic work. What is interesting is that when the man's attitudes towards the provision of income are entered, the woman's work status becomes insignificant. This could be because the man's attitudes and the woman's work status are correlated (as we have already seen).

Together, these variables form the base model (see table 6.3) upon which the work and life history variables are entered. On entering the work history variables, it became increasingly clear that none had any effect on the man's odds of having untraditional attitudes. This is surprising given the theoretical discussion earlier on in the chapter where it was assumed that there was an interactive effect between the man's experiences of his partner's participation in paid work and his attitudes. The lack of effect for these variables, when combined with the finding that the woman's attitude toward the responsibility for domestic labour has a significant effect, may suggest that the husband's attitudes are affected by his wife's employment experience through her attitudes. We will have evidence for or against this hypothesis after the next section which examines the structuring of the female partner's attitudes over time.

However, there is another hypothesis that could account for this relationship. It could also be that what we see here is the partnership of people with similar attitudes (a type of assortative mating as Becker (1974) might put it) rather than a coming together of attitudes through shared experiences. What is clear from past findings is that there is an interactive effect between partner's attitudes, but this could be because men and women with the same attitudes tend to pair up, or stay together at a higher rate than men and women with different attitudes.

All these theories are preliminary and impossible to confirm with this data, but it is clear that male partner's attitudes are not affected significantly by their partner's work life experiences, even if entered as interactions with the woman's present work status.

Table 6.3 Logistic Model of the Probability of the Male Partner Having Untraditional Attitudes Toward the Domestic Division of Labour

Variable		Odds	Significance
Woman's work status	Full time Houseworker	*Ref.*	
	Full Time	1.07	N.S
	Part Time	1.13	N.S
	Unemployed	1.36	N.S
	Non-Worker	2.16	N.S
Man's work status	Full Time	*Ref.*	
	Part Time	1.1	N.S
	Unemployed	1.5	*
	Full Time Houseworker	1.22	N.S
	Non-Worker	0.78	N.S
Woman's Age	51 to 60	*Ref.*	
	17-29	1.02	N.S
	30-50	0.72	N.S
Man's Age	51 to 60	*Ref.*	
	17-29	2.16	*
	30-50	2.1	**
Man's Attitude: Income Provision	Traditional	*Ref.*	
	Untraditional	6.6	***
Woman's Attitude:HW	Traditional	*Ref.*	
	Untraditional	2.9	***
Woman's Attitude: Income Provision	Traditional	*Ref.*	
	Untraditional	0.96	N.S
	Constant	0.07	***

N=1218   *=P<0.05   **=P<0.01   ***=P<0.001   deviance: 1192.8   df: 1202

What of the partners' early life history variables? On entering the variables that represented the partners' parents domestic division of domestic labour, neither the woman's or the man's variables were significant. As with the work history variables then, it seems as if his childhood experiences have very little, if any effect on the man's current attitudes controlling for the base model variables. In the same way, the variable that represents whether the respondent's mother worked during childhood was insignificant when entered into the model. Table 6.3 shows the significance and effects of the base model variables on the odds of the man having untraditional attitudes. Because the attitude variables have been left in the equation, almost all of the woman's work status variables are insignificant and the pattern of odds has changed from that reported above. Overall, this model has shown, fairly convincingly that work and life history variables have very little impact on the man's attitudes toward domestic work.

However, this may be because the male partner's attitudes are shaped through those of his partner and her work experiences over time. We may find more evidence for this hypothesis in the next section that examines the predictors of the female partner's attitudes.

A Model of the Effects of Work and Life History Variables on the Female Partners Attitudes

The model I will present in this section is almost identical to that in the last, except that the dependant variable this time is the woman's attitudes toward who should be ultimately responsible for domestic work. As such, I will not reiterate what I said about the base model variables in the last section. But, in this model, the work history variables that we will use as predictors stand in a much more direct relationship with the respondent's attitudes. Unlike in the last model where we were looking at the indirect effect of the woman's work activities on the man, here it is the effect of the woman's own experiences of paid work over certain periods that is of interest.

The Model As with the model of the man's attitudes, the woman's work status is very significant as a predictor of attitudes, whereas the man's is not (see 'base model' table 6.4). Thus, a woman working full time is over twice as likely to have untraditional attitudes as a full time housewife. In the opposite fashion to the last model, it is the woman's age group that is significant, rather than the man's. This confirms the direct effect of cohort upon attitudes, even controlling for the correlation between partner's ages. The effect is also in the expected direction with the youngest age group being more likely (1.21) then the second oldest age group (1.07) to have untraditional attitudes. Both the woman's attitude toward who should be responsible for the provision of an adequate income and the man's attitudes toward domestic work were significant predictors, but as in the last model, on entering the woman's attitudes toward income provision, the work status of the woman became insignificant, as did the age group variable. As, before, this may well be due to the co-linearity between these variables. When we enter the woman's views on income provision into the model, we are also fitting a term which closely mirrors the dependant variable, thus it is hardly surprising that this variable explains much of the variance and alters the significance of the work status variable. The man's attitudes toward the provision of income were insignificant. The significance of the variables and odds of the women having untraditional attitudes are reported in table 6.4.

Because the work history variables relate much more directly to the woman's than to the man's attitudes, it would seem more likely that there should be some significant relationship between them. As in the last model though, it soon became plain that this was not so and that none of the variables had a significant effect on the dependant variable. In the same way, it became apparent that, as in the model of the man's attitudes, that the life history variables did not exhibit a significant effect either. Thus, neither the variable that represents the woman's parents division of labour, nor whether the mother worked during childhood seemed to have any effect on the odds of the woman having untraditional attitudes.

Table 6.4 Logistic Model of the Probability of the Female Partner Having Untraditional Attitudes Toward the Domestic Division of Labour

Variables		Base Model		Full Model	
		Odds	Sig.	Odds	Sig.
Woman's work status	Full time HW	Ref.		Ref.	
	Full Time	2.11	***	2.11	*
	Part Time	1.08	N.S	1.08	N.S
	Unemployed	1.33	N.S	1.33	N.S
	Non-Worker	1.34	N.S	1.34	N.S
Man's work status	Full Time	Ref.		Ref.	
	Part Time	0.63	N.S	0.63	N.S
	Unemployed	1.62	*	1.62	**
Full Time Houseworker		0.85	N.S	0.85	N.S
	Non-Worker	0.92	N.S	0.92	N.S
Woman's Age	51 to 60	Ref.		Ref.	
	17-29	1.21	N.S	1.21	N.S
	30-50	1.07	N.S	1.07	N.S
Man's Age	51 to 60	Ref.		Ref.	
	17-29	1.05	N.S	1.05	N.S
	30-50	1.03	N.S	1.03	N.S
Woman's Attitude: Income Provision	Traditional	Ref.		Ref.	
	Untraditional	7.7	***	7.7	***
Man's Attitude: HW	Traditional	Ref.		Ref.	
	Untraditional	2.9	***	2.9	***
Man's Attitude: Income Provision	Traditional	Ref.		Ref.	
	Untraditional	1.15	N.S	1.15	N.S
Mother's HW %	low				
FT Work Last 10 yrs	<20 Months	-		5.6	**
N=1218	Constant	0.06	***		
	deviance & df:	1116.2	1202	1093.3	1185

*=P<0.05   **=P<0.01   ***=P<0.001

However, it may be that the effect of past life and work history experiences are complex and actually only emerge in interaction. One such interaction may be between the woman's early life experiences of parents division of domestic labour and her personal work history experience. It seems logical that the effect of paid work experiences on the woman's attitudes is negotiated through her existing attitudes which are partly dependent upon her early life experiences. To test for this effect, an interaction term between each of the work history variables and that representing the parents division of domestic labour was entered into the equation. Each of the work history variables represents different types of experiences of paid work on the woman's part, i.e. different mixtures of part time, full time and unemployment experience. Going back to our theoretical framework outlined earlier on, it would seem likely that experience of full time work is more likely to have an effect on attitudes than part time work since it is this status that demands the most changes in the organisation of domestic tasks (c.f. the discussions in this chapter and the last of the effects of the 'second shift' or 'double day'). Results show that this did indeed seem to be the case.

The 'full model' columns in table 6.4 show that women who come from households where the mother's proportion of domestic work was lowest and who have been working up to 20 months in full time work in the last decade before the survey have over five times the odds of having untraditional attitudes (controlling for age) than women who come from parental households with a more 'traditional' division of labour and who have not worked full time at all in the last decade (to save space non significant interaction terms in table 6.4 are omitted). The significance and size of the effect suggests that doing full time work has a large effect on attitudes if the woman already comes from a background where the parents practices were untraditional. Since the effect occurs in the group with up to 20 months of full time employment this might suggest that there is a fairly immediate affect on attitudes of starting full time work for this group of women.

The strength of the effect for the interaction term with the number of months the woman had spent in full time work in the last decade shows that a woman's entry into full time work (even if in a generalised sense over the last ten years) does have an effect on the way she perceives of the men's and women's roles on the issue of domestic work. What is most interesting is that it is only women that come from less traditional households that exhibit an effect on attitudes when they have worked full time for up to 20 months. This finding lends support to the hypothesis in the last section that men's attitudes toward domestic work are affected by his partner's work life history, but only indirectly through her attitudes.

Conclusions from the Models of Partners' Attitudes

We already know from past chapters that both male and female partners' attitudes are important predictors of how domestic work will be divided up. What was also clear though, was that the man's attitudes had a more direct impact on practices than the female partner's. The chapter investigated why this was so, but it is interesting from this chapter that although men's attitudes are crucial in determining the division of domestic work, his attitudes are formed in interaction with his partner and her own work and life history. However, from the evidence we have seen, past periods of part time employment do not seem to have any effect on women's attitudes compared to periods of full time house work, whereas there is a strong affect for having been employed full time. How should we interpret the interaction between the woman's parents' division of domestic labour and her work experience? We have already seen that women who work full time are more likely to have untraditional attitudes, thus it seems very likely that coming from a parental household that was itself 'untraditional' in the way it divided up domestic work further increases the probability that the woman will express untraditional attitudes. Thought of in another, perhaps more problematic fashion, it may be that all women from untraditional backgrounds are more likely to express untraditional attitudes, but only women who are working full time in the present feel that their own work position makes it sensible to have such attitudes.

Does the past paid employment of the female partner have any effect on the man's actual contributions to unpaid work time? Gershuny (1992) found that there was some adaptation on the part of the male partner to his wife's paid work time, and we have already seen that the woman's work history affects her partner's attitudes and these are crucial in determining the domestic division of labour. But can we detect a direct effect of the wife's work history on the male partner's behaviour? The last section of this chapter examines the effect of the woman's life experiences on the domestic work contributions of the male partner.

A Model of the Effects of Life and Work History Experiences on the Male Partner's Contributions to Domestic Work

Having looked at the effects of the female partner's work and life history variables on the attitudes of the partners, I now want to turn to the effects of these variables on how much time the male partner spends on domestic work. One of the main theoretical threads of this book is that we have to see the structure of domestic work as having a history (in terms of the partners lives), that is, it is structured by the path that partners have travelled along to get to their present situation, as well as being structured by the conditions that they experience in the present. This theoretical framework has been born out by the findings of this book so far. Chapter three has shown us that a simple model based on the present paid work contributions and marginal productivity of partners is a necessary, but not sufficient model within which to explain the patterns in the SCELI data. This was extended in chapter five which showed that the missing element was the male partner's attitudes which were crucial in determining the balance of domestic work between the partners. However, this chapter has shown that the male partner's attitudes themselves are shaped indirectly by their partner's paid work history and directly (or at least reciprocally) by their partner's attitudes. Can we complete the link between the attitudes of the partners, their present circumstances and their work histories by establishing a direct relationship between the male partners domestic contribution and his partner's work history?

Specifying a Model

As in chapter three, the measure of domestic work time will be the minutes per day that the male partner spends on domestic work tasks, rather than his proportion of domestic work. I have decided to use this measure, rather than a proportion so that we get a better idea of the direct effect that the independent variables have on the male partner individually in the easily understood metric of increased, or decreased minutes per day. When using this metric though, we face the problem of controlling for the total amount of domestic work accomplished in the household. Partners that have more children (or simply younger children), who have larger houses, or whose tastes are for a more ordered or cleaner home may do more domestic work. Unless we control for these variables, the size of any change will be impossible to judge. Since the model I will be using in this section is a simple OLS regression (because our dependant

137

variable is a continuous measure of minutes per day), the total amount of domestic work accomplished in the household will be entered as a control variable. The dependant variable in these models is also domestic work time net of childcare time. I have outlined the reasons for this before, but to reiterate, having children, especially young children, has large implications for how much domestic work there is and how this will be allocated. Rather than entering all work, including childcare, and then trying to control for the presence or not of a child, the models are more interpretable if we set childcare time aside and then control for the particular allocative differences made by the presence of children to general domestic work (c.f. the listing provided in chapter two). Since children can reduce the burden of work, as well as increase it, it makes more sense to look at the specific effects of children of different ages upon a generic measure of domestic work.

As outlined above, the base models for men's contributions to domestic work need to include those variables that represent the structural/economic constraints and costs that partner faces when deciding upon how they will allocate their time to unpaid work. Thus, the most important variables here are those that represent partners' paid work time. As in previous chapters, these variables are derived from the diary data and are split into quartiles to produce four categories for each partner which reflect their paid work time relative either to other men or other women. This is important since it is supposed in economic models of the allocation of time that people's decisions to enter the paid work force will depend upon their potential wage and thus the marginal productivity of paid work time over more time spent doing domestic work. There is a great deal of evidence that the labour market is segregated along lines of sex both vertically and horizontally, thus it makes more sense to make comparisons between the same sex, rather than between sexes. Since the models in this section will be using variables that look at the effects of the proportion of the woman's work life spent in different types of work and the woman's work history in more recent periods, it is necessary to control for the age of the partners. As in the last set of models, age is entered individually for both partners as a three-category variable.

Another variable that we need to control for is the difference in income between the partners. The full reason for this is outlined in chapter four, but we need to control for the difference made in the marginal productivity of paid work time by there being a large difference in income of the partners. The variable used here is the wife's income minus the man's, thus we should expect that as the difference becomes smaller, or positive, the marginal productivity of the man doing more domestic work time increases. Income from other sources may also have an effect on the productivity of partners. *A priori*, it is hard to make an assumption about how other types of income such as benefits or savings/windfall may affect the time that the man spends in domestic work, but the variables will be entered into the equation. Because we are not looking at childcare time, but at the general category of domestic work, we need to control for children-related variables that could affect partners times doing domestic work. Primary amongst these is the presence of a small child. This has been shown to increase male partners contributions as the female partner becomes more and more preoccupied with the care of the child and has little time to contribute to other types of domestic work. The effect would appear to be binary, i.e. having several small children is not as different from having one small child as it is from not having any. Thus a control variable is used that refers to the presence of any child under five. Though small children may increase the partners' domestic work time, the presence of older children may lead to a reduction as they begin to contribute to the overall work burden. To control for this, a set of dichotomous variables are entered into the model that refer to whether help is given by either a male or female child on four different activities - washing-up, cleaning and hoovering, cleaning clothes and cooking.

This type of domestic help to partners is one form of a more general effect that must be controlled for, that of commodity substitution. For instance, it could be that the household receives help from a member of the family that lives outside of the household (most usually a mother of one of the partners) or the household 'buys in' the services of someone by employing a domestic help. To control for these effects, two other sets of variables are entered that control for whether a relation from outside the household or a paid person helps with the same core domestic work tasks as outlined above. The last variables to be controlled for in the base model are those of the attitudes of the partners to both domestic work and the provision of an adequate income for the household. These are the same in structure as those outlined for the previous two models. As before, the comparison categories are those that are assumed to have the most 'traditional' work practices. In terms of the paid work variables this means that full time men and full time housewives are the base group, as are those that have traditional attitudes. For the other variables, those without a child under five are the base, as are those households where children, other adults and paid helpers do not help with the care domestic work tasks.

The work and life history variables used in the models are the same as those used in the previous two models, therefore I refer the reader back to table 6.3 which listed these in detail. Unlike in the previous models though, the effect of the variables in this model will be additive (as will be the effect of the base model variables), i.e. each variable will predict a positive, negative or null change in the quanta of domestic work minutes that the partner performs.

A Model of the Male Partner's Contributions to Domestic Labour

Before going on to examine the results of the work and Life history variables on the contributions of the male partner, I will briefly examine the results found for the base model variables (see table 6.5). As expected, the variables that represent the amount of paid work time that partners work are extremely significant (both $P<.001$) and tell the same story that was found in chapters three and five. Thus, men who do less paid work compared to the base category spend more time doing unpaid work (+100 mins. for the lowest quartile, +38 for the second and +11 for the third). If their partner works more hours than the reference category, men also do more unpaid work (+15 for the second woman's quartile, +46 for the third and +90 for the highest). Having a child under five in the household was also a significant and positive influence on the man's minutes per day ($P<0.01$, +7 mins). This also replicates past findings in this book and other studies (Pahl 1984). On the other hand, those variables representing the difference between the incomes of the partners and the household income form benefits and savings were not significant ($P=0.3$, $P=0.2$ and $P=0.9$ respectively).

After controlling for the presence of a child under five in the household, we also needed to test for the effect of any help in domestic work by the presence of children, other family adults and paid outside workers. Although all of the variables have been left in the equation, only those that represented a child's contribution to washing-up ($P=0.048$) and a paid outsiders contribution to the washing of clothes

Table 6.5 An OLS Model of the Man's Minutes Per Day of Domestic Work

Variables		Base Model B	Sig.	Full Model B	Sig.
Total Household Mins Per Day		0.51	***	0.51	***
Man's Paid Work Quartile	High	Ref.		Ref.	
	Low	100.3	***	98.5	***
	Medium Low	37.5	***	34.5	***
	Medium High	10.6		10.0	
Woman's Paid Work Quartile	Low	Ref.		Ref.	
	Medium Low	14.5	*	16.88	*
	Medium High	46.1	***	71.3	
	High	90.1	***	186.4	***
	Child <5 In Household	7.35	*	5.7	
	Child Does Washing Up	-12.6	*	-12.2	
	Paid Other Washes Clothes	-59.56	**	-49.1	*
Man's Attitude to HW	Traditional	Ref.		Ref.	
	Untraditional	24.8	***	25.4	***
Woman's Period in	<20 Months	Ref.		Ref.	
FT and PT Work	21-40 Months	-		-9.4	
In Last 10 Years	41-60 Months	-		30.7	
	61-80 Months	-		21.4	
	80+ Months	-		-8.4	
				16.7	
Interactions:					
W Work Quartile **Period In Work**	High + <20 Months	-		-142.1	**
W Work Quartile **Period In Work**	High + 21-40 Months	-		-121.8	***
W Work Quartile **Period In Work**	High + 41-60 Months	-		-133.7	***
W Work Quartile **Period In Work**	High + 61-80 Months	-		-83.5	***
W Work Quartile **Period In Work**	High +80+ Months	-		-106.8	***
	Constant	-159.3	***	-169.1	***

N=387 R^2 (adj)= 0.76 0.81

*=P<0.05 **=P<0.01 ***=P<0.001

(P<0.01 were significant. These are very interesting effects since both are negative influences on the number of minutes per day that the male partner performs, a child's contribution to washing-up having an effect of -13 minutes and the aid of an outside domestic worker in washing clothes, -57 minutes.

As in chapter five, the man's attitudes toward domestic work are more powerful predictors of the man's amount of domestic work than the female partner's when controlling for each in the model. Thus the man's attitude toward who should be ultimately responsible for domestic work is very significant (P<0.001) and leads to an increase of nearly twenty-five minutes per day, whereas the woman's attitude on this subject is insignificant (P=0.4). Both the partners' attitudes toward who should be ultimately responsible for the provision of an adequate income are insignificant (man's P=0.5, woman's P=0.2). To save space, table 6.5 gives the significance and estimates for the significant variables in the base model (at entry into the model: P<0.05) although all control variables were retained.

These findings are as expected from previous models and show the utility of the economic approach to the amount of domestic work time that men contribute, in as far as it can predict that there is some form of maximisation within households, as shown by the differential amounts of unpaid work that men do depending on their paid work time. As in chapter four though, an interaction variable between the paid work times of the partner's shows that men of the same work status do not do more domestic work if the female partner does more paid work.

As before, these results are from cross-sectional data, but we should expect that if men do respond to the amount of time their partners spend in paid employment, there should be a positive effect within each quartile of their paid work time the more paid work the female does. Moreover, the lack of significance of the variable that represents the income difference between the partners also shows that the imperative of maximising the marginal productivity of partners work is not as strong an influence as the new home economists might believe. Once again, it is hard to give an unequivocal edge to this finding when using cross-sectional data, but we should expect that if the incomes of the partners has an interactive effect on each others contributions to unpaid work then this variable should have a significant affect on the amount of time that the male partner spends in domestic work.

Again, as in previous chapters, attitudes may be a contributing factor here with men who have more untraditional attitudes toward domestic work doing more of it. We have seen from the model of men's attitudes that the length of time that the woman has been employed effects the male partner's attitudes indirectly through those of his partner, but does it affect the amount of unpaid work time that the man contributes directly? Gershuny has attempted to show that there is indeed a general increase in the amount of unpaid work time that men contribute to the household, but he maintains, this only occurs after the woman has been working for more than twenty months. As explained before, he sees this process as one of 'lagged adaptation', by which he means that either through argument and/or the readjustment of complicated structures of behaviour through consensual change, the male partner comes to do more domestic work. To test whether he does in the medium run and whether the woman's long run experiences make a difference, we need to build these variables into the equation.

As in the model of men's and women's attitudes, the work history variables of the female partner were added to the model and tested to see whether they explained a significant degree of variance in the OLS model. On the entering the different work history variables individually, all were initially insignificant. As before however, could it not be that the variables have effect but only in interaction with other characteristics of the female partner?

One particular candidate is the present paid work status of the female partner. The rationale behind this interaction is that, although the variable may not have a direct impact on the practices of the male partner when entered into the model alone, it could well be that it has an effect at specific levels of the woman's current work status. The significance of the woman's past full time work in the model of the woman's attitudes might suggest that it is full time work that may make all the difference in practices as well, thus it could be that only women working full time in the present who have also worked in the past have an effect on the behaviour of the male partner. This does indeed seem to be so. In interaction, the variable representing the woman's months of full and part time work in the last ten years has a strongly significant effect (P<0.001). Table 6.5 gives the significance and coefficients for the variables in the full model of the man's minutes per day of domestic work. For ease of interpretation I have only included the extra categories to the model that were significant. If we look at table 6.5, it shows that adding the interaction of the woman's present paid work group and the amount of full and part time work she has done in the last ten years has specific effects on the model overall. First of all, all of the woman's present paid work categories become insignificant apart from the lowest and highest quartiles (the latter roughly analogous to full time work). In the same way, the effect for the child's domestic help and the effect of having a child under five falls away to insignificance (compared to the base model).

The most interesting and important change in the full model is the effect of the interaction itself on the man's minutes per day of domestic work. Table 6.5 shows that, although the interaction itself was significant, only those categories that refer to the highest present paid work quartile of women partners has an effect in combination with work history. Thus, although there is indeed an effect here, it is not a generalised one that applies to all women who have worked full or part time. The effect is concentrated on those that have worked some periods part time in the past, but who are presently engaged in a higher number of hours (over 35 per week). There is also an interesting pattern of affect. Although all of the significant coefficients are negative, i.e. the number must be taken away from the grand mean of the partners of full time housewives with no paid work history plus effect of the female partner being in a certain paid work quartile, the greater the number of months that the woman was in full or part time work, the less negative the coefficient. There is a definite slope to the variables that suggests that there is some degree of adjustment by the male partner, the greater the number of months his full time partner is in employment. There is real evidence here, from a multivariate model that there is adjustment by men to the paid work time of their partners. This supports the lagged adaptation thesis of Gershuny (1994), but only in the more specific sense that there is adjustment only when the partner is now working full time. There is no effect for those working less hours, and it seems that the most direct effect (i.e. not an interaction effect) occurs after 21 months of employment.

Conclusions

Taken together, the models in this chapter show that there is a definite benefit to using work and life history variables when explaining the nature of households' division of domestic tasks. The models on women's attitudes showed that they bore the mark of their family background, but only in interaction with her experiences since childhood in her work life. If she had been working full time for at least 20 months in the last 10 years there is a much greater probability that she would have untraditional attitudes.

The woman's work history also affected the attitudes of her partner, but more indirectly through her own attitudes. The model of men's attitudes toward responsibility for domestic labour showed that having a partner with untraditional attitudes greatly increased the probability that his would be untraditional to. It could still be that this effect is due to homogamy, but the pronounced effects of the woman's work history on her own attitudes suggest that this may actually be the source. Another piece of evidence in this direction was the effect of the woman's past history of full and part time work on her partner's domestic time contributions. In interaction with the paid work quartile of the woman, the number of months that the woman had been in full or part time work did seem to have the effect of increasing the man's contributions, but only if the woman was presently employed in the highest quartile (roughly equal to full time work). This suggests that, as Gershuny (1994) proposed, there is some adjustment over time in the domestic work practices of partners as their commitments to paid work change

How do these findings fit in with the theoretical picture set out in chapter one of this book and its extension in the beginning of this chapter? The changes that have occurred in women's paid work practices in the last thirty years or so have made any analysis of the household a more complex business. As well as having to deal with a new set of economic factors we also need to account for a more complex ideological and cultural context. Researchers such as Dex (1988) have shown that many of the older attitudes toward women and work have now ceased to have much cultural salience, thus women have a far greater choice about how they combine paid work with family and domestic obligations. In some ways it is now expected that women will work, the only point of contention being how they will combine paid work with the care of children. Although there have also been changes in men's paid work patterns (notably the rise in unemployment in the last fifteen years) these have not impacted directly upon their domestic role simply because this was never seen as their realm of responsibility in the first place. In a sense, the tension that has come to emerge about men's domestic work practices has come via the new circumstances of their wives and partners who have found it increasingly difficult to reconcile their new paid work practices with the older structure of domestic work obligations.

Thus, when examining the patterns that emerge from the SCELI data, we have to bear in mind not only the increasing variety of work roles in the household, but also the subjective effects of this structural change on the attitudes or 'ideologies' of household members. Much of the empirical work in this book has gone into seeing the advantages and limits of using an economic perspective upon household work organisation. My main aim has been to show that this view of the household as a productive sphere is not incompatible with seeing it as the place where meaningful cultural interaction occurs. In fact, I have tried to show that we cannot understand the patterns in the data unless we augment the economic analysis of the 'maximising', 'single utility function' household with an analysis of the cultural and attitudinal perspectives from which people come when making decisions about the allocation of their time to different spheres of work. But, it is not enough to show that people with different attitudes have different preferences as to how they will arrange their time. If we do not attempt to see how these understandings are distributed across the population we will end up analysing behaviour as the outcome of people being more or less effected by the structural determinant of 'patriarchy'. Our theory of 'frames' states that specific attitudes will be more or less salient according to the 'background characteristics' of the person involved. That is, we should look to partners' work and life history, as well as their present circumstances for an explanation of where their attitudes come from, rather than looking to an over-arching social-structural variable. What this chapter has shown is that there is a definite effect in the data of the woman's upbringing and past experience of full time work on her attitudes, and via these to those of her partner.

People are knowledgeable about their present and past circumstances and we have to analyse this knowledge in quantitative analyses as based upon the probability that certain choices may be made given the paths that people have followed to get to their present position. This brings me to the subject of 'frames of reference' and their situational 'salience'. I outlined the idea of the framework earlier in this chapter and showed that the idea has already been put forward under a number of different guises, be that habitus (Bourdieu 1990), subjective rationality (Boudon 1989), life-world (Schutz 1972), index (Garfinkel 1967) or framework (Lindenberg 1985, 1986, 1989). We have to see a frame as a mix of cultural and material facets that allow people to discriminate among complex alternatives that have both economic and cultural value. Berk (1985) recognised this in her notion of the 'gender factory' where economic production went hand in hand with cultural production, but her interactionist framework was too present oriented, consensual and open to alternatives. Instead, we need to see partners' frames as being complex outcomes from past experience that are reciprocally related and sometimes in conflict or tension.

This perspective jettisons the handy, but ultimately dangerous concept of the single utility function and leads us into a more complex realm where empirical evidence must be used to assess the interaction of frames that cannot be known *a priori* (i.e. where it is assumed that preferences are uniform between individuals and unchanging). Given the changing nature of attitudes toward gender work roles (c.f. Hochschild 1990) and the increasing variance of experiences and situations that partner's and particularly female partners find themselves in, there is a good chance that conflict will occur between the 'frames' that have salience to partners. There was some evidence of this in chapter five when we examined the reasons why some partners saw their share of domestic work to be unfair. Quantitative data does not lend itself to the analysis of concepts such as satisfaction and conflict within the intimate confines of the household, thus the next chapter will look at these issues using work already carried out by more qualitative studies.

Notes

[1] An attempt was made to replicate the type of results obtained by Gershuny, but I could not find the upwardly linear pattern he shows. Instead, even without controls for partners paid work time, the pattern is indistinct.

7 Partners' SatisfactionWith and Conflict Over the Domestic Division of Labour

In chapter five I examined how equitable partners found their existing division of domestic labour when trying to understand the link between respondents attitudes and practices. The theoretical premise at the beginning of chapter five was that of social exchange theory; that is, when actors' notions of 'fair exchange' (Blau 1964) or the 'generalised norm of reciprocity' (Homans 1961) are violated, they react negatively toward the exchange partner who has not provide the equitable outcome. If true, this theoretical premise should have meant that women who worked full time, but who still did a large proportion of the domestic work would see their position as unfair. As chapter five showed this was not so, primarily because women's' ideas about equity seemed to be structured, at least in part, by their attitudes toward the proper work roles of men and women. To reiterate, the main findings were that although there was some linkage between the proportion of domestic work that the female partner was doing and her perception of fairness (41% of women believed that they did more than their fair share), this relationship was not direct since a majority of full time working women (53%) saw their proportion as fair, even though only a small number of these households would have divided their domestic tasks equally. The chapter showed that attitudes toward the proper work roles that men and women should fulfil have a large effect on the distribution of domestic labour, thus it may be that those women that have more traditional attitudes toward work roles do a greater proportion of the domestic division of labour quite freely, and see this situation as entirely fair. But it also appeared, from the findings of the models in that chapter, that it was the man's attitudes that were more efficient predictors of the domestic division of labour, irrespective of those of his wife. Moreover, from the tables presented of male and female respondents reasons for the unfairness of their practices, it appeared that there was a large amount of intransigence or disinterestedness amongst some husbands with regard to domestic work. It may be then that at least for households where the female has untraditional attitudes, that it is the man's unwillingness to take on domestic tasks that leads to the inequitable distribution of domestic tasks.

The question is, does the position of the male partner lead to dissatisfaction by the female partner, and perhaps to conflict between the partners? According to the theoretical position that I tentatively laid out in the opening chapter of this book and fleshed out more fully in the last chapter, we have to see the division of domestic labour as the consequence of partners decisions concerning the allocation of time and material circumstances with each partner's attitudes and beliefs about the proper roles that men and women should fulfil in the household. The 'ongoing' nature of this relationship is vitally important because it supplies us with the explanatory device for the nature of the attitudes and constraints that are now faced by partners in the household. Previous choices have, in this respect, shaped those available now, just as they have shaped the perspective or 'framework' through which the present situation is viewed. Evidence for this 'processual' account of the domestic division of labour has been put forward in the proceeding chapters, as has evidence for another vital point: that partners frameworks are not necessarily in perfect agreement. On one level, this statement seems somewhat obvious - of course partners will sometimes disagree. On another though, the idea of frameworks offers us the link, or 'sociological imagination' (Mills 1959) to see social and economic patterns in what would otherwise be random disagreements between partners and hopefully offer some sociological explanation for them. We are not solely interested in whether conflicts occur within the household, but whether there is a systematic 'contradiction' which means that conflict is to a certain extent built in. The increase in the number of women now in paid employment is a macro level economic and social change that has had profound effects at the level of the household. There is some evidence (Wilkie 1988; England and Kilbourne 1991) that the increasing participation of married women in full time paid work in the US. has, combined with the lack of participation of husbands in domestic work, contributed to the rise in divorce and separation rates. This suggests that there is a large amount of dissatisfaction with this element of marriage that lacks study and needs investigation. What we need is to outline the processes that lead to dissatisfaction and conflict: this is the aim of this chapter.

Unfortunately, there are grave methodological problems involved in getting information from married or cohabiting partners about their satisfaction with domestic work and levels of conflict. Although it may be possible to ask respondents how satisfied they are with the present organisation of domestic work tasks in their household, the question comes loaded with assumptions about the nature of their relationship with their partner. Moreover, satisfaction is a complicated issue: I may well express satisfaction with the way tasks are organised at the moment, but I may do so because I see no practical alternative, not because I necessarily like the situation. When investigating conflict between partners, these problems are even more acute. To ask questions about the degree of conflict that exists between partners is to ask them indirectly about how good their relationship is. In that situation there are big incentives for them to give their answers a positive spin. Evidence of the existence of these problems has already been offered in this book in relation to Arlie Hochschild's notion of the 'family myth' by which overt conflict is avoided because the partners come to perceive the domestic division of labour as something other than it actually is. The important point is though that the conflict did not disappear, but was transformed into resentment. I will come back to Hochschild's study later as it provides a very insightful analysis of the tensions and conflict inherent in some kinds of household work practices.

The problems listed above mean that any research in this area is liable to problems of validity. This is true of both qualitative and quantitative data, but these problems are especially acute when using standardised questions and closed responses. More qualitative methods such as the unstructured interview are better methodological alternatives since the investigator can probe more deeply and attempt to contextualize respondents answers from interviews, which can be more respondent led and therefore naturalistic. Hochschild used observational techniques within the respondents homes to gather data upon relations and work practices that goes someway toward getting round the problems presented by the 'family myth'. These methods do not guarantee the validity of data since the researcher is still present and thus exerting some effect, but they do open up a much richer source of data. On the other hand, qualitative methods have their own problems (such as unreliability), which mean that it would be useful to look at quantitative evidence as well. Although qualitative methods will yield richer, more valid results and give us a deeper understanding of satisfaction and conflict between partners, there should still be relative differences between groups using more quantitative methods. That is to say, although we may not trust the results from a structured survey to give us a full understanding of how satisfied partners are with their present situation and the degree of conflict between them, we may nonetheless be able to perceive patterns in the quantitative data that will reassure us that the qualitative data is presenting us with a reliable picture. Using different sources derived from both of the methodologies, we should be able to 'triangulate' our findings to a certain a degree. As explained in chapter two, this is an essential part of the book. In the same way that it is imperative that we try to combine the theoretical insights of economics as well as sociology in the analysis of the causes of the domestic division of labour, we also need to combine the reliability of the large-scale survey with the detailed hermeneutic accounts of more qualitative researchers. In this chapter, I will combine the findings of a number of published qualitative and quantitative studies with the evidence from the SCELI data set. In this way, we should be able to get a better picture of the relationship between the division of domestic labour and partners level of satisfaction with it, and thence to the levels of conflict that might ensue.

It is also difficult with quantitative data to get evidence rich enough to allow us to investigate the nature of the relationships between partners' 'frameworks' and the changes that occur within an individual's framework over time. We have already looked at how some life and career variables shape women's attitudes and domestic work practices, but the examination has been mostly statistical and needs to be fleshed out with more qualitative examples that reveal the meanings women attach to their choices. In the first part of this chapter, I want to use evidence from Arlie Hochschild's study *the Second Shift* (1990) to embellish the theoretical stance I have already discussed and pave the way for the quantitative evidence that I will bring on later. Hochschild's study is not the only qualitative study to include partners' dissatisfaction with the domestic division of labour and the sources of conflict, but it is the most perceptive. Although she only studies ten families, she brings to these families situations the 'sociological imagination' that links their personal troubles (Mill 1959) and experiences to macro phenomenon and movements.

The Stalled Revolution

Hochschild's (1990) book examines the situations of ten families where the woman works outside the home in paid employment. Rather than looking at the causes of the increase in the amount of time that women in the US. now spend in paid employment, Hochschild examines the 'gender strategies' of the household and how they cope with the demands of domestic work and childcare now that the wife cannot look after these full time. She shows that in almost all of the households, the wife does far more domestic work than the husband, such that she does what Hochschild calls the 'second shift', the first shift being her paid employment. Over one year, this second shift means that the wife does a month's extra work. I have described and criticised the concept of the gender strategy in chapter five, but to briefly reiterate, Hochschild identified two ideal type gender strategies: the 'traditional' where the woman was seen as the homemaker and the man as the breadwinner and the 'egalitarian' where both partners identify with both the breadwinner and domestic, or homemaker roles. In the middle lie the 'transitional' men and women who have elements of both traditional and egalitarian ideologies. Although she doesn't attempt to rigorously analyse the reasons for the changes in US society and economy that have led to the situation whereby more women are working outside of the home, she shows how this development is only half completed, and is in her words a 'stalled revolution'. What is most interesting about the book is the way that Hochschild links the macro picture of the effects of the stalled revolution with the micro level interactions. At the macro level women are being attracted into the workforce in ever greater numbers by the changing nature of technology and the economy, changing their attitudes and their approach to family life, whilst at the micro level the everyday processes of production and reproduction in the home are fraught because 'traditional' or 'transitional' men are finding it very hard to come to terms with the new roles and expectations that are being made of them by egalitarian women. Hochschild sums this situation up thus

> Problems between husbands and wives, problems which seem "individual" and "marital", are often individual experiences of powerful economic and cultural shock waves that are not caused by one person or two. Quarrels that erupt....result mainly from a friction between faster-changing women and slower changing men, rates of change which themselves result from the different rates at which the industrial economy has drawn men and women into itself (Hochschild 1990, p11).

At first glance this typology sounds very much like the exchange theory outlined earlier, that is, women start doing more paid work and men don't respond by doing more domestic work, but Hochschild goes on to describe and explain the narrative histories of each of the partners in her ten families in the study to show the processes that underlie the woman's dissatisfaction and the subjective bases of each partner's belief in their own position.

Gender Strategies, Frameworks and Life History

On one level, all of the households have to cope with the everyday tasks of domestic work and childcare whilst both partners have full time paid work outside of the household. But, different households cope with these demands in different ways depending on their gender strategies, or frameworks as we have come to talk about them

> When I sat down to compare one couple that shared the second shift with another three that didn't, many of the answers that would seem obvious - a man's greater income, his longer hours of work, the fact that his mother was a housewife or his father did little at home, his ideas about men and women - all these factors didn't really explain why some women work the extra month a year [the second shift] and others don't. They didn't explain why some women seemed content to work the extra month, while others seemed deeply unhappy about it. When I compared a couple who were sharing and happy with another couple who were sharing but miserable, it was clear that purely economic or psychological answers were not enough. Gradually I felt the need to explore how deep within each man and woman gender ideology goes (Hochschild 1990, p14).

Thus, Hochschild's 'traditional', 'transitional' and 'egalitarian' ideal types form the backdrop onto which she paints very detailed accounts of the childhood and formative experiences of the individuals involved, their interactions and the history of these interactions. In essence, Hochschild uses detailed description and historical explanation to lay out the frameworks that the men and women in the study use when they think about how much of, and which types of domestic work they will, or more importantly should do. In this respect, Hochschild's work is very similar to that of Kathleen Gerson (1985). In a useful study, Gerson shows how women's work and family decisions in the United States now take place within a much more complex social and economic framework than they did at the start of the 'subtle revolution' in the late 1950s and early 1960s. She has shown that the factors that influence women to move, or 'veer towards or away from the domestic role' are complex and constantly changing

> .... change is a dominant motif. Although a minority of the women in this study had the luxury (or, viewed from a different perspective, the misfortune) to carry through the plans and expectations they initially took into adulthood, the more typical experience involved encounters with new, unanticipated situations that deflected women from their early goals....In the long run, the life patterns of these women grew out of a series of decisions that interacted in surprising ways.....; even the most carefully calculated choices often had unintended consequences that led in unanticipated directions (Gerson 1985, p191-2)

Gerson's approach is very similar to Hochschild's, except that Hochschild concentrates much more upon the interaction of the partners in her study and looks solely at domestic work and childcare. Hochschild's frameworks are of a much more detailed kind than those that were laid out in the previous chapter, since for Hochschild, most of the people in her study were 'transitional'. People can have both 'shallow' ideologies (ideologies that were contradicted by deeper feelings) and 'deep' ideologies (which were reinforced by such feelings). What is important here is that people are complex and can have multiple, even contradictory orientations to gender roles. For example, although someone may want to be egalitarian in their practices and may profess to having a surface ideology that supports a woman's paid work role as just as important as the paid work role of her husband, this may be contradicted by how they 'feel' about that role. Hochschild gives a good example of this

> Ann Myerson's surface ideology was egalitarian; she wanted to feel as engaged with her career as her husband was with his. This was her view of the 'proper experience' of her career. She thought she should love her work. She should think it mattered. In fact, as she confessed in a troubled tone, she didn't love her work and didn't think it mattered. She felt a conflict between what she thought she ought to feel (according to her surface ideology) - emotionally involved in her career - and what she did feel - uninvolved with it (Hochschild 1990, p16).

I give the above quote as an example to show that Hochschild does not lose sight of the fact that women, like men can be transitional, or semi-traditional as well as being egalitarian depending on their childhood experiences, work and life history. The fact is though that, as chapter three and five of this book have shown, women will tend to be more egalitarian than men (at least in their surface ideology), and reflect this in their demand for their male partners to be more involved in the domestic work. In the 'Second Shift' study as a whole (around 50 couples) Hochschild found that around 60% of the women thought that domestic work should be the responsibility of both partners, whereas only 25% of the men believed this. In practice, Hochschild's study found that even if men stated that they believed that domestic work should be shared between the partners, it did not actually happen (amongst her very small sample), a finding that gains some support from this book.

What kind of experiences shape peoples gender role attitudes and frameworks and thus their perception of inequity? Attitudes are not formed deterministically by specific circumstances, so is it possible to point to certain kinds of experiences that may have effects upon people? The last chapter showed that women's attitudes towards men's and women's work roles were significantly affected by the type of division of domestic labour in the parental home. Thus women who come from homes where the mother did a relatively low proportion of the domestic work (relative to other households) are more likely to have untraditional attitudes (depending on their current and past paid work experiences) than women who come from households where the mother did a larger proportion of the domestic work. But this statistical relationship is not simple. As Kathleen Gerson has shown

> Daughters...., do not passively receive and adopt the personalities and orientations of their mothers. They can separate themselves from these examples and make both conscious and unconscious judgements about them....Over time, daughters choose to confirm or deny particular aspects of their mothers' behaviour in their own lives. It is not enough to know what a mother did or how she felt; we must take into account how a daughter evaluated her mothers' behaviour when she was young and how she consciously or unconsciously responds to her mothers model as her own life develops (Gerson 1985, p49).

Hochschild (1990, p191) has examples of childhood experiences that had opposite effects on attitudes and frameworks in adulthood. One respondent's experiences as the child of a single mother had instilled in her a belief that women should find male protection through submission to them. Another's experiences as the daughter of a very traditional woman had left her with a fear of becoming a 'doormat' like her mother. Both found negative elements in experiences that we would predict would be positive influences on the adoption of certain frameworks.

But attitudes gained in childhood are not static and may well change drastically with experiences during adulthood. I discussed Gerson's (1985) study of women's choices about motherhood and work in chapter five and showed there how fragile personal relationships and marriages, economic squeezes in the household, domestic isolation and expanded work opportunities lead women to identify with and spend more time doing paid work. On the other hand, a stable relationship coupled with blocked work opportunities and/or an unsatisfactory job led some women to make the decision that the domestic role was a better alternative. Identification with one realm would effect the way in which the division of domestic tasks was perceived, even if, 'objectively' the division seemed to unfair and thus ripe for the development of dissatisfaction.

Gender Strategies, Frameworks and Interaction

It is in her descriptions of the interactions between the ideologies, or frameworks of the partners that Hochschild's account is most valuable since she shows how dissatisfactions occur and then develop over time. Hochschild shows how the burden of the second shift brings out the woman's dissatisfaction, which then impacts on her relationship with her partner. These dissatisfactions can either be resolved by one or both partners changing their practices, or they can linger on and just become endemic in the relationship. Alternatively, the partners' can develop a family myth between them that transforms explicit conflict into a deeper, more covert resentment. Hochschild saw 'family myths' develop in households where the partners' practices were at odds with their ideologies about the proper work roles that men and women should fulfil, or where partner's ideologies were different. Finally, the woman can decide that enough is enough and leave the household and her spouse. In an analogy to Fred Hirsch, Gershuny (1994) has labelled these possibilities those of loyalty, voice or exit. Although this is a useful analogy, in reality, the outcome is often much less decisive. The woman may decide that the alternatives are not good enough to leave the relationship, but this does not necessarily mean that the situation is resolved. If no adjustment is made, the 'family myth' may staunch open resentment on the issue of domestic work, but dissatisfaction with the second shift comes through in other ways. As Hochschild remarks (p189), if men share the second shift it affects them directly, but if they don't share, it affects them through their wives, telling on both the partners 'through their fatigue, sickness and emotional exhaustion'. Amongst the ten couples in Hochschild study there were examples of marriages breaking up, adjustments being made and dissatisfaction lingering on, but each outcome is intrinsically linked to the narrative of the partners that precedes it.

Hochschild found however, that these narratives could be grouped into three main types: those marriages in which the gender ideologies of the partners clashed (and thus they tried to undertake different kinds of gender strategies); those where economic circumstances clashed with the partners' gender ideologies (even though they agreed amongst themselves about the way they wished to organise household work); lastly, those where the role of the 'homemaker' was devalued by both partners (primarily because both had high-flying careers).

The first type of tension is the most obvious from the theoretical framework that I have been laying out in this chapter so far. With the increasing number of women working and women whose mothers would have worked, we can expect to see a strain arise between traditional or transitional men and more egalitarian women. Hochschild found that one third of the couples in her study had gender role ideologies that disagreed. That couples with such differing world views should get married is interesting in itself, but the *Second Shift* study shows that some couples entered marriage without discussing the possibilities of their future together or agreeing upon a clear bargain before they married. In the main, both partners to these marriages knew that the others ideology differed, but hoped that the other would change. Other couples married with the same kinds of approaches toward the problems of combining work with family life, but one partner then changed. Tensions set in these relationships when the other partner (usually the man) could not adapt to the new understanding of the situation. In some instances, men were not wholeheartedly against their wives doing paid work. As I mentioned earlier, peoples gender role ideologies are rarely coherent. Thus, some men respected their wives wish to work, but nonetheless wanted them to fulfil the obligations they took them to have toward the home and family (i.e. be the person mainly responsible for domestic work and the more diffuse tasks of 'caring').

Hochschild talks of a 'scarcity of gratitude' in couples where gender strategies disagree (i.e. ideology and practice) that can lead to friction. Each partner made sacrifices that they presumed the other would be grateful for, but because they had differing gender strategies, this gratitude did not emerge leaving each feeling 'taken advantage of'. This example from Hochschild (p206) gives a good account of this:

The big gift that Jessica Stein offered Seth was to give up working full time. For Seth,
the big gift was to give up leisure to work overtime. Their problem was not, I think, that

they could not give. It was that, given their gender ideals, Seth wanted to "give" at the office, and Jessica wanted to "receive" at home - to have Seth play catch with their younger son, play piano with the older one, while she escaped to "catch up" on her career. A gift in the eyes of one was not a gift in the eyes of the other.

Thus, although each thought they were being selfless and sacrificing, this was not seen in the same light by the other because of the framework through which they perceived the situation. In a sense, what brought tension to the relationship were the differential valuations that each made of a particular form of work. This point goes right back to the theoretical discussion of chapter one where the economic or 'rational choice' approaches to the division of domestic labour were criticised for being unable to account for the differing perceptions of utility that cultural frameworks bring to choice situations. Thus, although people may subjectively see their actions as self-sacrificing and in the best interests of the household / partners, their actions are not of a universal currency since they only have value when viewed through a person's cultural viewpoint and feelings about the proper work roles of the sexes.

Hochschild's second reason for tension in the household revolves around the changing economic situations that partners have to face, irrespective of their gender role attitudes. Thus, even though partners may agree between themselves on the proper work roles that men and women should fulfil, their ideas may not coincide with the finite resources that are available to them. Hochschild (p59-74) gives the example of a couple whose gender ideology is distinctly traditional, but where the wife has to work through economic necessity. This leads to dissatisfaction for both since the husband feels guilty for not providing the breadwinners wage that he feels he should be able to do and the wife dislikes working and feels resentful toward the husband because she needs to. This type of tension has been commented on in British literature on the domestic division of labour, though in a more abstract fashion. Susan Yeandle (1984, 169) discusses the tension between the dual forces of patriarchy and economic rationality in the negotiations of partners over how domestic work and childcare will be divided. She suggests that where either patriarchy or 'economic interests' are dominant in the negotiations between partners about where and when the woman should work, negotiations will tend toward consensus, but where the two forces have equal importance, negotiations may tend toward conflict. In her account though, all Yeandle's examples point to the man's attitudes being the most important factor in dictating whether negotiations will be conflictual, and she shows that it is the man who feels drawn between the economic benefits of his wife's wages and his cultural belief that women should primarily be domestic workers. This suggests that when economic interests recede (e.g. when the household can live on the man's income alone) then the household will be in consensus, which implies that the woman doesn't have a preference about how she allocates her time, irrespective of the pecuniary rewards (which would be contrary to most research [c.f. Dex 1988] in this area and other findings from her own book). In reality, I think that Yeandle may really have meant that partners ideologies can also clash, thus causing tension and that the extension of the other point may have come about through the use of the patriarchy/economics theory that lacked discrimination in empirical application (c.f. chapter one of this book).

This question of the intersection of economic imperatives and gender ideology does raise the issue of how class affects dissatisfaction and conflict over the division of domestic labour. I have not examined class much in this book, except in chapter four, where I examined the patterning of attitudes around the issues of gender work roles. This is because explanation is often better served by using specific mechanisms rather than general socio-economic indicators. Thus, although class may have been a statistically significant addition to many of the models in the chapters after chapter four, it would have acted largely as an umbrella variable for a host of more specific effects that happened to be highly correlated with class measures. There is some evidence that partners' dissatisfaction with the domestic division of labour may be directly linked to class. Firstly, it may be linked indirectly through the level of income and resources that partners' have available to cushion the effects of the combining two jobs. The effects could be bi-directional: middle class and professional women are more likely to have full time jobs than are working class women (Martin and Roberts 1984) and thus may be under greater pressures at home in trying to cope with the second shift. On the other hand, middle class and professional households will be in a much better position to ameliorate the effects of both partners being employed because they have higher levels of resources available that allow them to buy in the labour power necessary. 'Commodity substitution' may not though always be a possibility since money cannot buy a person more hours in the day. Ann Oakley (1974) found that although there were 'superficial' differences in the tendency of working class and middle class women to say that they were dissatisfied with being a housewife, this difference was actually an artefact of the working class women's 'restricted code' (Bernstein 1971). There could be some truth in this because there are distinctive linguistic/cultural differences between middle class and working women that may mean that working class women are more likely to revert to a traditional role ideology and thus state that they are 'satisfied' with the housewife role (as chapter four showed), but it may also be that Oakley was trying very hard to get a coherent story from her respondents who were relatively few in number.

The last type of tension outlined by Hochschild is that which occurs when both of the partners value work and career above domestic responsibilities and the family. This tension is altogether different from the two just outlined, except in the fact that it bespeaks a problem with combining paid and unpaid work in a 'family' or 'marriage' friendly manner. As Hochschild states

> Men and women may gradually come to share the work at home more equitably, but now they may be doing altogether less of it. The latent deal between husband and wife is "I'll share, but we'll do less". A strategy of "cutting back" on the housework, the children, the marriage may be on the rise, with correspondingly reduced ideas about what people "need" (Hochschild 1990, p209).

There certainly seems to be some evidence of this in this book so far. Chapters two and three show that as women come to do more paid work, they do correspondingly less domestic work in the home, as do their husbands. This could be because, as Hochschild states, there is an explicit agreement between the partners, or that the process is more unconscious as partners find less and less time to do the tasks that they once did. In the Second Shift study, the households that experienced this third type of pressure tended to be those where both of the partners were professional people. They could thus afford to buy in the labour power to clean the house and look after the children. Hochschild shows unfortunately that these couples experience a more subtle impairment:

Their homes were neater; there were fewer paintings stuck to the refrigerator door, fewer toys in the hallway. The decor in the living room and dining rooms was more often beige or white....Not until the couple separated did the wife look back at this [situation] with regret and devote real attention to her son (Hochschild 1990, p210).

This review of Hochschild's study and the few others I have mentioned indicate that the issue of dissatisfaction around the division of domestic labour is one that is structured in particular ways. Moreover, we can link them back to the theoretical schema that I have been laying out throughout this book. A set of hypotheses emerges from this qualitative data that we can now go on to examine in the findings of the more quantitative studies in this area and the SCELI data set. The perception of satisfaction is not directly linked to the proportion of domestic work that the woman does. Instead, satisfaction seems to be the result of the persons proportion of domestic work as refracted through their attitudes or gender role framework. Thus, we should see some differentiation between women according to their paid work status, but this is unlikely to be chiefly determinate. Instead, the woman's paid work time and proportion of domestic work should interact with her attitudes toward gendered work roles.

Social Surveys of Dissatisfaction and Conflict

For the reasons outlined in the first section of this chapter there have been relatively few quantitative studies of the consequences of the 'second shift' for partners within a household. Most have concerned themselves with explaining why imbalances in partners' domestic work contributions exist. But, those that exist have shown, as did chapter five in this book that the perception of fairness where household work is concerned is only slightly linked to the actual amounts (or proportions) of domestic work that the female partner does (Blair and Johnson 1992; Thompson 1991; Wilkie, Ratcliffe and Ferree 1992). A majority of women believe that their proportion is fair, even where they are doing roughly the same number of paid work hours as their husbands. Other studies have taken this finding and tried to link it to partners' dissatisfaction with the division of domestic work or with family life as a whole, suspecting, as I have in this book, that 'fairness' is refracted through a persons gender ideology, and only develops into dissatisfaction if the ideology and experience are incompatible. Thus, as both Wilkie, Ratcliffe and Ferree (1992) and Blair (1993) have found, it is not the difference in the amount of domestic work that is important but men's and women's expectations and meanings regarding time demands and the division of paid and unpaid work that predicted marital satisfaction. Blair's (1993) work also showed that the wife's perception of fairness was the strongest predictor of both husbands' and wifes' perceptions of marital conflict. These findings are similar to those of the more qualitative studies and reinforce the idea that the 'framework' through which the person sees the allocation of work tasks has a great deal of effect on whether they see it as equitable.

An area that has not been covered at all by the qualitative literature, although it has been examined by some US. social surveys is the differential effect of responsibility, or management of domestic work and actually doing it on perceptions of fairness and dissatisfaction. A number of researchers (Brannen and Moss 1991; Berk 1985; Yeandle 1984) have remarked upon the amount of work that researchers miss when they exclude responsibility for the planning of meals etc. It seems that an article by Mederer (1993) is the only systematic study of the issue. Helen Mederer (1993) has used data from a study of 652 female, full time state employees from Rhode Island in the US. to model the effects of these two different types of 'work' (i.e. management and allocation) and has found that whereas both the management of, and the allocation of tasks contribute independent negative effects to the woman's perception of 'fairness', her scales depicting the balance of management 'work' did not predict the amount of conflict that women reported between themselves and their partners. Since most studies have not found a link between the division of domestic work and whether the woman feels that her proportion is fair, it is interesting that Mederer does. What is more interesting though are the implications that her finding may have for how female partners see their role. Although female partners may be dissatisfied with their responsibility for the management of domestic work tasks, it could be that this responsibility is not seen as serious enough to lead to conflict. It could also be that demanding and getting help from male partners with the accomplishment of tasks is easier and requires less negotiation and conflict than the reallocation of management responsibility. Thus women can set standards for how specific tasks are done, but lose this control if they hand over responsibility to their partners. The division of domestic tasks on the other hand seems to be directly linked to the amount of conflict between the partners. Unfortunately, Mederer's study, by its very nature cannot give us a very clear picture of the mechanisms that underlie the different effects of management and allocative responsibility.

One explanation for the discrepancy between Mederer's study and those of Wilkie, Ratcliffe and Ferree (1992), Blair (1993) and Barnett and Baruch (1987) might be found in Perry-Jenkins and Folk's (1994) article about class differences in women's perception of fairness and marital conflict. For households where both partners were middle class, both working class or the wife was middle class and the husband working class, the more equal the division of what they termed 'feminine' tasks (mostly cleaning and cooking), the more equitable the woman found the division. But, in households where the husband was middle class and the wife working class, her perceptions of equity were unrelated to the proportion of domestic work that she does. It may be, as Perry-Jenkins and Folk suggest that husbands and wives may pay attention to the status of their spouses job when deciding what is equitable. Thus, in households where the man is middle class and the women working class, it may be that she sees her own job as less important than her husband's, even though she may work as many hours. Taken to its logical end though, this answer if true would imply that an exchange theory explanation was apt when our investigations have already shown that it is rather inadequate to the task. A paper by Layte (1998) however offers evidence against a social exchange interpretation of Perry-Jenkins and Folk's findings. Also using the SCELI survey, Layte showed conclusively that women's satisfaction with the division of domestic labour was not significantly effected by differences in the status of partner's jobs or their dependency on their husband. Their satisfaction was defined through their attitudes to the proper roles of men and women and the interaction of these attitudes with their proportion of domestic work.

Taken together, these studies show that the patterns pointed to by the qualitative studies do indeed seem to exist. As in Hochschild's study, it is clear from those of Wilkie, Ratcliffe and Ferree (1992), Blair (1993), Barnett and Baruch (1987), Mederer (1993) and Layte (1998) that perceptions of equity and fairness over the division of domestic labour are crucially influenced by the persons framework or type of gender ideology. Perceptions of fairness and dissatisfaction are still affected by the proportion of domestic work that the women does, the proportion affecting the level of satisfaction via the attitudes of the women (an interaction effect). Most importantly, the effect of the second shift on dissatisfaction and fairness does seem to be directly linked to the paid work status of the woman. Thus, we see from both the qualitative and quantitative studies that it is full time women and to a certain extent, part time women who find that combining unpaid domestic work with paid work provokes dissatisfaction when the male partner does not become involved more fully with domestic work. As predicted in the qualitative studies, conflict also arises in the above situation, but the quantitative studies where less helpful about the specific processes that occur in these situations.

These findings support the set of hypotheses presented at the end of the last section. We can now apply these to the SCELI data set to see whether they gain support there. Thus, in the next section I will examine to what extent the findings of the qualitative and quantitative studies are supported by the data used so far in this book. Unfortunately, the SCELI data set contains no questions that can be used to assess the levels of conflict between the partners, thus we have to rely upon the evidence already presented to give us information on this. A model will be presented that looks at the predictors of dissatisfaction on the woman's part with the domestic division of labour.

Two Models of Women's Satisfaction With The Domestic Division of Labour

In this section I want to build and examine a model of the female partner's level of satisfaction with the division of domestic work tasks within her household. The SCELI Household and Community Survey (1987) included a number of questions on the partners satisfaction with several situations such as 'family life', 'present job', and most importantly, how work around the house was divided up. The respondents were asked to answer by selecting a box on a ten point scale between very dissatisfied (0) and very satisfied (10). As expected from the discussion in the first section of this chapter, the majority of respondents answered the question on their satisfaction with domestic work positively (i.e. toward satisfaction) such that only 12% of female respondents ticked a category on the dissatisfaction side of the scale. It could be that this distribution reflects the reality of a sample who are mostly satisfied with the distribution of domestic tasks, but it could also be that these women are giving their answers to this personal question a positive spin. In practice the absolute value of their response does not matter since we are interested in the relative differences between women with different characteristics. Even if we assume that this question does not tap the truly complex nature of women's level of satisfaction with the division of work in their household and that few will give us a truly valid response, we could still expect that these effects are normally, or evenly distributed throughout the population of women within the survey, in which case we should still expect to see relative differences between women with different characteristics. When examining the parameter estimates from the models, we are more interested to see which characteristics are associated with negative effects on the satisfaction of the woman. Although we have already looked at some of the data from the SCELI data set that referred to whether men and women thought their contributions were fair, we cannot, unfortunately combine this with the data on satisfaction since they come from different surveys. The questions on fairness were asked as part of the area specific studies of the main survey in 1986 whereas the questions on satisfaction all come from the 1987 Household and Community Survey.

Specifying a Model

In accordance with the findings of the research that we have been looking at throughout this chapter, we will need to control for the paid work status of the woman in the model since this is one of the main variables around which the issues we have been discussing revolve. To reiterate, it is the strains associated with the increasing amount of time that women now spend in paid work that we are seeking to assess. Thus two variables will be added to control for (and see the effect of) the partners work statuses. As we have seen, these strains can be hard to cope with, even where partners are doing equal amounts of domestic work (and thus we should expect women's dissatisfaction will increase as they do more paid work), but the proportion of domestic work that the woman performs will be an important factor in how intense these strains are. We should see a negative relationship between the woman's proportion of domestic work and her satisfaction after controlling for both partner's paid work status. Rather than use the diary based measure of the woman's proportion of domestic work, in these models I have used the woman's self-estimate of her proportion. Since we are looking at the woman's perception of her situation, this more subjective measure should be more valid than the perhaps more objective measure from the diary sample. This estimated proportion was categorised into three groups defined by the values half a standard deviation away from the mean of the sample. By doing this we can look at the effect of being in a category of women that do a large proportion of domestic work (or at least perceive they do) relative to those that do a smaller proportion. Using this measure of domestic work has the added advantage of allowing us to use the larger sample derived from the Household and Community Survey. Time constraints do not lead immediately to dissatisfaction though. The woman's framework, or at least the gender role attitude part of it will determine to a certain extent the level of dissatisfaction since it may legitimate the distribution of domestic work, irrespective of her own paid work status. Two variables representing the partners' attitudes to who should have responsibility for domestic work and another two representing those toward responsibility for obtaining an adequate income for the household are included in both models. Both sets of variables are dichotomous and refer to the partner being either traditional or untraditional. As I have explained before, this typology is a very simplistic model of the 'true' attitudes of the partners, but the patterns that this type of data uncovers are the important objective since, although crude, an untraditional response, as chapter five showed is highly related to increases in the man's amount of domestic work time. Our theory of frames also suggests another more specific hypothesis. Having untraditional attitudes and doing a high proportion of domestic work should individually decrease the woman's satisfaction, but the theory also suggests that together, a woman with an untraditional frame of reference, doing a high proportion of the domestic work should produce an additive, or interactive effect, further decreasing satisfaction. To test for this, we can add an 'interaction' term into the model.

If we look at the theories outlined and evidence presented so far in this chapter it also seems logical that the distribution of leisure time between the partners could have an effect on how satisfied women are with the division of domestic work. If the man has a great deal more leisure time, even though he works just as many hours, this may have negative effects on the woman's satisfaction. The SCELI Household and Community Survey included a question that allows us to look at the effects of imbalances in leisure time, as perceived by the woman. The question asks who has most leisure time between the partners and has three response categories (man, woman, both).

One of the themes of the last section of this chapter was the effect that class may have on the woman's satisfaction. To look at this variables representing each partners class position were created and a household class derived using the dominance principle (Goldthorpe 1983). The variable uses the Goldthorpe (1980) collapsed five-class scale and refers either to the present or last occupation of the partners. Lastly, control variables were entered for the age of the partners. This variable was categorised into three groups: those aged 17 to 29, 30 to 50 and 51 to 60.

As the dependant variable in this analysis is a ten point scale of dissatisfaction, the model uses an ordered logit model rather than a standard OLS regression. This type of model allows us to estimate relationships between an ordinal dependent variable (i.e. a categorical variable which nonetheless has a specific order to it) and a set of independent variables. The model estimates an underlying score as a linear function of the independent variables and a set of cut points. Thus, we will be estimating the probability that the estimated linear function, plus random error, falls within the range of the cut points, where the cut points are our ten levels of satisfaction.

In the model, the base category used for comparison is that which was taken to be the most 'satisfied'. Thus the full time housewife from class five (working class) who is over 50 with traditional attitudes and who does a low proportion of the domestic division of labour is the category to which the other coefficients are compared. The model thus looks at factors which make women more dissatisfied with their division of domestic labour. Variables were added to the model and retained if they reached a significance level of P>0.05. Unlike in the models in the previous chapters, there is no base model for these variables since we simply want to see whether a range of variables have an effect in the directions outlined in the previous sections of this chapter, but the work statuses of the partners and their age groups were retained in the models as controls even if they did not reach significance. The interaction of the variables in this model are very important to the interpretation, thus I will present the model at different stages of construction, i.e. after entering major groups of variables.

Table 7.1 displays the coefficients and significance of the variables for five different models of the woman's satisfaction with the domestic division of labour. Moving from left to right, table 7.1 shows the development of the full model and the effect that new variables have on those already in the model. This allows us to get a better view of the relationship between the variables just discussed.

To begin, the work status variables and age group variables were added to the model. As expected, the woman's work status was very significant whereas the male partner's was not. Both the part time and full time categories of the woman's work status had negative effects on her satisfaction with the domestic division of labour. One important test/control variable that had to be entered was that of class. The main hypothesis from the section on existing quantitative studies of satisfaction was that working class women who had middle class husbands would be more satisfied, even when doing higher proportions of domestic work than women of the same, or 'higher' social class than their husbands.

Table 7.1 An Ordered Logit Model of Women's Satisfaction with the Distribution of Domestic Work

Variable		Model 1 B	Sig.	Model 2 B	Sig.	Model 3 B	Sig.	Model 4 B	Sig.	Model 5 B	Sig.
Woman's Age	51 to 60	Ref.		Ref.		Ref.		Ref.		Ref.	
	17 to 29	-0.52		-0.50		-0.65	*	-0.58	*	-0.58	*
	30 to 49	-0.47	*	-0.47	*	-0.51	*	-0.47	*	-0.48	*
Man's Age	17 to 29	Ref.		Ref.		Ref.		Ref.		Ref.	
	17 to 29	-0.64	*	-0.63	*	-0.56	*	-0.54	*	-0.56	*
	30 to 49	-0.34		-0.32		-0.25	*	-0.24		-0.25	
Woman's work status FT Houseworker	Full Time	Ref.		Ref.		Ref.		Ref.		Ref.	
	Full Time	-0.31	*	-0.23	*	-0.5	**	-0.45	**	-0.48	**
	Part Time	-0.34	*	-0.32	*	-0.44	**	-0.43	**	-0.44	**
	Unemployed	0.48		0.52		0.36		0.33		0.29	
	Non-Worker	0.66		0.71		0.64	**	0.62		0.55	
Man's work status	Full Time	Ref.		Ref.		Ref.		Ref.		Ref.	
	Part Time	0.01		0.00		-0.2		-0.14		-0.15	
	Unemployed	0.10		0.12		-0.07		0.06		0.05	
	Full Time Houseworker	0.35		0.23		0.26		0.16		0.25	
	Non-Worker	-0.26		-0.25		-0.32		-0.18		-0.18	
Woman's Attitude:HW	Traditional	-		Ref.		Ref.		Ref.		Ref.	
	Untraditional	-		-0.21		-0.42	**	-0.47	***	-0.27	*
Woman's %HW	Low	-		-		Ref.		Ref.		Ref.	
	Medium	-		-		-0.44	**	-0.39	**	-0.36	*
	High	-		-		-1.24	**	-1.2	***	-1.0	***
Who Has Most Leisure Time?	Woman	-		-		-		Ref.		Ref.	
	Man	-		-		-		-0.42	**	-0.37	*
	Both Same	-		-		-		0.22		0.25	
Interactions:											
Woman's %HW Medium / HW Attitude Untraditional		-		-		-		-		-0.02	
Woman's %HW High / HW Attitude Untraditional		-		-		-		-		-1.13	**
Log Likelihood		-2111.1		-2109.7		-2078.0		-2065.1		-2059.4	

N=1136   *=P<0.05 **=P<0.01 ***=P<0.001

159

This did not emerge from the model where the class measure was insignificant and was thus excluded. Surprisingly, on entering the model, the woman's attitude toward who should have responsibility for domestic work was not significant. However, model 3 in table 7.1 shows why this was so. Only once we had controlled for the woman's perceived proportion of domestic work did her attitudes become a significant predictor of satisfaction, with untraditional attitudes having a negative effect. The woman's attitude toward who should be responsible for the provision of an adequate income was not significant and was thus dropped from the model. Did the woman's proportion of domestic work also support the thesis outlined earlier? Upon entry into the model, the variable representing the woman's proportion was very significant and showed that if the woman did the highest proportion of the domestic division of labour this had a very negative effect on her satisfaction. We can even see a gradient to the effect for the woman's proportion of domestic work with the 'high' category having nearly three times the effect of the 'medium' category.

Our hypothesis earlier on suggested that we should see a relationship between the perceived division of leisure time between the partners in the household and the female partners' satisfaction with domestic work. Model 4 in table 7.1 shows evidence that supports this hypothesis. If the woman perceives that her husband has more leisure time, this has a very significant negative effect on her satisfaction with the domestic division of labour.

Lastly, do we see an interactive effect between the woman's proportion of the domestic division of labour and her attitudes as the frame working theory suggests we should? It appears so. Model 5 in table 7.1 shows that if the woman has untraditional attitudes, but does a high proportion of the domestic division of labour this has a large and significant negative effect on her satisfaction. Interestingly, when this interaction is entered into the model, the main term for the woman's attitudes becomes insignificant.

This seems perfectly understandable since untraditional attitudes on their own would not necessarily lead to dissatisfaction with domestic work. It is only when the women holds these attitudes, but also perceives that she is in a traditional domestic work role that dissatisfaction emerges. Overall then, the ordered logit model supports our hypotheses about the relationship between the woman's employment status, gender role attitudes and domestic work practices and lends weight to the findings of the qualitative studies examined earlier in this chapter.

Conclusions

The combination of qualitative and quantitative evidence in this chapter has shown that dissatisfaction and conflict over the domestic division of labour is complex, but also structured in particular ways. The qualitative evidence presented from researchers such as Hochschild, Yeandle and Gerson show that the changes in the paid work participation of women over the last thirty years has had dramatic effects on the relationships between partners within households, even if not on the allocation of domestic work. Changes in women's paid work practices have been accompanied by important changes in women's attitudes (c.f. Dex 1988) that mean that the once taken for granted roles of housewife and breadwinner are now problematic. The changes have happened so quickly that the majority of people still inhabit the 'transitional' space that Hochschild proposes lies between the 'egalitarians' and 'traditionals'. Yet in this space, men are closer to the traditional and women the egalitarian. The complex reasons for this difference in attitudes have been outlined in this chapter and in the last, but its existence can lead to differences between partners that are difficult to bridge. Partners are not cultural dopes who are shackled to simplistic attitudes, but complex, often contradictory economic and social actors who seem, on the whole to be trying to make their relationships work. Unfortunately, the contradictions in the structure of socio-economic life in this period mean that the project is difficult because it requires that we change our conceptions of gender roles as well as alter the habitual structures of behaviour that come to us most readily. The qualitative evidence has shown that partner's dissatisfaction with the domestic division of labour and often the relationship as a whole results from three different, but equally important contradictions involving partners frameworks and economic circumstances. One is illustrated by Hochschild's work which shows how partners with different gender role attitudes (derived from the past work and life experiences) can often find themselves disagreeing over the relative values of different types of work, or commitments to the family. A second stems from the contradictions brought out when partners ideal gender role is made impossible by the economic circumstances that they find themselves in. A partner may want to stay at home and take on the role of the 'care-giver' or home maker, but this may be made impossible by the households need for a larger income that can only be made if that partner works in the labour market instead of in the home. A third contradiction is far less common, but may emerge where both partners frameworks agree, but both agree that they are breadwinners in the face of home circumstances that require more input from the partners. This contradiction is of a more general nature since it effects the ability of the partners to uphold a relationship at all, as well as limiting their ability to deal with the organisational needs of the household in terms of domestic work.

The quantitative evidence has also confirmed the importance of partners' frameworks for understanding the roots of dissatisfaction and conflict, but shows how these interact with the paid work status of the woman and the division of domestic tasks in the household. It is clear that 'equity' is not quite as simple as social exchange theory suggests since we have to try to factor the life and work history of the partners into the equation before we can begin on constructing a preference schedule that is coherent and takes into account the position of the other partner. To understand the emergence of dissatisfaction we need to know, as dictated by the exchange theorists, what the relative balance of work is between the partners and how this relates to their individual resources usable both inside and outside the relationship. But, this is not the end of the story, we also need to examine the cultural framework from which the individual partner views the exchange relationship since the price of the bargain is set as much by this factor as it is by the relative availability of resources. To gain even a probabilistic understanding of a person's framework using quantitative data we have to examine their experiences from childhood. This complexity means that we gain a great deal of conceptual understanding if we use qualitative evidence to highlight the meanings that partners give to their actions.

The theoretical stance of this book has been to try to combine the insights of some of the economic literature on the household which emphasises choice in situations of scarcity and differential cost with the sociological insight that behaviour is often given value by the meanings that it has for actors. This chapter has highlighted once again why this is necessary. Previous chapters have shown that households do attempt to maximise their productivity by allocating labour in different ways in different circumstances. But, as this chapter has shown, what partners see as valuable and therefore worth doing varies according to the gender role frameworks that they believe in. Thus, as Hochschild showed, partners may subjectively feel that they are doing their best to 'care' for the family and their partner by doing certain kinds of work. Yet to their partner, this is not seen as useful or necessary since they believe, via their framework or ideology that other types of activities take precedence. The 'rationality' that should govern the allocation of time differs between the partners and leads to dissatisfaction and conflict. Moreover, we can see from the evidence presented that these 'rationalities' are patterned in certain ways - thus the 'private troubles' of the households in Hochschild's study are closely linked to macro economic and social changes that have occurred in the last half-century.

8 Conclusions

This book has explored the relationship between attitudes toward the work roles of the sexes and the domestic division of labour between partners within households. I have asked three simple questions: first, what effect does an increase in the woman's paid work participation have on the division of domestic work between her and her partner? Previous research on this subject has shown that it has little redistributive effect, raising the further issue of why this is so. Finally, I asked what effect this inequitable division of domestic tasks has on the woman's satisfaction with the division of domestic tasks, and the level of conflict between the partners. The introduction to the book made it clear however, that before we could answer these questions we needed to examine our theoretical approach to the household. Thus, before going on to look at the answers this book has offered to these questions, we should first go back to the theoretical problems that have hamstrung previous studies.

A New Theoretical Framework?

Previous quantitative studies of the domestic division of labour have generated inconclusive results, because the theoretical approaches they have adopted have been inadequate to the task. This inadequacy could be traced to the problem of combining a model of behaviour based upon scarcity related/cost benefit analysis with one based upon the study of processes of legitimation and value orientations. Thus, if we look at past quantitative studies (Berk 1985; England & McCreary, 1987; Brines 1993), Gary Becker's (1976) economic model of time allocation is used as the main analytical engine of their theory since this allows the researcher to construct substantive predictions about data. However, this model of how paid and unpaid work is distributed provides a necessary, but not sufficient explanation for the patterns found in data. In an attempt to explain this discrepancy, Berk *et al* invoke a sociological theory of normative orientations (that is, people have an overriding normative preference for a certain type of household organisation), but, rather than augmenting the economic theory, this theory is an alternative, deterministic, 'value' theory of choice (Parsons 1954) that mixes poorly with the economic theory. Berk *et al* know that respondents are making choices based upon their notions of the proper division of labour between male and female partners in the household, but they lack an adequate account of how these socially structured notions relate to the economic, or rational choice model with its simple assumptions and powerful predictive ability. Thus, if respondents are not 'rationally maximising' along the lines that the economic theory predicts, then they must be enacting structures of gender norms that act internally to shape their preferences and 'push' them toward certain modes of behaviour.

This dualistic approach is not a good basis upon which to build empirical models or interpret results. Neither the economic or the sociological theory is adequate on its own and yet the structure of each makes integration difficult. On the one hand, the economic theory is powerful in application, but relies upon unrealistic assumptions about actors having perfect information and ordered preferences. Moreover, it cannot accommodate preferences that are social or cultural in origin, unless they are invoked as constraints on otherwise 'rational' decisions. The sociological approach on the other hand does not permit us to make predictions about the way that behaviour changes given different circumstances since actors are motivated by the 'value orientations' of the society. If the theories could be usefully combined, these problems would not be so bad, but there is no real integration between the two theories.

Chapter one examined the theoretical problems inherent in the theories currently in use in the literature and outlined the effects that these problems have caused past empirical research. It then put forward a new theoretical approach to the analysis of the division of domestic labour that allowed us to see individuals and households as maximisers, but maximisers who had social, as well as economic goals. The theory is based upon the 'discrimination' model of choice proposed by Siegred Lindenberg, which has a similar structure to the subjective expected utility theory that underpins past economic models, but unlike these models, it sees individuals as maximising along one dimension alone. This sounds a rather unimportant, even retrograde change, but it allows us to build a more realistic theory which can encompass cultural factors and social structure into the decision making process. Unlike the standard economic model of choice, the alternatives seen as acceptable in discrimination theory are those that are seen as important given the 'frame of reference' that the person is attempting to maximise. Unlike economists, sociologists have always seen a person's definition of the situation as crucial to their understanding of the rationality of their behaviour, and thus the explanation for it. The definition of the situation is given by a sociological understanding of the context and social location in which the behaviour occurs. As was explained, the standard economic or rational choice model of choice has to assume that people see a situation in the same way and that preferences are identical, otherwise a radical indeterminacy sets in to the models. If people can see different aspects of a situation as important, or can perceive it in different ways, how are we supposed to be able to build models of how they will respond to changes in costs/alternatives? The answer is that we use sociological understanding of their present situation (social location) and past experiences as a means to construct ideal-type understandings of their motivations.

If individuals are maximising along one dimension though, doesn't this mean that we have reverted to the determinist, value models of choice that were criticised above? Luckily not, for although the person defines the situation in a particular manner and pursues a particular goal, this does not stop them choosing the means to that goal that maximises their utility. Moreover, the model also specifies the circumstances in which the framework itself or the definition of the situation to the individual may change, thus stopping the actor being locked into a particular definition of the situation. These circumstances are defined by the 'situational salience' of the framework that the person is using to discriminate amongst the alternative courses of action open in the pursuit of their main aim (maximand). If in trying to maximise amongst a number of alternative courses of action, the individual finds that the existing 'definition of the situation' does not differentiate amongst the alternatives, the 'situational salience' of the framework falls and it may be replaced by a new one that defines a new goal and criteria for judging whether it has been attained.

The study of the domestic division of labour is particularly in need of an approach that can integrate a theory of choice with social structural variables, but there is a more general need in sociology. In the 1980s for example, sociologists and economists sought to understand the ways in which people respond to and in turn, mould the wider economic situation by studying the activities of households.

Researchers soon found that they needed new theoretical tools to understand the innovatory ways in which people responded to unemployment and economic insecurity. One answer was put forward by Ray Pahl (1984) in the concept of the 'household strategy'. This was derived from studies of the urban poor in the third world, particularly Latin America, where the idea of the 'survival strategy' was used to illustrate the resourcefulness of people striving to survive urban poverty (Roberts 1978). Claire Wallace (1993, p95), one of Pahl's co-authors, has stated that the concept of the household strategy was used because

> ....in the 1970s the dominant academic paradigm in urban sociology had been Marxist structuralism, which saw individual actors as irrelevant or at best reflections of dominant structural forces. The focus on household strategies allowed a more humanistic interpretation and enabled us to recognise the sources of power and rationality existing within households, which could not necessarily be predicted from structural analysis. A further advantage was that this perspective enabled us to look at 'work' in a much wider sense, in terms of what people actually do rather than by examining institutions in the labour market or some forms of formal employment.

It is plain from this quote that Pahl (1984) and Pahl and Wallace (1985) wanted to be able to look at households as productive units and explain how the organisation of this production was related to the local social and economic context. More importantly, they wanted to get away from the sociological approach that saw the choices of individuals and households as mere epiphenomena subordinate to structural forces. This aim parallels that of this book. In practice, the theoretical approach remained largely implicit in their work (see chapter one), but it is clear that an approach similar to the one outlined in this book would be appropriate to studies such as that of Pahl.

There were however problems with the notion of the household strategy. First of all, the idea that the household had a strategy implied (though this was never directly addressed) that it also had some form of collective decision making process. The indirect consequence of this is that differences of interests and power imbalances amongst members of the household are ignored. I mentioned this tendency in chapter one, and tried to show in the framework that I put forward how individual interests should never be subsumed under those of the household, even when assuming that there is some (all be it vague) tendency for households to 'maximise'. I will discuss this at greater length below when examining the results from chapters three and five. The second problem with the notion of the household strategy is the extent to which this implies 'rational' action on behalf of actors (putting aside the problem of collective decision making). This is one of the main criticisms that Graham Crow (1989, p12) makes of the concept of 'strategy'.

> In various instances it proves difficult to speak of the rationality of household strategies, either because it is hard to detect anything resembling rational-decision making having preceded actions, or because there is no one standard of rationality by which it is appropriate to judge the strategies that have been developed.

By his first remark, I think that Crow is stating that people do not assess all of the possible avenues of action before making a decision, rather than saying that people do not 'think' about a decision before they make it. This was one of my criticisms of subjective expected utility theory and one of the points that made Lindenberg's 'discrimination model' of choice a more realistic, and more sociological alternative.

The second criticism that Crow makes is I think a misunderstanding of what Pahl and Wallace, as well as much rational choice theory attempts to do. Most do not decide on an 'objective' definition of rationality appropriate to the situation and then after comparing all behaviour to this, dismiss as irrational any behaviour that doesn't agree with the definition (though some may do, c.f Goldthorpe 1998). If we believe that actors actually make choices and are not simply the puppets of social structure, we need to assume unless given information to the contrary, that they make choices for their own reasons. As such, our task as sociologists is to try to find these reasons, to find out why they behaved as they did, or made the decision that they did. This does not mean that social action is unconstrained, nor that it takes place in a cultural vacuum. As chapter one showed, the theoretical schema that we developed takes material and institutional constraints seriously because these are an integral part of the discrimination theory in terms of the costs (in the most general sense) involved in any decision. A person's decisions and alternatives are also subjectively related to their social location via their life and work history. This location can be seen as, and is both a constraint and a resource that constructs individual life experiences and forms social groups (Giddens 1984; Bourdieu 1990). Thus, on the one hand, our choice of alternatives is limited by our knowledge of the alternatives available. Information is costly and no individual could ever have complete knowledge of any choice situation or its future consequences. On the other, behaviour will be constrained by the relative costs of alternatives and the institutional context. However, these choice situations are the resources from which people as individuals, households or social groups construct their lives.

In the same way, social action also takes place within an environment which is shaped by past choices of the actor and those around them, and the social and economic environment in which they live. Because this environment is one of the 'background characteristics' (see chapter one) that are constitutive of any choice situation and thus the rationality involved, they are not determinant, though they may be constraining in the ways just proposed. Therefore, although the rationality of any decision or action may not always be found, it should be an empirical question as to whether it will be or not. Of course, our theory should help us to create hypotheses about the rationality of the situation (i.e. the actors intentions as well as the social, economic and institutional environment) that can then be tested using data and as the section at the end of the first chapter showed, this is true of the theoretical framework that we developed from the discrimination model of choice. In developing a theory which links choice situations to individual biographies and household circumstances I have not sought to directly address the institutional and societal context in which these processes occur. This is a lamentable, but necessary omission, given the limit on space available, but does not reflect the importance of these contexts. Thus, in discussing how individuals and households make decisions about how to allocate labour time, it must be remembered that these decisions occur within local labour markets which are structured extensively along lines of gender (Burchell et al, 1994) and local social networks which consolidate or undermine certain patterns of domestic organisation (Bott 1957; c.f. Morris 1990, pp176-188). Similarly, although almost all the chapters in this book discuss the factors which shape individuals attitudes toward the proper work roles of the sexes, these processes need to be located within a society in which women are still predominantly identified with the domestic role (Walby 1986, 1989).

Having reviewed the theoretical work of this book, we can now go on to look at whether it answered the three simple questions set out in the introduction.

Finding the Limits of the New Home Economic Theory

Chapter two made it clear that the 'traditional' division of domestic work between partners was still the dominant pattern in the SCELI data set. Even in those households where the woman worked full time, the female partner still did over 60% of the total amount of domestic work time and tasks. Moreover, the male partners of women who work full time actually did fewer minutes per day of domestic work than the partners of women who were full time housewives. These patterns are very interesting since they suggest that there is no reciprocal relationship between the paid and unpaid work contributions of the partners. Although the data are cross-sectional rather than longitudinal, it seems from this initial analysis that if a woman moves from full time housework to being a part time worker to doing full time work, she decreases the frequency that she does tasks (though not the overall number of different tasks) and thus spends less time doing domestic work overall. On the other hand, the man's contribution seems to remain stable as the women does more paid work. How do we explain these patterns? Chapter one of the book showed that, although flawed, the NHE theory advocated by Gary Becker is, theoretically speaking, a better alternative than any of the other theories reviewed and the theory has had some success in explaining the distribution of domestic work in other studies (Berk 1985; England & McCreary 1987; Brines 1993). However, the theory has to assume that partners within a household will change their work arrangements in response to a change in work practices on behalf of the other partner if this change alters the marginal productivity between the partners. The findings of chapter two do not sound promising for this theory, but we could not be sure that the theory is wrong unless we perform a much more rigorous analysis controlling for those variables that Becker has suggested may confound the effects of a change in paid work practices by the female partner. For example, the analysis in chapter two does not control for the income difference that may exist between the partners that may influence their contributions to unpaid work. In essence, we need to construct a multivariate model of partners paid and unpaid work contributions, that takes account of a number of confounding variables. This was the task of chapter three.

Chapter three sought to find out whether the NHE theory offered a sufficient explanation for the patterns found in the SCELI data, or whether there was a large amount of unexplained variance as found in the studies by Berk (1985), England & McCreary (1987) or Brines (1993). Chapter two found very little evidence of a relationship between the work contributions of partners, thus it seemed unlikely that the NHE theory of the household would be a sufficient explanation for the data. Chapter three attempted to see how close actual data from the SCELI surveys approximated an ideal type model, controlling for different variables that may superficially confound the theory's predictions. The theory predicts that households 'on the margin' will attempt to find the best configuration of time and resources, given opportunity costs and productivity in their search for the greatest possible well-being. What this means in practice is that we should see an increase in the amount of time that the male partner spends doing domestic work if the female partner's productivity in paid work, and concomitantly, her time in paid work increases (since, according to the theory, households will not increase the amount of time that an individual spends in paid employment unless their relative productivity increases). Although this prediction was wrong, the theory did gain some support from the data.

Initial results for the model showed, as in chapter two, that men's contribution to domestic work does not increase when the women's productivity and time in paid work increases. The NHE theory was correct, however, in suggesting that we should see differentials in the domestic work contributions of men according to their time in paid work. Thus, men who did more paid work time did less domestic work on average than men who worked a smaller amount of time in paid employment. Thus, men's contributions to unpaid work are related to their paid work time, but, contrary to the theory on test, they are not related to their wives since there was no increase the men's domestic contributions, controlling for their own paid work time, as their wives did more paid work.

Could other variables not be confounding the predictions of the theory? There are three main variables that Becker states may alter the productivity's of the partners and thus the distribution of work. The marginal difference between the incomes of the partners may be such that the increase in the woman's paid employment time is not enough (i.e. her productivity in paid work is not as high as the man's in paid employment) to change the marginal productivity of the husband and thus tempt him to do more domestic work for the good of the household. The second variable is the number of children in the household. Becker states that women have a natural advantage in nursing that makes the women's marginal productivity in domestic work greater than the male partner's, if there are young children in the household, since she can do domestic work and nurse at the same time. The last variable that may confound the model is the purchase of 'commodity substitutes', such as an outside domestic worker, to replace the unpaid work of the woman. Of these variables, only the difference in marginal incomes of the partners had any effect on the male partners contribution to domestic work, suggesting again that the NHE theory is correct in its assumption that the time the partners spend in domestic work will be endogenously determined by other work commitments and productivity, but the contributions of partners are not reciprocally related (the husbands are not affected by the wives). Unless we can find reasons why the wife is agreeing to do more domestic work than the male partner, this latter point implies that the NHE assumption of the single utility function that I have criticised so much in this book is wrong, and that partners (probably male partners) pursue their own interests, sometimes over those of the household. If this is true, we should examine more closely the processes of negotiation that underlie the distribution of domestic work. I will come back to these points shortly while discussing the conclusions from the last three chapters.

The Political Economy of the Household

It is clear from chapter three that the NHE theory of time use is a necessary, but not sufficient explanation for the patterns in the SCELI surveys. There are more processes at work in the distribution of domestic work in the household than are suggested by the theory - but what are these? One of the prime contenders must be the cultural beliefs and attitudes that men and women have of the proper division of domestic labour in the household. As chapter one explained, much past research has attempted to conceptualise and measure the effect that attitudes and beliefs have on practices in the household, but none have put forward a coherent picture of how attitudes are related to the 'productive' or economic aspects of the household. As either 'patriarchy', the 'enactment of gender roles' or 'normative values', culture has been conceptualised as a homogenous and determinist system of beliefs. Although chapter one went on to discuss a better conceptualisation of the 'culture' of gendered work roles, it was in chapters four and five that we examined the actual patterning of attitudes toward the proper work roles of men and women, and the relationship of these attitudes to practices within the household. Chapter four showed that paid work has an important place in the lives of many women and that they do not, in general, see themselves as less suited than men to this role in terms of their own abilities and aspirations. This belief and associated attitudes is complicated by the issue of how this role combines with household responsibilities and with the role that the male partner will fulfil. Although women express the belief that they have a legitimate place in paid work, a majority in all work status groups still feel that the male partner should be the main breadwinner in the household. The extent to which women express this belief differs widely between women of different work status', thus it is more common amongst part time workers, full time domestic workers and non-working women. Women's attitudes are also shaped strongly by their birth cohort with younger women being far more untraditional in their attitudes than older women. Attitudes were also related to class and education with women from higher social classes with more qualifications being more likely to express untraditional attitudes. The pattern of attitudes amongst men is similar to that amongst women, but more interestingly, there is a strong reciprocal relationship between the work status of the woman and the attitudes of both her and her partner. If attitudes and beliefs are constitutive of domestic work practices, this reciprocal relationship suggests that the household has to be seen as an interactive system in which the aspirations, attitudes and circumstances of both partner's react with and upon each other to produce the behavioural outcome of a substantially inequitable division of household labour. We will see some evidence of this relationship in the discussion of the results from chapter five.

The first section of chapter four explored the relationship between behaviour and attitudes and concluded that we can see attitudes as autonomous orientations to certain types of social action or cognitive choices that are conceptually separate from, but which nonetheless interact with present practices to produce behaviour. This interaction may operate along the 'as if' lines presented in chapter one in Lindenberg's discrimination model. Thus, attitudes will operate as orientations to social action, as long as they allow the person to discriminate among alternatives that are presented to them. As other factors rise in importance to match the primary factor (e.g. as the dissonance between present practices [done for whatever reason] and the existing framework increases), the choice probability of the frame moves toward non-discrimination and the frame itself is re-evaluated and possibly replaced with another if the person can no longer discriminate between the alternatives that they face. It sounds from this that we would expect that those with more untraditional attitudes, *ceteris paribus*, would divide domestic labour along more egalitarian lines - chapter five set out to see whether this was so.

It would seem that for attitudes to have an effect on domestic practices, partners would need to be aware of how they divide up domestic work tasks. Yet, Arlie Hochschild (1990) has shown that partners' actual domestic work practices can diverge dramatically from the way partners say they divide unpaid work. Hochschild argues that this divergence occurs because partners are trying to resolve the dissonance between their actual domestic practices and their beliefs about how they think they *should* divide domestic work by developing an agreed story between them. Chapter five examined the relationship between both partners' estimates of their practices and between these estimates and their attitudes. It found, like Hochschild, that partners' do have an agreed understanding of their practices that differs substantially from our measures using the diary evidence and that the degree of disjunction was clearly related to the attitudes of partners. But, the model of the 'family myth' in chapter five showed that this gap between the partners' estimates and the diary evidence was more likely to be a result of the inadequate knowledge that people have of the amount of domestic work that they and their partners do, rather than being a result of the psychological process that Hochschild outlines in her book. Correlation coefficients between partners' estimates and the diary totals showed that full time working women and unemployed women were much better at estimating their proportion of domestic work than were part time or non-working women (and part time were better than non-working women). A clearer test of the 'strong' hypothesis of the family myth (i.e. the psychological process) also failed to support Hochschild's work.

Even with this disjunction between the partners' self-estimates and the diary evidence, it was clear that inequitable divisions of domestic labour do not go unnoticed. However, chapter five showed that this does not necessarily lead to practices being seen as unfair. Controlling for the work status of the woman, the majority of men and women saw their household arrangements as fair. It seems then that some women see their main role as that of the main 'homemaker', even where they work full time themselves. The reasons why female partners saw their share of domestic work as unfair were, however illuminating. Many women saw this inequity being due to their partners' greater involvement in paid work, but a large proportion also cited their partners ineffectiveness and disinterestedness as a major reason why they did more of the domestic work. This finding was supported by evidence from multivariate models in chapter five that showed that male and female partners' attitudes had differential affects on domestic work practices. Where the female partner has untraditional attitudes, their effect on practices was negligible. On the other hand, the male partner's attitudes are much more powerful predictors of the woman's proportion of domestic work. These statistical patterns seem to indicate, for households where the female has untraditional attitudes at least, that it is the man's unwillingness to take on domestic tasks that leads to problems experienced by the NHE models in chapter three.

Chapters three, four and five show that the NHE theory of the household is correct in its assertion that households and the individuals within them will attempt to 'maximise', even if only loosely, the productivity of their members. As such, its economic framework is a vital component of any model that attempts to explain the division of domestic labour in households. However, the respondents to the SCELI survey have cultural concerns as well as economic ones, as can be seen from the effect that attitudes have on practices and on how these practices are perceived. Contrary to the literature outlined in chapter one though, chapter four showed that these beliefs about the proper division of domestic tasks between men and women are not homogenous but vary widely. If partners are acting 'as if' to maximise household productivity and equity, they are doing it with an eye to their cultural understandings of what 'equity' means. Where these understandings differ between partners, there is definite evidence that the man is more able to make his attitudes count in practice than the woman. This last point is extremely important. Doubts have been expressed about the assumption of a single utility function in the NHE thesis in a large body of literature, but the findings of chapter five show that the assumption is untenable. There is clear evidence here that individual partners often have different agendas and that these lead to an inequitable division of domestic labour.

If men do generally seem to be able to make their attitudes count over their partners' in situations where attitudes differ, it would seem necessary to offer some explanation of why this is so. If we look back to chapter one, this was the aim of exchange theory where researchers such as John Scanzoni (1972, 1979) attempted to explain many patterns in the relationship between married partners through the concept of 'power'. We discarded Exchange theory as our general theory of choice because of it's inattention to the productive aspects of the partnership, but without a concept of power, how do we account for this imbalance between partners? One way would be to try to reintroduce some of the notions of power through resources that are usable outside the home that were used in exchange theory. To do this we would have to reconstruct our NHE theory around multiple utility functions and the differential resources and opportunity costs of partners, a task well beyond the scope of this book. On the other hand, the widespread nature of this imbalance, even where the woman works full time suggest that differential resources may interact with cultural structures that have not been fully investigated in this book. This is unsurprising given the limited number of attitude measures available and the difficulty of fully investigating any complex attitude using quantitative data. For instance, both Yeandle (1984) and McRae (1986) have shown that women often feel guilty about asking their partner to do more domestic work, even when they have more demanding jobs (in terms of time) and untraditional attitudes because they sense that such beliefs are not held widely elsewhere in society. As such, they do not feel they have a legitimate right to demand more domestic work from their partner. In many respects this may be correct since older relatives and friends are more likely to have traditional attitudes, as shown by chapter four.

However, we still need to explain where these attitudes emerge from, and what affect this difference in attitudes has on the satisfaction of partners if we are to answer the questions I laid out in the introduction to this book. These tasks were undertaken in chapters six and seven.

Attitudes, Practices and Work and Life History

Before examining the results of chapters six and seven, it would be useful first quickly go back over the ground we have covered so far since these chapters rest on what went before. Chapter one concluded with a request that we take work and life histories seriously as an important route through which to recover the rationality of decisions made in the present. We have seen that the homo economicus put forward by various shades of economic theory is not a good model of the social actor that we see in the SCELI surveys, but it is hard to reassert the rationality of the actors involved if all we have by way of an explanation for their lack of 'maximisation' is a socio-cultural belief about the proper work roles for men and women. This is not to say that this is not a viable type of explanation. In the end, this is what social theorists such as Weber (1978), Giddens (1975) or Stinchcombe (1968) have confirmed gives the social sciences any measure of the 'cause' of an act, in the sense that a person believing something to be true about the world decided to act thus. The question is really, what set of circumstances in the person's life and its history shaped the grounds upon which the belief came to have truth for them. In essence, what made this belief, this intention to act in the present, understandable as a form of rationality. Putting the point this bluntly underplays the epistemological problems involved in getting knowledge of other minds and the complexity of multivariate causality. Nonetheless, if we want to recover the rationality of the present situation we have to look to a persons past circumstances. This was the aim of chapter six.

The chapter constructed four different models that looked at the effect of work and life history variables on the attitudes and domestic work practices of partners in the household. A number of different variables were used to tap the early life experiences of the partners such as their experiences of their parents division of domestic work, and others that examined the affect of different kinds of paid work at different points in the woman's work history. The results showed that, although we could not discern any early life history effects, or effects through the female partner's work history on the man's attitudes, there was a definite evidence that the man did a greater amount of domestic work if the woman had been employed for over a year and a half in part time, and crucially, full time employment, and was presently in full time employment. This latter effect seems to suggest a slow process of adjustment between the woman's paid work time and the man's domestic work contributions, but it is impossible to say with quantitative data how such changes come about since we know nothing off the negotiation that accompanied the changes. I will speculate more fully about this process a little later in my discussion of chapter seven.

Although there was no direct relationship between the female partner's work history and the male partner's attitudes, the model of the male partner's attitude toward domestic work in chapter six showed that they were reciprocally related to those of his wife, and her attitudes did bear the mark of her early life experiences and past work life. If the woman comes from a background where there was an untraditional division of domestic work between her parents, she is no more likely than a woman from a traditional background to have untraditional attitudes. However, if the same is true and she had worked in full time employment for over 20 months, she is over five times more likely to have untraditional attitudes than a woman from a traditional background who has not worked full time. This suggests that the experience of working, coupled with the background knowledge that men are just as capable of doing domestic work as women reduces the traditionalism of a woman's attitudes. Since her attitudes are a major predictor of the male partner's, it seems at least likely that his attitudes have been shaped through exposure to his wife's experiences and her attitudinal development.

Unfortunately, it is very difficult to be anything more than tentative about such a conclusion. As with the issue of changes in male partners' attitudes, it will be possible to answer such questions using data from the British Household Panel study where there is longitudinal data on attitudes and paid and unpaid work that could be used to analyse processes of change. As such, we should treat findings from these cross-sectional data as tentative at best.

This evidence suggests, as did the evidence from chapter five, that there is more than an element of negotiation between partners around domestic work. More importantly though, it is clear that past experiences alter the woman's perception of the partners' roles in the household and these changed perceptions may then impact on the male partner, forcing some change in his behaviour. A change in behaviour may not, however mean that he has undergone a change in attitudes. If not, this may mean that the changes that we see in the behaviour of partners in the SCELI sample is proceeded by, and continues with conflict occurring between the partners. As chapter five showed, many women see the inequity in domestic work being due to reluctance on behalf of their partners to become involved. Does this situation lead to conflict and dissatisfaction on the part of the female partner? This question was examined in chapter seven.

Conflict and Dissatisfaction

At various points throughout this book I have made use of the findings of qualitative studies in an attempt to get a better understanding of the processes that underpin the domestic division of labour. Qualitative evidence is especially important to chapter seven, since it examines the female partners satisfaction with the domestic division of labour, and whether this leads to conflict between her and her partner. This is a delicate subject and comes loaded with value judgements about the people concerned and the quality of their relationship. However, by combining qualitative and quantitative evidence, chapter seven showed that there are some essential contradictions between the frameworks of attitudes and beliefs that partners' hold and the economic circumstances that they face that mean that there is a greater chance that the woman will be dissatisfied with the partners' domestic practices and that this will develop into conflict. The quantitative evidence showed clearly that the female partners' framework of attitudes and beliefs interacts with her paid work status and the level of inequity in practices to produce different levels of dissatisfaction on her part. Thus a woman may do a large proportion of the domestic work and work full time, but this does not mean that she will necessarily be dissatisfied with the situation, nor see it as inequitable (as shown by chapter five), if the framework through which she sees the situation legitimates it to the necessary level. However, as our theoretical approach from chapter one makes clear, this situation can change if other background factors begin to take on more importance. In such a situation, e.g., such as when the male partner becomes unemployed, yet still not become involved in domestic work, the woman's 'frame of reference', may switch and with it her satisfaction with present circumstances. In talking about 'frames of reference' and their relationship with satisfaction however, we should not forget, as was hinted at in the above example that the processes underlying the division of domestic labour are pervaded by power relations. Men may refuse to do more domestic work and be able to uphold this position in the face of the female partner's dissatisfaction and probable overwork. At various points in this book I have discussed the material constraints that can lead partners to make certain types of decisions, but I have also tried to make it clear that these decisions, or even the definition of the material situation, may not always be shared between the partners, primarily because of different cultural perceptions of their positions. In this situation, the distribution of work and resources that result can be heavily shaped by the struggle that then ensues between the partners. By using the work of Hochschild, I have made it clear that there is a structural contradiction in the 'frameworks' through which many male and female partners see their domestic situation, and that this contradiction can and does cause marital conflict. Looking back all the way to chapter one, I discussed the problems Blood (1963) had coming to terms with the exchange theorist's assumption that couples take explicit account of the possibility of divorce when negotiating the division of domestic labour. Exchange theory may be a bad overall model of the division of domestic labour, but as researchers such as Wilkie (1988) and England & Kilbourne (1991) have shown, it was correct in asserting that the ultimate response to a partner's inactivity can be (and increasingly is) divorce. Women's increasing participation in paid work, even if only part time, has meant that life outside of a relationship or marriage is now possible if persuasion and conflict do not invoke changes in behaviour on behalf of the other partner. It would be interesting to use currently available longitudinal data to establish whether female partners are using divorce or separation more frequently because of this increased power on their part.

What overall conclusions can we draw from this book? First of all, it is clear that the changes that have occurred in women's work patterns over the thirty years have led to increasingly complex patterns of attitudes amongst men and women as to the proper roles of the sexes in the household and in paid work. These changes have been the subject of a number of works (Dex 1988; Jowell, Witherspoon & Brook 1988), but this book has shown how these patterns are related to the domestic work practices and satisfactions of partners.

Secondly, it is also clear from this book that the present debate on the degree of 'choice' that women exercise or 'constraint' that they face is rather basic in the sense that no account has been given so far of the long run determinants of the situations that women find themselves in (Hakim 1995, 1996; Ginn *et al* 1995; Bruegel 1995). More seriously, little has been done to disentangle the notions of choice and constraint as they apply to actors making choices in a cultural and economic environment. This book has shown that if we wish to explain the distribution of domestic work in households we need to see the individuals within as a complex mix *of homo economicus* and *homo sociologicus*. The former tries to maximise the 'productivity' of the household, but does so under the influence of the latter, who makes sense of certain types of work organisation and thus either heightens the sense of injustice with it, or legitimates and normalises it. Which ever occurs, it is not then set in stone, but becomes the basis upon which changing circumstances are judged.

However, such findings that have been found by this book uncover new questions that need to be examined. Although we have established a coherent theoretical picture of the relationship between partners' attitudes and the negotiation of domestic work over the long run, our empirical findings have been sketchy due to inadequacies in the data. New data sources, such as the British Household Panel Study or the Family and Working Lives Survey are now available and as a longitudinal surveys they will be very useful for further research in this area. Likewise, this book has not been able to look at the relationship between the partners, the household, the local social network and the division of domestic labour. This would be a fruitful area of research, especially if it could relate patterns of domestic work to institutional structures outside of the home.

Appendices

Appendix A

Time	What were you doing?		Who was involved with you in the **main** activity? (Tick and/or write in)				Where were you during the **main** activity? (Please tick)				Time
	Main activity in each quarter hour	Anything else in the quarter hour	Alone	Husband Wife	Own Children	Other Person(s) (Please write in the relationship of the person to you)	Own Home or Garden	Own Work-Place/School	Travel-ling	Else-where	
4a.m.											**4a.m.**
.15											.15
.30											.30
.45											.45
5a.m.											**5a.m.**
.15											.15
.30											.30
.45											.45
6a.m.											**6a.m.**
.15											.15
.30											.30
.45											.45
7a.m.											**7a.m.**
.15											.15
.30											.30
.45											.45
8a.m.											**8a.m.**
.15											.15
.30											.30
.45											.45
9a.m.											**9a.m.**
.15											.15
.30											.30
.45											.45

177

Appendix B

HCS (UK 1987) Time Budget Coding Frame Devised by Jay Gershuny, University Of Bath

A. Formal Work

1. At Work

0101   Normal work
0102   Unscheduled break at work
0103   Scheduled break at work (eg meal)
0104   Other work-related activities

2. Paid Work at Home

0201   Childminding
0202   Running a catalogue
0203   Jobseeking paperwork at home
0204   (Other) Jobsearch activities
0206   Other homeworking (non-computer)
0207   Other homeworking (computer)
0208   Work 'brought home' (non-computer)
0209   Work 'brought home' (computer)

3. Second Job

0301   Second, third etc. job (for money)
0302   Other informal economic activity

4. School/Classes

0401   Educational activities - unspecified
0402   Lunch break at educational establishment - school
0403   Student at educational establishment
0404   Other educational activities
0405   Night and privately tutored classes for hobbies

5. Travel to/from Work

0501   Jobseeking activities outside home
0502   Travel to/from work
0503   Education travel
0504   Job search - travel
0505   Other work-related travel

B. Domestic Work

6. Cooking/Washing up

0601   Food preparation
0602   Baking, freezing foods, making jams, pickles, preserves, drying herbs
0603   Washing up, putting away dishes

178

0604 Making a cup of tea, coffee, etc.
0605 Set table

7. Housework

0701 Washing clothes, hanging washing out to dry, bringing it in
0702 Ironing clothes
0703 Making, changing beds
0704 Dusting, hoovering, vacuum cleaning, general tidying
0705 Outdoor cleaning
0706 Other manual domestic work
0707 Housework elsewhere unspecified
0708 Putting shopping away

8. Odd Jobs

0801 Repair, upkeep of clothes
0802 Heat and water supply upkeep
0803 DIY, decorating, household repairs
0804 Vehicle maintenance, car washing etc.
0805 Home paperwork (not computer)

0806 Pet care, care of houseplants
0807 (Other) tasks in and around the home, unspecified
0808 Tasks - unspecified
0809 Feeding and food preparation for dependent adults
0810 Washing, toilet needs of dependent adults
0811 Shopping for others
0812 Fetching/carrying for others
0813 Other care of adults
0814 Doing housework for someone else (unpaid)
0815 Care of adults - unspecified
0816 Services for animals (eg animals to vet)
0817 Fetching, picking up, dropping off
0818 Home paperwork on computer

9. Gardening

0901 Gardening

10. Shopping

1001 Everyday shopping, shopping unspecified
1002 Shopping for durable goods
1003 Services for upkeep of possessions
1004 Money services
1005 Attending jumble sales, bazaars etc.
1006 Video rental or return
1007 Other service organisations or use (eg travel agents)

11. Child Care

1101 Feeding and food preparation for babies and children
1102 Washing, changing babies and children
1103 Putting children and babies to bed or getting them up
1104 Babysitting (ie other people's children)

1105   Other care of babies
1106   Medical care of babies, children & adults
1107   Reading to, or playing with babies, children & adults
1108   Helping children with homework
1109   Supervising children
1110   Other care of children
1111   Care of children and babies - unspecified

12. Domestic Travel

1201   Accompanying adult or child (eg to doctor)
1202   Shopping/services (travel to or from)
1203   Care of others (travel)
1204   Posting a letter

C. Personal Care

13. Dressing/Toilet

1301   Personal hygiene and self-care, dressing, 'got ready to go out'
1302   'Got up', 'went to bed'

14. Personal Services

1401   Personal medical, dental, paramedical care
1402   Other personal care/need activity - not specified
1404   Personal services (eg hairdresser)
1405   Other medical services (eg sick note)
1406   Welfare services, counselling
1408   Personal services not elsewhere specified

15. Meals/Snacks

1501   Eating at home
1502   Drinking non-alcoholic beverages

16. Sleep/Naps

1601   Main sleep
1602   Short naps and snoozes
1603   Being sick, ill in bed

D. Outdoor Leisure

17. Leisure Travel

1701   Going for a drive
1702   Travel to/from leisure activity
1703   Travel for religious, political, community, voluntary activity
1704   'Arrived home', 'went out'
1705   Other travel
1706   Travel - not specified

18. Excursions, Trips

18. Excursions, Trips

1801 Camping, caravanning
1802 Day trips to towns or cities
1803 Visiting beauty spots, the seaside etc.
1804 Zoos, museums, galleries, stately homes, exhibitions
1805 Unspecified active leisure outside home
1806 Going to a library

19. Playing Sport

1901 Outdoor team games
1902 Non-team ball hitting sports
1903 Running, jogging, cross-country, track and field
1904 Golf
1905 Fishing
1906 Bowls
1907 Martial arts
1908 Swimming and other water sports
1909 Keep fit, yoga, aerobics, dance practice
1910 Cycling
1911 Other outdoor sports
1912 Other indoor sports
1913 Horse rides
1914 Hunting, shooting, fishing etc.
1915 Other participation in sport and active leisure activities

20. Watching Sport

2001 Watching sport live at the event

21. Walks

2101 Walks, rambles
2102 Other outdoor hobbies (eg painting, collecting mushrooms)

22. At Church

2201 Religious practices

23. Civic Organisations

2301 Legal services, dealing with police
2302 Community/political, trade union meetings
2303 Activities as councillors, officials
2304 Voluntary tutoring
2305 Organising sports/coaching
2306 Providing meals/refreshments
2307 Paperwork associated with voluntary activity
2308 Other voluntary/organisational work
2309 Other political/community activities (eg demonstrations)
2310 Other religious, political, community, voluntary activities

E. Out-of-Home Leisure

24. Cinema/Theatre

2401 Watching films at the cinema (incl. other public viewing of recorded material)
2402 Going to theatre

2403   Other live entertainment (eg concert, opera)
2404   Pop concert etc.

25. Dance/Party etc.

2501   At a party/dance
2502   Meeting friends, relatives outside respective homes
2503   Gambling (ie at betting shop, casino)
2504   Driving lessons
2505   Other - leisure and entertainment activities out of home
2506   Leisure and Entertainment - not specified
2507   'Went dancing' (ie disco or dance hall)
2508   Scouts/Guides etc

26. Social Clubs

2601   At a social or night club

27. Pubs

2701   At the pub
2702   Playing pub games (eg darts, billiards, video games)
2703   Wine bar, drinking at restaurant

28. Restaurants

2801   Eating out at restaurants, cafes
2802   Eating out at a fast food or takeaway
2803   Eating out not specified
2804   Eating meal at pub (not snack)

29. Visiting Friends

2901   Eating out at a colleague's, relative's, friend's house
2902   Visiting friends, relatives

F. Passive Leisure

30. Listening to Radio

3001   Listening to radio

31. Watching T.V.

3101   Watching broadcast TV
3102   Watching video tapes and discs
3103   Programming video, rewinding tapes

32. Listening to Music etc.

3201   Listening to tapes, records etc.

G. Other Home Leisure

33. Study

3301 Studying
3302 Computer activities (educational, programming)

34. Reading Books

3401 Reading books

35. Reading Papers/Magazines

3501 Reading newspapers, magazines
3502 Reading letters

36. Relaxing

3601 Relaxing, pottering around
3602 Sitting in garden, sunbathing
3603 Kissing, cuddling, fondling
3604 Other leisure activities
3605 Leisure - unspecified

37. Conversation

3701 Talking, chatting, arguing, discussing
3702 Telephoning

38. Entertaining Friends

3801 Entertaining at home
3802 Alcohol, tobacco (smoking) and drugs consumption

39. Knitting/Sewing

3901 Knitting, sewing, dressmaking

40. Pastimes/Hobbies

4001 Homebrewing, wine making
4002 Watching home movies, slides
4003 'Playing'
4004 Playing video/computer games
4005 Playing games, cards
4006 Artistic and music activities
4007 Hobbies, collections not shown elsewhere
4008 Writing - longhand or typewritten (default)
4009 Writing on word processor
4010 Filling in time budget diary

41. Unknown activity.

9999 Entry missing or indecipherable

Bibliography

Acker, J.(1988), Class, Gender, and the Relations of Distribution, Signs, Vol.13, pp473-97.

- (1989), The Problem With Patriarchy, *Sociology,* 23, pp235-40.

Allport, G.W.(1935), Attitudes, in C. Murchison (Ed), *A Handbook of Social Psychology,* Clark University Press, Worcester, Mass.

Amsden, A. (Ed.), *The Economics of Women and Work,* St Martins Press, New York.

Anderson, M., Bechhofer,F. and Gershuny, J.I. (1994), The Social and Political Economy of the Household, Oxford University Press, Oxford.

Archer, M.S. (1988), *Culture and Agency: the Place of Culture in Social Theory,* Cambridge University Press, Cambridge.

Bahr, S.(1974), Effects on Power and Division of Labor, in L.Hoffman & F.I.Nye (Eds), *Working Mothers,* Jossey-Bass, San Francisco.

Barnet, R. C. & Baruch, G.K. (1987), Determinants of Fathers' Participation in Family Work, *Journal of Marriage and the Family,* Vol. 49, pp29-40.

Becker, G.S.(1974), A Theory of Marriage, in T.W. Schultz (Ed), *Economics of the Family,* Chicago University Press, Chicago.

- (1976), A Theory of the Allocation of Time, in G.S.Becker (Ed), *The Economic Approach to Human Behaviour,* University of Chicago Press, Chicago.

- (1981), *A Treatise on the Family,* Harvard University Press, Cambridge.

Benin, M.H. & Agostinelli, J.(1988), Husbands' and Wives' Satisfaction with the Division of Domestic Labor, *Journal of Marriage and the Family,* Vol. 50, p349-361.

Ben-Porath, Y.(1982), Economics and the Family - Match or Mismatch? A Review of Becker's 'A Treatise on the Family', *Journal of Economic Literature,* Vol.20, pp52-63.

Berk, R.A.(1980), The New Home Economics: An Agenda for Sociological Research, in S.F.Berk, *Women and Household Labour,* Sage, Beverly Hills, CA.

Berk, R.A. & Berk, S.F.(1978), A Simultaneous Equation Model for the Division of Household Labour, *Sociological Methods and Research,* 1978, Vol.6, pp431-68.

Berk, S.F. (Ed) (1980), *Women and Household Labour,* Sage, Beverly Hills, CA.

- (1985), *The Gender Factory: The Apportionment of Work in American Households,* Plenum Press, New York.

Bernard, J.(1964), The Adjustments of Married Mates, in H.T. Christensen, *Handbook of Marriage and the Family,* Rand McNally, Chicago.

- (1973), My Four Revolutions: An Autobiographical History of the ASA, *American Journal of Sociology, Vol. 73, pp773-91.*

Bernstein, B.(1971), *Class, Codes and Control: Volume One, Theoretical Studies Towards a Sociology of Language,* Routledge Kegan Paul, London.

Blair, S.L. & Johnson, M.P.(1992), Wives' Perceptions of Fairness of the Division of Labor: The Intersection of Housework and Ideology, *Journal of Marriage and the Family,* Vol. 54, pp570-581.

Blau, P.M.(1964), *Exchange and Power in Social Life,* Wiley, New York.

Blood, R.O.(1963), Rejoinder to 'Measurement and Bases of Family Power', *Journal of Marriage and the Family,* Vol.25, pp475-78.

Blood, R.O. & Wolfe, D.M.(1960), *Husbands and Wives,* Free Press, Glencoe, Ill.

Blossfeld, H.P. & Rohwer, G.(1995), *Techniques of Event History Modelling: New Approaches to Causal Analysis,* Erlbaum, Mahwah, N.J.

Blumer, H.(1955), Attitudes and the Social Act, *Social Problems,* Vol. 3, pp59-65.

Bott, E.(1957) *Family and Social Network,* Tavistock, London.

Boudon, R.(1989), Subjective Rationality and the Explanation of Social Behaviour, *Rationality and Society,* Vol.1, No.2, pp173-196.

Bourdieu, P.(1990), *The Logic of Practice,* Translated by R.Nice, Polity Press, Cambridge.

Brannen, J. & Moss, P.(1991), *Managing Mothers: Dual Earner Households After Maternity Leave,* Unwin Hymen Ltd, London.

Brickman, P.(1974), *Social Conflict,* Heath, Lexington, Mass.

Brines, J. (1993),The Exchange Value of Housework, *Rationality and Society,* Vol.5,No. 3, pp302-40.
- (1994), Economic Dependency, Gender, and the Division of Domestic Labor at Home, *American Journal of Sociology,* Vol.100, No.3, pp652-88.

Bruegel, I.(1996), Whose Myths Are They Anyway?: A Comment, *British Journal of Sociology,* Vol. 47, no 1, pp175-177.

Buchanan, J.M.(1969), *Cost and Choice,* University of Chicago Press, Chicago.

Budd, R.J. & Spencer, C.(1984), Latitude of Rejection, Centrality and Certainty: Variables Affecting the Relationship Between Attitudes, Norms and Behavioural Intentions, *British Journal of Social Psychology,* Vol. 23, pp1-8.
- (1985), Exploring the Role of Personal Normative Beliefs in the Theory of Reasoned Action: the Problem of Discriminating Between Alternative Path Models, *European Journal of Social Psychology,* Vol. 15, pp299-313.

Burchell, B., Elliot, J. & Rubery, J.(1994), Perceptions of the Labour Market: An Investigation of Differences by Gender and by Working Time, in J.Rubery & F.Wilkinson (Eds), *Employer Strategy and the Labour Market,* Oxford University Press, Oxford.

Burr, W.R.(1973), *Theory Construction and the Sociology of the Family,* Wiley, New York.

Burr, W.R., Hill, R., Nye, F.I. & Reiss, I.L.(Eds) (1979), *Contemporary Theories About the Family - Vol.1,* Collier Macmillan, London.

Charles, N. & Kerr, M.(1988), *Women, Food and Families,* Manchester University Press, Manchester.

Christensen, H.T.(Ed) (1964), *Handbook of Marriage and the Family,* Rand McNally, Chicago.

Coleman, J.S.(1979), *Qualitative and Quantitative Social Research: Papers In Honour of Paul F. Lazerfeld,* Free Press, New York.

Coser, R.L.(Ed)(1964), *The Family: Its Structure and Functions,* St Martin's Press, New York.

Crompton, R. (1989), Class Theory and Gender, *British Journal Of Sociology,* Vol.40 No.4, Pp565-587.

Crompton, R. & Harris, F.(1998), Explaining Women's Employment Patterns: 'Orientations to Work' Revisited, *British Journal of Sociology,* Vol.49, No. 1, pp118-136.

Crompton, R. & Mann, M.(Eds)(1986), *Gender and Stratification,* Polity Press, Cambridge.

Cromwell, R.E. & Olsen, D.H.(Eds)(1975), *Power in Families,* Wiley, New York.

Crow, G.(1989), The Use of the Concept of 'Strategy' in Recent Sociological Literature, *Sociology,* Vol.23, pp1-24.

Delphy, C. & Leonard, D.(1986), Class Analysis, Gender Analysis and the Family, in R.Crompton & M.Mann (Eds), *Gender and Stratification,* Polity Press, Cambridge.

DeMaris, A. & Longmore, M.A.(1996), Ideology, Power, and Equity: Testing Competing Explanations for the Perception of Fairness in Household Labour, *Social Forces,* Vol.74, No.3, pp1043-1071.

Dex, S.(1988), *Women's Attitudes Towards Work,* Macmillan, London.

Doeringer, P.B. & Piore, M.(1971), *Internal Labour Market and Manpower Analysis,* D.C. Heath and Company, New York.

Duke, V. & Edgell, S.(1987), The operationalisation of Class in British Sociology: Theoretical and Empirical Considerations, *British Journal of Sociology;* 1987, Vol.38, 4, pp445-463.

Eisenstein, Z.(1979), *Capitalist Patriarchy and the Case for Socialist Feminism,* Monthly Review Press, New York.

Eiser, J.R.(1980), *Cognitive Social Psychology,* Cambridge University Press, Cambridge.
- (1987), *The Expression of Attitude,* Springer-Verlag, New York.
- (1988), *Attitudes and Decisions,* Routledge, London.
- (1990), *Social Judgement,* Open University Press, Milton Keynes.

England, P. & Farkas, G.(1986), *Households, Employment, and Gender: A Social, Economic and Demographic View,* Aldine, New York.

England, P. & McCreary, L.(1987), Integrating Sociology and Economics to Study Gender and Work, in A.H.Stromberg, L.Larwood & B.A.Gutek (Eds), *Women and Work: An Annual Review,* Sage, CA.

England, P. & Kilbourne, B.S.(1991), Markets, Marriages and Other Mates, In R.Friedland & S.Robertson (Eds), *Beyond the Marketplace: Rethinking Society and Economy,* New York, Aldine.

Fazio, R.H. & Zanna, M.P.(1981), Direct Experience and Attitude-Behaviour Consistency, in L.Berkowitz (Ed.), *Advances in Experimental Social Psychology, Vol. 14,* Academic Press, New York.

Ferree, M.M.(1976), Working Class Jobs: Housework and Paid Work as Sources of Satisfaction, *Social Problems*, Vol.23, pp431-41.
- (1980), Satisfaction with Housework: the Social Context, in S.F.Berk (Ed), *Women and Household Labour*, Sage, Beverly Hills, CA.

Ferreira, A.J.(1967), Psychosis and Family Myth, *American Journal of Psychotherapy*, Vol.21, pp186-225.

Festinger, L.(1957), *A Theory of Cognitive Dissonance*, Peterson, Evanston, Ill.

Finch, J. & Groves, D.(Eds)(1983), *A Labour of Love*, Routeledge and Kegan Paul, London.

Finch, J.(1987), The Vignette Technique In Survey Research, *Sociology*, Vol.21, No.1, pp105-114.
- (1993), Conceptualising Gender, in D.H.J.Morgan & L.Stanley, *Debates in Sociology*, Manchester University Press, Manchester, England.

Finnegan, R., Gallie, D. & Roberts, B.,(1985), *New Approaches to Economic Life: Economic Restructuring, Employment and the Social Division of Labour*, Manchester University Press.

Fishbein, M.(1982), Social Psychological Analysis of Smoking Behaviour, in J.R. Eiser (Ed.), *Social Psychology and Behavioural Medicine*, Wiley, Chichester.

Fishbein, M. & Ajzen, L.(1975), *Belief, Attitude, Intention and Behaviour: An Introduction to Theory and Research*, Addison-Wesley, Reading Mass.

Fox, G.L. (1973), Another Look at the Comparative Resource Model: Assessing the Balance of Power in Turkish Marriages, *Journal of Marriage and the Family*, Vol.35, pp718-30.

Freiberg, J.W.(Ed)(1979), *Critical Sociology*, Irvington Publishers, New York.

Friedland, R. & Robertson, S.(Eds)(1991), *Beyond the Marketplace: Rethinking Society and Economy*, New York, Aldine.

Gallie, D. (1986), *The Social Change and Economic Life Initiative: an overview*, Economic and Social Research Council, London.

Gallie, D., Marsh, C. & Vogler, C.(Eds)(1994), *Social Change and the Experience of Unemployment*, Oxford University Press, Oxford.

Garfinkel, H.(1967), *Studies in Ethnomethodology*, University of California Press, CA.

Geerken,M. & Gove,W.R.(1983), *At Home and At Work: The Families Allocation of Labor*, Sage Publications, Beverly Hills.

Gershuny, J.I.(1982), *Household Work Strategies*, ISA Conference, Mexico City.

Gershuny, J.I., Godwin, M., Jones, S.(1994), The Domestic Labour Revolution: A Process of Lagged Adaption?, in M.Anderson, F.Bechhofer & J.Gershuny (1994), *The Social and Political Economy of The Household*, Oxford University Press, Oxford.

Gershuny, J.I. & Marsh, C.(1994), Unemployment in Work Histories, In D.Gallie, C.Marsh & C.Vogler (Eds), *Social Change and the Experience of Unemployment*, Oxford University Press, Oxford.

Gershuny, J.I., Miles, I., Jones, S., Mullins, C., Thomas, G. & Wyatt, S.M.E. (1986), Preliminary Analysis of the 1983/4 ESRC Time Budget Data, *Quarterly Journal of Social Affairs*, Vol.2, pp13-39.

Giddens, A. (Ed) (1975), *Positivism and Sociology*, Heinemann, London.
- (1978), *Central Problems in Social Theory*, Macmillan, London.
- (1979), *The New Rules of Sociological Method*, Hutchinson, London.
- (1984), *The Constitution of Society*, Polity Press, Cambridge.

Ginn, J., Arber, S., Brannen, J., Dale, A., Dex, S., Elias, P., Moss, P., Pahl, J., Roberts, C., Rubery, J. (1996), Feminist Fallacies: A Reply to Hakim on Women's Employment, *British Journal of Sociology*, Vol. 47, No.1, pp167-173.

Goldin, C.D.(1990), *Understanding the Gender Gap: an Economic History of American Women*, Oxford University Press, New York.

Goldthorpe, J.H.(1980), *Social Mobility and Class Structure In Modern Britain*, Oxford University Press, Oxford.
- (1983), Women and Class Analysis: In Defence of the Conventional View, *Sociology*, Vol.18, No.4.
- (1998), Rational Action Theory for Sociology, British Journal of Sociology, Vol.49, No.2, pp167-192.

Goode, W.J.(1964), *The Family*, Prentice-Hall, Englewood Cliffs.

Gouldner, A.W. & Gouldner, H.(1960), *Modern sociology; an Introduction to the Study of Human Interaction*, Harcourt, Brace & World, New York

Gregson, N. & Lowe, M.,(1994), Waged Domestic Labour and the Renegotiation of the Domestic Division of Labour Within Dual Career Households, in *Sociology,* Vol. 28, No.1, pp 55-78.

Gronau, R.(1977), Leisure, Home Production and Work: The Theory of the Allocation of Time Revisited, *Journal of Political Economy,* Vol. 4, pp1099-1124.

Haferkamp, H. (Ed.)(1989), *Social Structure and Culture,* de Gruyter, New York.

Hakim, C.(1979), *Occupational Segregation,* Research Paper No.9, Dept. of Employment, London.

- (1993), The Myth of Rising Female Employment, *Work, Employment and Society,* Vol.7, No.1, pp97-120.

- (1995), Five Feminist Myths About Women's Employment, *British Journal of Sociology,* Vol. 46, No.3, pp429-455.

- (1996), *Key Issues in Women's Work: Female Heterogeneity and the Polarisation of Women's Employment,* Athlone Press, London.

- (1998), Developing a Sociology for the Twenty-first Century: Preference Theory, *British Journal of Sociology,* Vol. 49, No. 1, pp137-143.

Hannan, M.T.(1982), Families, Markets, and Social Structures: An Essay on Becker's 'A Treatise on the Family', *Journal of Economic Literature,* Vol. 20, pp65-72.

Harris, C.C.(1969), *The Family,* Allen and Unwin, London.

- (1983), *The Family and Industrial Society,* Allen and Unwin, London.

- (1987), *Redundancy and Recession in South Wales,* Basil Blackwell, Oxford.

Hartmann, H.(1979), Capitalism, Patriarchy and Job Segregation by Sex, in Z.Eisenstein, *Capitalist Patriarchy and the Case for Socialist Feminism,* Monthly Review Press, New York.

Hawrylyshyn, O.(1977), Towards a Definition of Non-Market Activities, *Review of Income and Wealth,* Vol.32,1.

Heer, D.(1963), The Measurement and Bases of Family Power: An Overview, *Journal of Marriage and the Family,* Vol.25, pp133-39.

Hochschild, A.(1990), *The Second Shift,* Piatkus, London.

Hoffman, L. & Nye, F.I.(Eds)(1974), *Working Mothers,* Jossey-Bass, San Francisco.

Hollis, M. & Nell, E.J.(1975), *Rational Economic Man; A Philosophical Critique of Neo-Classical Economics,* Cambridge Univerity Press, Cambridge.

Hollis, M.(1977), *Models Of Man: Philosophical Thoughts On Social Action,* Basil Blackwell, Oxford.

- (1989), *The Cunning Of Reason,* Cambridge Univerity Press, Cambridge.

- (1991), Why Elster is Stuck and Needs to Recover His Faith, *London Review of Books,* 24th January.

Homans, G.C.(1961), *Social Behaviour: its Elementary Forms,* Routledge and Kegan Paul, London.

Horrell, S.(1994), Household Time Allocation and Women's Labour Force Participation, in M.Anderson, F.Bechhofer and J.Gershuny, *The Social and Political Economy of the Household,* Oxford University Press, Oxford.

Hunt, A. (1968), *A Survey of Women's Employment, Vol. I & Vol. II,* HMSO, Aldershot.

Jenkinson C, Layte R, Lawrence K.(1997) Development and testing of the medical outcomes study 36-item short form health survey summary scale scores in the United Kingdom: results from a large scale survey and a clinical trial. *Medical Care* Vol.35, No.4; pp410-16.

Jowell, R. & Airey, C.(1984), *British Social Attitudes: The 1984 Report* (Gower, Aldershot).

Kahneman, D. & Tversky, A.(1984), Choice, Values and Frames, *American Psychologist,* Vol.39, No. 4, pp342-350.

Kandel, D. & Lesser, G.(1972), Marital Decision Making in American and Danish Urban Families: A Research Note, *Journal of Marriage and the Family,* Vol.34, pp134-38.

Kimmel, P.R & Havens, J.W.(1966), Game Theory V's Mutual Identification: Two Criteria for Assessing Marital Relationships, *Journal of Marriage and the Family,* Vol. 28, pp460-65.

Kleinke, C.L.(1984), Two Models for Conceptualising the Attitude-Behaviour Relationship, *Human Relations,* Vol. 37, No.9, pp 813-26.

Komarovsky, M.(1962), *Blue Collar Marriage,* Random House, New York.

Lamouse, A.(1969), Family Roles of Women: A German Example, *Journal of Marriage and the Family,* Vol.31, pp145-52.

Layte, R.(1996), Gendered Equity: The Material and Cultural Determinants of the Domestic Division of Labour, DPhil Thesis, University of Oxford, Oxford.

- (1998), Gendered Equity? Comparing Explanations of Women's Satisfaction with the Domestic Division of Labour, *Work, Employment and Society,* Vol. 12, No. 3.

Lindenberg, S.(1985), An Assessment of the New Political Economy: Its Potential for the Social Sciences and Sociology In particular, *Sociological Theory*, Vol. 3, No 1, pp99-114.
- (1986), *Rational Choice and Framing: the Situational Selection of Utility Arguments*, World Congress of Sociology.
- (1989), Choice and Culture: The Behavioural Basis of Cultural Impact on Transactions, Social Structure and Culture, H.Haferkamp (Ed), *Social Structure and Culture*, de Gruyter, Berlin.

Luxton, M.(1980), *More Than a Labour of Love*, Women's Press, Toronto.

Mann, M.(1979), Idealism and Materialism In Sociological Theory, In J.W.Freiberg,(Ed), *Critical Sociology*, Irvington Publishers, New York.

Marsh, C.(1982), *The Survey Method: The Contribution of Surveys to Sociological Explanation*, George Allen and Unwin, London.

Martin, J. & Roberts, C.(1984), *Women and Employment*, Report on the Dept. of Employment/OPCS Survey, HMSO, London.

Maynard, M.(1990), The Re-shaping of Sociology? Trends in the Study of Gender, *Sociology*, Vol.24, pp269-90.

McRae, S.(1986), *Cross-class families : A Study of Wives Occupational Superiority*, Clarendon Press, London.

Meissner, M., Humphries, E. , Meis, S. & Scheu, W.(1975), No Exit for Wives, *Review of Canadian Sociology and Anthropology*, Vol.12, pp424-39.

Merton, R.K.(1967), *On theoretical sociology: five essays, old and new*, Free Press, New York

Michel, A. (1967), Comparative Data Concerning the Interaction in French and American Families, *Journal of Marriage and the Family*, Vol.29, pp337-44.

Morgan, D.H.J. (1985), *Family, Politics and Social Theory*, Routeledge, London.

Morgan, D.H.J. & Stanley, L.(Eds)(1993), *Debates in Sociology*, Manchester University Press, Manchester, England.

Morris, L. (1985a), Renegotiation of the Domestic Division of Labour, in R.Finnegan *et al* (Eds), *New Approaches to Economic Life*, Manchester University Press, Manchester.
- (1985b), Local Social Networks and Domestic Organisation, *Sociological Review*, Vol.33, pp327-42.
- (1988), Employment, Households and Social Networks, in D.Gallie (Ed.), *Employment in Britain*, Blackwell, Oxford.
- (1990), *The workings of the Household*, Basil Blackwell, Oxford.
- (1993), Domestic Labour and Employment Status among Married Couples: A Case Study in Hartlepool, *Capital and Class*, Vol. 49, pp 37-52.

Murchison, C. (Ed)(1979), *A Handbook of Social Psychology*, Clark University Press, Worcester, Mass.

Murdock, G.P.(1949), *Social Structure*, Macmillan, New York.

Nerlove, M. (1974), Toward a New Theory of Population and Economic Growth, in T.W.Schultz (Ed.), *Economics of the Family*, University of Chicago Press, Chicago.

Nunnally, J.C.(1978), *Psychometric Theory*, McGraw-Hill, New York.

Oakley, A.(1974), *The Sociology of Housework*, Robertson, London.

Pagel, M.D. & Davidson, A.R.(1984), A Comparison of Three Social Psychological Models of Attitude and Behavioural Plan: Prediction of Contraceptive Behaviour, *Journal of Personality and Social Psychology*, Vol. 47, pp517-33.

Pahl, J.M.(1983), The Allocation of Money and the Structuring of Inequality within Marriage, *Sociological Review*, Vol.31, pp 237-62.

Pahl, J.M. & Pahl, R.E.(1971), *Managers and Their Wives*, Allen Lane, London.

Pahl, R.E.(1984), *Divisions of Labour*, Basil Blackwell, Oxford.

Pahl, R.E. & Wallace,C.D.(1985), Household Work Strategies In An Economic Recession, in N.Redclift, & E.Mingione (Eds.), *Beyond Employment: Household, Gender and Subsistance*, Basil Blackwell, Oxford.

Parsons, T. & Bales, R.F.(1956), *Family, Socialisation and Interaction Process*, Routeledge and Kegan Paul, London.

Perry-Jenkins, M. & Folk, K.(1994), Class, Couples and Conflict: Effects of the Division of Labor on Assessments of Marriage in Dual-Earner Families, *Journal of Marriage and the Family*, Vol. 56, No 1, pp165-180.

Piore, M.(1980), Economic Fluctuation, Job Security, and Labour Market Duality in Italy, France and the United States, *Politics and Society*, Vol.9, pp379-407.

Pitts, J.R.(1964), The Structural-Functional Approach, in H.T. Christensen, *Handbook of Marriage and the Family*, Rand McNally, Chicago.

Pleck, J.H.(1985), *Working Wives/Working Husbands*, Sage, Beverly Hills, CA.

Redclift, N. & Mingione, E.(Eds.)(1985), *Beyond Employment: Household, Gender and Subsistence*, Basil Blackwell, Oxford.

Reid, M.G.(1934), *Economics of Household Production*, John Wiley, New York.

Roberts, B.(1978), *Cities of Peasants: The Political Economy of Urbanisation In the Third World*, Sage, London.

Robinson, J.P., Converse, P. & Szalai, A.(Eds)(1972), Everyday Life in Twelve Countries, in A. Szalai *et al.*(Eds), *The Use of Time*, Mouton, The Hague.

Robinson, J.P.(1977), *How Americans Use Time: A Social Psychological Analysis of Everyday Behaviour*, Praeger, New York.

Rosenberg, M.J. & Hovland, C.I.(1960), Cognitive, Affective and Behavioural Components of Attiudes, in M.J.Rosenberg & C.I.Hovland(Eds.), *Attitude Organisation and Change: An Analysis of Consistency Among Attitude Components*, Yale University Press, New Haven.

Ross, C.E.(1987), The Division of Labour at Home, *Social Forces*, Vol. 65,No. 3, pp816-33.

Rossi, P.H.(1979), Vignette Analysis: Uncovering the normative Structure of Complex Judgments, in J.S.Coleman & R.Merton (Eds.), *Qualitative and Quantitative Social Research: Papers In Honour of Paul F. Lazerfeld*, Free Press, New York.

Rubery, J. & Wilkinson, F.(Eds)(1994), *Employer Strategy and the Labour Market*, Oxford University Press, Oxford.

Safilios-Rothschild, C.(1967), A Comparison of Power Structure and Marital Satisfaction in Urban Greek and French Families, *Journal of Marriage and the Family*, Vol. 29, pp345-52.

- (1976), A Macro and Micro Examination of Family Power and Love: An Exchange Model, *Journal of Marriage and the Family*, Vol.38, pp355-61.

Sawhill, I.(1980), Economic Perspectives on the Family, in A.Amsden (Ed.), *The Economics of Women and Work*, St Martins Press, New York.

Scanzoni, J.(1970), *Opportunity and the Family*, Free Press, New York.

- (1972), *Sexual Bargaining: Power and Politics in American Marriage*, Prentice-Hall, New Jersey.

- (1979), Social Processes and Power Within Families, in W.R.Burr, R.Hill, F.I.Nye & I.L.Reiss (Eds), *Contemporary Theories About the Family - Vol.1*, Collier Macmillan, London.

Schutz, A.(1972), *The Phenomenology of the Social World*, Heinemann, New York.

Schultz, T.W. (Ed.) (1974), Economics of the Family, Chicago University Press, Chicago.

Sprey, J.(1979), Conflict Theory and the Study of Marriage and the Family, In *W.R. Burr et al, (Eds), Contemporary Theories About the family, Vol.2*, Free Press, New York.

Stinchcombe, A.(1968), *Constructing Social Theories*, Harcourt Brace Jovanovich, New York.

Stromberg, A.H., Larwood, L. & Gutek, B.A.(Eds)(1987), *Women and Work: An Annual Review*, Sage, CA.

Stromberg, A.H & Harkess, S.(Eds)(1988), *Women Working: Theories and Facts in Perspective 2nd Edition*, Mountain View, CA: Mayfield.

Szalai, A., Converse, P.E., Feldheim, P., Scheuch, E.K. & Stone, P.F.(Eds)(1972), *The Use of Time: Daily Activities of Urban and Suburban Populations In Twelve Countries*, Mouton, The Hague.

Tam, M., (1997), Part Time Employment: A Bridge or a Trap?, Avebury, Aldershot.

Thibaut, J.W. & Kelley, H.H.(1959), *The Social Psychology of Groups*, Wiley, New York.

Thompson, L.(1991), Family work: Women's Sense of Fairness, *Journal of Family Issues*, Vol. 12, No. 2, pp181-196.

Thorne, B. & Henly, N.,(Eds)(1975), *Language and Sex: Difference and Dominance*, Newbury House, Mass.

Vanek, J.(1974), Time Spent in Housework, *Scientific American*, Vol.231, pp116-120.

- (1980), Household Work, Wage Work and Sexual Inequality, In S.F. Berk (Ed.), *Women and Household Labour*, Sage, Beverly Hills, CA.

Vogler, C. & Pahl, J.(1993), Social and Economic Change and the Organisation of Money Within Marriage, *Work Employment And Society*, Vol.7 No.1 pp71-95.

189

Walby, S.(1986), *Gender, Class and Stratification: Toward a New Approach, in Gender and Stratification*, R.Crompton & M.Mann, Polity, Cambridge.

    - (1988), Gender, Politics and Social Theory, *Sociology,* Vol.22, pp215-32.

    - (1989), Theorising Patriarchy, *Sociology,* Vol.23, pp213-34.

Walker, K. & Woods, M.(1976), *Time Use: A Measure of Household Production of Goods and Services*, American Home Economics Association, Washington.

Wallace, C. (1993), Reflections on the Concept of Strategy, in D.Morgan & L.Stanley (Eds), *Debates in Sociology*, Manchester University Press, Manchester.

Ware, J.E., Kosinski, M.A. & Keller, S.D.(1994), *SF-36 Physical and Mental Health Summary Scales: A User's Manual*, The Health Institute, New England Medical Center, Boston, Mass.

Weber, M.(1978), *Economy and Society, 2 Vols.* Edited by G.Roth and C.Wittich, University of California Press, Berkley, California.

Wheelock, J.(1990), *Husbands at Home: the Domestic Economy in a Post-Industrial Society*, Routledge, London.

Wicker, A.W.(1969), Attitudes Versus Actions: The Relationships of Overt and Behavioural Responses to Attitude Objects, *Journal of Social Issues,* Vol. 25, pp41-78.

White, M.(1983), *Long-Term Unemployment And Labour Markets*, Policy Studies Institute, London.

Whitherspoon, S.(1988), Interim Report: A Woman's Work, in R.Jowell *et al* (Eds), *British Social Attitudes: the 5th Report*, Gower, Aldershot, Hants.

Wilkening, E.A. (1968), Toward a Further Refinement of the Resource Theory of Family Power, *Sociological Focus,* Vol.2, pp1-19.

Wilkie, J.R.(1988), Marriage, Family Life and Women's Employment, in A.H.Stromberg & S.Harkess (Eds), *Women Working: Theories and Facts in Perspective 2nd Edition*, Mountain View, CA: Mayfield.

Wilkie, J.R.,Ratcliff, K.S & Ferree, M.M.(1992), Family Division of Labor and Marital Satisfaction Among Two Earner Married Couples, *Journal of Marriage and the Family*, Vol. 56, No 1, 1994, pp165-180.

Yeandle, S.(1984), *Working Women's Lives*, Tavistock, London.

Young, M. & Willmott, P.(1957), *Family and Kinship in East London*, Routledge and Kegan Paul, London.

    - (1973) *The Symmetrical Family*, Routeledge and Kegan Paul, London.

Zimmerman, D. & West, C., (1975), Sex Roles, Interruptions, and Silences in Conversation. In B.Thorne & N.Henly (Eds), *Language and Sex: Difference and Dominance*, Newbury House, Mass.